22111306

CORPORATE MOBILITY
AND
PATHS TO THE
TOP

Corporate Mobility and Paths to the Top

STUDIES FOR
HUMAN RESOURCE AND
MANAGEMENT DEVELOPMENT
SPECIALISTS

J. Benjamin Forbes
AND
James E. Piercy

Q

Quorum Books
New York • Westport, Connecticut • London

Library of Congress Cataloging-in-Publication Data

Forbes, J. Benjamin.
   Corporate mobility and paths to the top : studies for human
resource and management development specialists / J. Benjamin Forbes
and James E. Piercy.
     p.   cm.
   Includes bibliographical references and index.
   ISBN 0–89930–524–5 (alk. paper)
   1. Chief executive officers—United States. 2. Executives—United
States. 3. Career development—United States I. Piercy, James E.
II. Title.
HD38.25.U6F67   1991
658.4'09—dc20   90–42967

British Library Cataloguing in Publication Data is available.

Library of Congress Catalog Card Number: 90–42967
ISBN: 0–89930–524–5

First published in 1991

Quorum Books, 88 Post Road West, Westport, CT   06881
An imprint of Greenwood Publishing Group, Inc.

Printed in the United States of America

The paper used in this book complies with the
Permanent Paper Standard issued by the National
Information Standards Organization (Z39.48–1984).

10 9 8 7 6 5 4 3 2 1

Copyright Acknowledgments

The authors gratefully acknowledge permission to quote the following:

J. B. Forbes (1987). Early intraorganizational mobility: Patterns and influences. *Academy of Management Journal*, 30, 110–125. Reprinted by permission of The Academy of Management.

J. B. Forbes & J. E. Piercy (1983). Rising to the top: Executive women in 1983 and beyond. Reprinted from *Business Horizons*, 26(5), 38–57. Copyright 1983 by the Foundation for the School of Business at Indiana University. Used with permission.

J. B. Forbes, J. E. Piercy, & T. L. Hayes (1988). Women executives: Breaking down barriers? Reprinted from *Business Horizons*, 31(6), 6–9. Copyright 1988 by the Foundation for the School of Business at Indiana University. Used with permission.

J. E. Piercy & J. B. Forbes (forthcoming). The phases of the chief executive's career. Reprinted from *Business Horizons*, forthcoming. Copyright forthcoming by the Foundation for the School of Business at Indiana University. Used with permission.

J. E. Piercy and J. B. Forbes (1986). The functional backgrounds of chief executives: Differences across time and industries. *Akron Business and Economic Review*, 17, 27–32. Used with permission.

This book is dedicated to Lark and Ursula and five sons, Tommy and Michael, and James, Richard, and Jeffrey, for their support and love.

Contents

Illustrations

Preface

The preparation of this book began when we realized that two research efforts, initially focused on either end of the management career, had expanded to the extent that they met in the middle. In the late 1970s, we began studying the backgrounds of chief executive officers (CEOs). We were particularly interested in the differences that existed across industries. Later, while we were studying other issues concerning CEOs, such as changes in functional backgrounds over time, we began working on the other end of the business career with a study of early intra-organizational mobility. The early mobility study was then extended upward with a policy capturing study of the general management promotion decision. At about the same time, we decided that studies of CEOs only did not answer all of our questions about top executive backgrounds and careers. For example, to merely ask whether the new CEO came from inside or outside, or from a particular functional area or from general management is not highly enlightening because of the frequent change of positions that often precedes appointment as chief executive. The following is a typical scenario. An executive comes into the company from outside as vice president of finance; one year later he becomes an executive vice president; after two more years he is appointed president and chief operating officer; and three years after that, he is elected chairman and CEO. Is this person an insider or an outsider? Is he a functional specialist or a general manager? To gain a better understanding of these issues, we studied a large number of top executive promotions, from the vice president/general management level all the way up to CEO.

Of particular interest today are the positions of women executives. We conducted two detailed analyses of the backgrounds and placement of America's top female executives, and noted the progress made from the early to the late 1980s. To tie all the previous research together, we gathered data on the entire careers of CEOs in the manufacturing, utility, transportation, banking, insurance, and retailing industries, noting different patterns within these various settings. Finally, we cycled back to the start and updated our earlier research on the demographic backgrounds of CEOs. Now, in this book we have attempted to integrate the results of over ten years of research.

The primary audience for this work is the management practitioner, particularly the human resource specialist concerned with designing and implementing executive development programs. However, the material should be valuable for everyone with an interest in management careers, from the CEO, who is responsible for developing his successors, to the young person still tentatively planning his or her career.

We also hope that the academic community will find our data useful. As suggested by Edgar Schein (1986), we have tried to describe the realities of managerial careers. With the exception of our early career study, we have not tried to test particular theories or models from career-related academic fields such as psychology, sociology, or anthropology. We have, however, considered empirical data from these areas as well as from the many practitioner-oriented descriptive studies in this field. Theories relating business strategy to career systems were found to be particularly useful, and we have tried to relate our findings to these models. However, we have found that the reality of executive careers is much too complex to be captured by any current academic theory.

This research has been generously supported by numerous institutions and individuals. The John Carroll University School of Business has provided summer funding and released time for this research; and we wish to thank our past and present deans: Ray Alford and Frank Navratil. The funding was provided by grants from the Wasmer family and the Mellen Foundation, and we are in their debt. A John Carroll University Grauel Faculty Fellowship made possible the final preparation of the book.

Faculty collaborators to be thanked include Marian Extejt, who assisted with the policy capturing study, and Tom Hayes, who worked with us on our second study of women executives. We are also very grateful for the research assistance on several studies provided by a former MBA student at John Carroll, Dan Talarcek. Fifteen top executives, who were members of the Board of Trustees of John Carroll University, participated in the general management promotion simulation and we thank them all. We also wish to thank Robert Ginn, Chairman Emeritus of Centerior Energy for sharing with us information about his career and about careers in the public utility industry. Finally, we are extremely grateful to the former "Chief Academic Officer" at John Carroll University, Art Noetzel, for continually sharing materials and ideas, and for his interest in and encouragement of this research.

CORPORATE MOBILITY
AND
PATHS TO THE
TOP

1

Introduction

This book is primarily intended for practicing business people—especially those who aspire to top management positions and those responsible for developing future business leaders. Our research over the past ten years has focused on the complexity of upward mobility in today's ever changing business organizations. The result of this research is presented here in the hope that it will prove useful to business people.

One of the most critical tasks facing human resource professionals in the 1990s and beyond will be identifying and developing aspiring top executives. The information presented in this book will provide useful data, options, and recommendations for the development and implementation of such programs. This will not be an easy task. Imagine the following mythical fable.

A FABLE

Once upon a time there existed a land in which most of the people worked on the rich farmland at the foot of a range of semi-active volcanoes. While their lives were comfortable, many were attracted to the challenge of climbing the volcanic mountains in the hope of finding great riches and power at the top. It was a very difficult climb and only a small number ever reached the peaks.

Eager young climbers often studied the methods used by the older successful climbers in the hope that, by following proven paths and using proven techniques, they too might reach the summit. Unfortunately, these volcanic mounts were constantly changing; sometimes in subtle, almost imperceptible ways, sometimes violently and catastrophically. Relatively easy paths to the top became very difficult, almost vertical ascents, or led into impassable chasms. At the same time, new, previously unknown routes to the top were created.

The nature of the mountains was such that some whose specialized climbing techniques had proven unsuccessful on one peak found that the exact same methods worked extremely well in another location.

It was a very long and difficult climb and many grew tired. About halfway up the mountains, some discovered a lush and apparently safe plateau. Here they often stopped to rest and many chose to stay. This was a dangerous decision, however. There occasionally occurred periods of increased volcanic activity during which the middle sections of the mountains were completely destroyed while the tops and bottoms were left relatively unscathed.

Because of the uncertain nature of these times, the older leaders became concerned. Perhaps those who reached the top would be foolhardy adventurers who just happened to have luck on their side. How could they train and counsel young climbers so that the most competent would reach the peaks?

THE CURRENT BUSINESS ENVIRONMENT

The environment in which today's business managers operate is even more volatile and unpredictable than the mythical situation described above. Twenty years ago, a young businessperson entered the world of work with the expectation that there were certain well defined rules that, if followed, would allow them to pursue a successful career. Today, the young manager or professional does not know what to expect. The young person, however, can probably deal with this uncertainty and adapt. They never thought that they knew what the rules were. The older, mid-career manager may be the true victim of change; his or her world is crumbling or, to return to the volcano analogy, is being blown apart.

In 1982, John Naisbitt correctly identified ten "Megatrends" that were transforming our society. We are still experiencing the effects of these forces—and others. American businesses have been forced to try to adapt to powerful economic, technological, and societal changes.

With the Reagan years we saw runaway inflation tamed and government regulations eased. However, these were two bogeymen behind which many American firms had been hiding. No longer could costs be easily passed on to the customer. Foreign competition has increased tremendously. We have lost our position as the leading industrial power in the world. The Japanese have driven many industries out of existence and are now busy acquiring many of those that remain. Our own financial community has seen profits to be made in the weakened condition of many firms. The merger and acquisitions mania of the 1980s has caused many firms to restructure or be restructured. The power of corporate top management has been significantly weakened. Outside money managers have more influence over business strategy and structure. Economic uncertainties will continue to increase with the rise of the newly industrialized countries in Asia and Latin America. The European Community will be more of a threat after 1992 and opportunities for development will appear throughout Eastern Europe and China.

The major technological change of the 1980s was the development and application of powerful personal computers and work stations. That revolution has only just begun and will surely continue to change our lives and the way we do business into the twenty-first century. In addition, the 1990s will surely bring other major technological shifts. For example, it is likely that patterns of energy usage will be altered as applications of super-conductivity and cold fusion are developed.

A significant demographic shift which will continue to change our society, our business practices, and surely the career paths within businesses is the aging of the baby boom generation. Within hierarchical organizations of all sorts, there will be a greater supply of candidates for middle and upper level positions. At the same time, because of the economic and technological changes discussed above, there will be fewer such positions in the organizations of the future. In addition, there will be fewer candidates for entry-level positions. This will result in major disruptions in the traditional, seniority-based promotion systems of many organizations. It will also open up opportunities for many classes of people who have been under-utilized in the past, such as women, minorities, and handicapped people.

A major premise of this book is that career paths evolve and change in relation to the needs of the organization as reflected in its strategy and structure. There is growing documentation of this point (Nystrom & McArthur, 1989). It is generally well accepted that successful firms adapt their strategy and structure to match the demands of the external environment (Lawrence & Lorsch, 1969; Miles & Snow, 1978). Thus as the external environment (economic, technological, and social) changes so must organizations modify, or in some cases revolutionize, their goals and their traditional means of doing business. These changes will mean that historically well established career paths will be disrupted and new ones created.

Similar ideas about management have been popularized recently by Tom Peters (1987). Peters documents the sources of the chaos facing American industry today and claims to have written (at least in preliminary form) a "Handbook for a Management Revolution." He describes the changes that many firms have already successfully made, such as down-sizing, de-layering, and decentralizing, and urges those who have not yet started to adapt to hesitate no longer.

The impact that all of this will have on management careers is still not clear. Our goals for this book are to 1) review empirical data on executive career paths (there will be an emphasis on our own work but other studies will be covered as well); 2) discuss existing and emerging theoretical models that attempt to describe and explain the data; and finally, 3) recommend how individual and organizational career planners should prepare for the future.

CONVENTIONAL WISDOM ON MANAGEMENT CAREERS

We believe that many career decisions are based on invalid information. The data that will be presented in this book will question much of the conventional wisdom concerning corporate upward mobility. For example, while some believe that every American has a chance to rise to the top of major business organizations, others contend that only those born with the proverbial "silver spoon" have a real shot at the top. Of course the truth lies somewhere in between, as we will show in the following chapters.

Many people, including human resource managers, are not aware of the realities of career paths within large corporations. Vroom and MacCrimmon (1968) conducted a study of the promotion system in one large company. They were able to predict promotion chances based on career histories and determined that those in finance and marketing had significantly greater opportunities to move up than employees in manufacturing; and that those in personnel had very little chance for upward mobility. This information came as a shock to many in the company—especially to the senior personnel manager who had recently given a talk to lower level managers about the Horatio Alger-type opportunities that existed within the firm. Other studies indicate that lower and middle level managers typically overestimate their chances for promotion (Rosenbaum, 1984).

Many people are aware of the studies of top executives that identify the functional areas from which they came and conclude that most chief executives have backgrounds in marketing and finance (Burck, 1976) or, more recently, that banking is the most common background of CEOs (Boone & Kurtz, 1988). These conclusions are widely cited and readily accepted, however, they are overgeneralizations. Our research indicates that it is not meaningful to lump together firms from different industries when examining career paths. Different industries have different needs for technical expertise at the top and the most common functional background found at the top varies quite a bit across industries. In addition, the distribution of functional backgrounds of chief executives has varied over the years as the need for critical technical skills has changed.

Recent books and articles have charged that women have been barred from the executive suites by a "glass ceiling" at the general management level and by the even more formidable "wall" behind which top management status lies (Morrison, White, & Van Velsor, 1987). Our research shows that women have, in fact, made significant, albeit slow, progress in climbing the corporate ranks. Unfortunately, until recently their numbers have been very small in relation to the number of men in middle and upper management positions. Therefore, although the probability that they will be promoted may equal or exceed that for a man in the same position, it will still take a great deal of time before we see women in large numbers at the top of business organizations.

Many people still believe in the myth of the "mobile manager" (Jennings, 1971). That is, they think that one must make frequent changes in employers in order to reach higher levels in the business world. This has never been true and in fact numerous studies, including our research, show that in most industries the successful top executive may make a few moves early in his career but then settles down and spends most of his life working for the same firm.

Recent work by John Kotter (1982, 1988) has focused on the importance of developing general management skill (specifically, an intimate familiarity with the firm and the industry) among the leaders and future leaders of business firms. While we generally agree with this prescription, we have found evidence that many functionally specialized leaders are chosen to head major corporations. This is often in the best interest of the firm and we must recognize that there are actually numerous paths to the top in many industries.

Finally, the career management literature recommends that future top executives need a fast start. They need lots of early challenge and responsibility (Berlew & Hall, 1966) in order to experience a cycle of success. They must also receive early promotions or they will fall behind in the "tournament" which determines who will reach the top (Rosenbaum, 1984). Again we believe that this is an overgeneralization. We will review the existing research on this topic and show that different early experiences may be appropriate in different situations.

LOOKING AHEAD: AN OVERVIEW

This book is built around a series of studies that we have conducted over the past ten years. Our presentation of the various executive career studies and issues will follow a rough chronological sequence.

First, we will examine the early career experience. The critical issues in Chapter 2 include the socialization process, the importance of a fast career start, and the question of whether what happens in the first few years of a career strongly influences success in later years. Our research, which is presented in Chapter 3, consisted of a study in which 180 newly hired employees were followed for 12 years. The various factors that influenced their upward mobility were identified.

In Chapter 4, we will present two studies dealing with mid-career issues. Our first study in this chapter focused on the promotion decision making process and examined the criteria used for promotion into a general management position. Here we had 15 top executives, as well as a group of lower level managers and professionals, rate hypothetical candidates for this position. In this "policy capturing" study, the relative importance of breadth of experience, functional background, and early pattern of upward mobility (slow or fast) was evaluated.

In the second study, we analyzed almost 700 management promotions as announced in *The Wall Street Journal*. The data revealed two general paths to top management. The first is an insider, general management track with little inter-firm or inter-industry movement. The alternative path involves greater functional specialization but requires less firm or industry specialization. There is greater opportunity to move among different firms and industries.

Chapter 5 will deal with the special problems and opportunities for women in management. Here we will be comparing the positions and backgrounds of a group of almost 1,300 women in executive positions in the early 1980s with data for a group of 1,945 women in similar positions gathered five years later.

In the next three chapters we will focus on the backgrounds and careers of CEOs. In Chapter 6 we will look at personal characteristics of CEOs as established even before they entered the workplace. Such issues as family background, region of birth, and education will be discussed. We will compare studies of the backgrounds of top executives conducted at different points in time. Chapter 7 will deal with business background, particularly functional area. Here the data will be from two comprehensive studies—one involving approximately 800 CEOs, the other over 1,300 chief executives. We will show that different industries prefer different backgrounds and that in general the relative emphasis on various functional areas has changed over time.

Chapter 8 will investigate the entire career paths of 230 CEOs in manufacturing firms. In this study, we identified eight different paths to the top and also discovered six distinct phases of the top executive's career. We will also describe top executive career paths in five other industries (utilities, transportation, banking, insurance, and retailing).

Our conclusions and the implications of our analyses for career planning, human resource planning, and executive selection and development will be covered in Chapter 9. We will discuss the need for change in how executives are identified and developed, and will show how organizational-level strategic planning techniques may be used to help individuals make career planning decisions in today's complex and unpredictable world.

2

The Early Years

Although it may take 25 to 30 years for a person to reach the top of a major corporation, there is considerable evidence that the early years are a critical phase. Much like the launching of a satellite into orbit, unless the powerful booster works perfectly to overcome the force of gravity, the space vehicle will fall back to earth.

CAREER STAGES

The nature of human development and maturation is such that we pass through various predictable stages. These stages are identifiable by the challenges that must be met in order to develop further. Behavioral scientists have mapped out these phases in childhood (Erickson, 1963) and in adulthood (Levinson, Darrow, Klein, Levinson, & McKee, 1978). Careers also seem to consist of regular stages during which certain tasks must be accomplished.

Douglas Hall (1976) has identified five career stages: entry, socialization, advancement, maintenance, and withdrawal. During the entry or exploration stage, the individual is still searching for the right occupation and organization. Once a choice has been made, the socialization or establishment stage begins. This is a time of learning, testing, and evaluation for the individual and for the employer. Having learned the ropes of the new occupation and organization and finding a positive evaluation of the match by both the new employee and the employer, attention usually turns to moving up in the organization. This indicates movement into the advancement stage. For many people advancement starts to level off eventually. When a career plateau is reached the individual has entered the maintenance stage. At this point, career paths diverge. Some people continue to advance in their careers, some plateau, and others begin to decline. Finally, at the end of the career comes the withdrawal stage.

In this chapter we will examine early career issues; that is, those occurring during the socialization and advancement stages. Later chapters will be concerned with mid-career and late-career issues. However, since we will be focusing on those who did not plateau, who instead reached the top, we will later introduce a new set of stages that seems to better describe the career of the top executive.

STARTING A CAREER

The early years of any career can be a critical period. Both the individual and the organization are learning about each other. As is true with any new relationship, first impressions are very important. The individual may be overwhelmed with new information. Whether planned or unplanned the new employee will experience a period of socialization during which he or she will learn not only the official requirements of the job but also the unwritten expectations of their new role. The new employee will be evaluating this information in an attempt to determine whether or not the decision to join this particular organization was the correct choice. Often the individual actually experiences a feeling of "reality shock" or "culture shock." The first sensation occurs primarily among those just entering the business world from school (Louis, 1980); the latter to those more experienced people moving to a radically new corporate culture (Sathe, 1985).

The shock occurs because of the gap between expectations about the job and the world of work and the reality of the situation. The change between school and a work organization brings with it many differences: differences in tasks, differences in schedules, differences in relationships with people, differences in time horizons, differences in evaluation criteria. However, the greatest problem encountered at this time is disappointment with the quality of the job. Many college graduates expect to be given jobs with more responsibility, more freedom, more interesting work, and more challenge, and also shorter and more convenient working hours than provided by the typical entry-level position (Feldman, 1988; Greenhaus, 1987).

The organization is often disappointed with the new recruit, who they find to be overly ambitious and unrealistic in their personal expectations, too theoretical in their approach to work, and naive with respect to knowledge of how things really work in the business world (Schein, 1964). They often need to be "broken in."

While this phase may result in some dissatisfaction and often turnover among those who did not have a realistic preview of the job (Wanous,

1980), it is also a time during which the individual is especially suscep-
tible to major change in behavior, attitudes, and even values. In fact,
many organizations intentionally create an environment which causes
the new recruit to question past behaviors, feelings, and beliefs (Sathe,
1985). Consider the rigors of Marine Corps boot camp or the experiences
of new members of certain religious cults. It has recently been noted
that many business firms with strong corporate cultures do much of the
same thing. Pascale (1984) describes a process in which "hazing" and
"debasement," and working in the "trenches" is combined with exposure to strong role models, folklore, tradition, and corporate values to
mold the new recruit into the corporate image.

What kinds of experiences should the business firm provide for the
new employee so that his or her career within the organization is not
derailed before it begins? There is general consensus that the following
human resource management practices will help to make the transition
a successful one.

- Recruitment and selection programs that are based on an understanding of the personal characteristics required for successful
  performance in the entry-level position as well as on later jobs
  to which promotion is likely.
- Selection using valid measures of these personal characteristics.
- The use of realistic job previews to acquaint the prospective employee with the negative as well as the positive aspects of the job
  and the company.
- The design and use of effective orientation programs.
- If necessary, the use of effective training programs.
- The development and consistent use of appropriate socialization
  practices.

Since it has received less attention in the human resource literature
than the other points listed above and because of its great importance
in helping to launch young careers, we will discuss the meaning of
"appropriate socialization practices." Organizational socialization may
be defined as, "The process by which individuals are transformed from
total outsiders of companies to participating, effective members of them"
(Feldman, 1988, p. 71). This process actually begins for many people
before they enter the organization. "Anticipatory socialization" refers
to the fact that individuals may begin to change their habits and attitudes
even before they start working (Van Maanen, 1976). For example, business students often start to dress, talk, and perhaps even think like
business people as a result of their educational programs and part-time
and summer work experiences.

The second stage of socialization is referred to as "encounter" or "breaking in" (Feldman, 1988). This phase lasts three or four months and involves learning new tasks and organizational practices, and establishing new social relationships. The final stage is known as "change and acquisition" (Greenhaus, 1987) or "settling in" (Feldman, 1988). During this phase the "metamorphosis" of the individual is completed. This stage typically begins during the third or fourth month and ends by the sixth or seventh month (Feldman, 1988), although in some situations it may well last longer. By this time the individual should have settled down, adjusted to the new situation, and be ready to make more meaningful contributions to the organization. The new person is now able to play a more active role—they have "learned the ropes" and been accepted by the organization. This acceptance is often marked by some symbolic action that signifies passage through the probationary testing period. The newly initiated member may receive a change in job title, a transfer, a promotion, a raise, or a party; or the shift in status may be signaled more subtly by sharing more "secret" information with the new person. Successful socialization results in mutual acceptance. Not only does the organization accept the individual but the junior member of the organization agrees to a "psychological contract" in which he or she accepts the demands and expectations of the job and the organization (Schein, 1978).

Organizational socialization should be a mutual influence process. A business organization must not try to make every new recruit into an exact clone of their stereotype of the successful manager. Clearly, the new employee must fit in; however, too much conformity is harmful to the individual and to the organization. Youthful enthusiasm and fresh ideas will soon be forgotten in an environment that discourages or punishes them. A capability that is critical for survival in today's business world is the ability to be innovative and to change and adapt to ever-changing threats and opportunities. Organizations must nurture this natural talent of youth and try to re-awaken it in older employees.

Schein (1978) has noted that there exist two types of norms within organizations: pivotal and peripheral. Pivotal norms are essential for successful performance within the particular organization. For example, a businessperson must not be opposed to the existence of the free market system. In a strong corporate culture he or she should accept a small number of core values. However, he or she need not accept the firm's short-term goals or current product line as the only way to achieve those goals within that system. The latter would be more peripheral norms. With respect to these norms, there are three individual responses to socialization: "rebellion" (the complete rejection of all organizational norms), "conformity" (the complete acceptance of all norms), and "creative individualism" (the acceptance of only the most pivotal norms).

Today more than ever creative individualism is the most desirable outcome for both the individual and the firm.

The individual should not see the first year of employment as a period of "brainwashing" or as a "sink or swim" trial; rather, he or she should be made to feel that they are members of a fraternity/sorority pledge class; and that they have been selected because they are outstanding individuals and may have much to contribute to the group. First, however, they have to learn the values of the current sisters and brothers; decide whether they fit in and whether the benefits of membership are worth the costs; and prove their commitment to the group by suffering through a somewhat uncomfortable initiation process.

There are other social and psychological benefits of this process. Human decision processes are such that an uncomfortable feeling of "cognitive dissonance" (Festinger, 1957) occurs when we perceive discrepancies among our behaviors, feelings, and beliefs. Such a feeling is very likely to occur during group initiation or during organizational socialization. Having chosen to join a frat or a firm and then discovering that the initial experience is very dissatisfying creates an unsettling state of mind. The cognitive dissonance may be resolved by changing the decision (that is, leaving the situation). However, if one chooses to stay, then the decision is often justified by changing the perception of the worth of the group. We develop more positive feelings toward the group and are more likely to accept the beliefs and values of the group in order to justify our suffering through the initiation/socialization process.

In addition, new recruits are often put through the socialization process as a group. The more demanding the experience, the more likely that this group will become a tight knit, cohesive unit whose members trust one another, can openly communicate with one another, and can depend upon one another throughout their careers. In order to facilitate this group identification, the firm should provide adequate opportunities for the new recruits to communicate, commiserate, and coalesce as a unit.

While there are many similarities, the end of the socialization period may not be as clear in the business firm as it is in the sorority or fraternity. Schein (1978) has identified four continuing issues to which the junior businessperson must attend. First, there must continue to be improvement in performance on the job. Second, the employee typically must increase his or her technical competence in a specialized functional area (e.g., accounting, computers, marketing). Third, the new employee must be willing to still accept a relatively junior role in the organization. Fourth, this is the time to re-evaluate the choice of profession and organization. Incorrect career decisions are often made; however, the sooner they are altered the sooner the individual may begin making progress on a more satisfying and productive track.

THE IMPORTANCE OF EARLY MOVEMENT

While often described as following the socialization or establishment stage, the advancement stage (Hall, 1976) actually may begin sooner. "Fast track" or "high potential" employees are expected to start proving their worth to the organization immediately.

Research within the former Bell System indicated that early job challenge could have a long-lasting, positive effect on an individual's career. Berlew and Hall (1966) studied management trainees over a four year period. Those who were given more demanding initial assignments were more successful than those who received less demanding jobs. Initial job challenge led to quicker promotion to higher management positions (Bray, Campbell, & Grant, 1974). Also, Bell System managers who experienced greater job challenge during their first eight years had reached higher levels in their companies after 20 years (Howard & Bray, 1988).

This phenomenon is generally explained as a socialization effect. The early challenge, which is successfully met, causes the new employee to internalize high standards of work behavior (Berlew & Hall, 1966). They experience a sense of psychological success which boosts their self-esteem and their feelings of competence and motivates them to seek even more challenge (Hall, 1976). This creates a self perpetuating "success cycle."

While individual ability and motivation are related to career success in large organizations (Howard & Bray, 1988), there are alternative explanations for the early job challenge results and there are other factors which strongly affect career attainment. Promotion decisions are not (and should not be) made solely on the basis of individual characteristics such as ability, personality, and motivation. Such information is extremely valuable for selection decisions and for identifying high "potential" employees. However, potential and performance are two quite different things. In their very impressive 20 year study of managers in Bell System companies, Howard and Bray (1988) found that of those predicted to reach middle management (high potential managers) by the initial assessment center evaluation, 60 percent had been successful. Of course, that means that 40 percent of those with potential did not actually perform as predicted.

In business organizations, most promotions are based on performance—primarily most recent performance, but also past performance. In fact there is evidence that one's entire career history (performance, promotions, transfers, etc.) has a significant impact on ultimate career success. Our position in this book is that promotions are made in the hope that the manager being moved up will have the ability and motivation to perform in the new job. The ability and motivation are not typically measured directly, instead they are inferred from "signals" in the candidate's track record—his or her career history. What signals are important, long-term predictors of upward mobility? We will look at research studies that have attempted to answer that question.

RESEARCH ON EARLY MOBILITY

Movement in a hierarchical organization may be described in a number of ways. An individual may move laterally: from job to job within the same functional area (for example, production management); across different functions; even across different divisions or businesses. Researchers may record the number of such moves, the frequency of moving, or the average time in each job. Of course, a member of the organization may move upward. The velocity of upward movement may be determined by examining the rate of such movement over time. We can also examine changes in the speed of vertical movement—does the movement accelerate or decelerate at different points in the career? There is also a third type of movement which is very important but not easily measured.

This is "radial" movement within a career cone (Schein, 1978). Using this model, one may move vertically—from the base of the cone toward the point, horizontally—changing position on the surface of the cone (at the same height between base and point), and radially—toward the inner core of the cone. Radial movement implies that greater trust is being placed in the member and that they will be given access to special privileges and more confidential information. This typically accompanies vertical movement but not always. Sometimes people are "kicked upstairs"—being promoted to a less critical, and probably dead-end activity (Schein, 1978). Unfortunately, access to this type of information is difficult to obtain and therefore there has been little empirical research on this kind of movement.

The research on early career issues includes the Bell System studies described above (Berlew & Hall, 1966; Bray, Campbell, & Grant, 1974). In this research, the positive effects of early job challenge were explained as the result of improvement in the confidence and motivation of the new employees. However, an alternative explanation is that successful performance on these challenging jobs sent a positive signal to higher management about the ability of the new member, and that this signal influenced later promotion decisions. In fact, both effects were probably in action. Other research on the early career phase has focused on the signaling explanation.

The Tournament Mobility Model

The importance of early promotions was made clear by the research of Rosenbaum (1979, 1984). He found that those who were promoted early rose to higher levels than those who were not. The first group remained in the "tournament," but those not promoted in the early rounds were effectively eliminated from later competition. If this model accurately describes promotion patterns in most business firms, the implications for individuals and for organizations are that success in the early years is critically important—without it the career is dead.

The ramifications may be appreciated by considering two earlier "ideal" sociological models of occupational mobility: contest and sponsored mobility (Turner, 1960). Our nation in general, and the business community in particular, values the norm of open opportunity. Everyone, regardless of origins or past positions, should have an equal opportunity to continue to compete for advancement. This is the contest mobility norm. In this system, decisions about who will move up are delayed as long as possible and individuals are allowed maximum freedom of career mobility. This model would create high levels of employee motivation since everyone—the mailboy as well as the Harvard MBA—has a shot at promotion. It provides continuing opportunity for "late bloomers," assures a large pool of candidates from which to choose when filling positions, and would result in better quality management selection decisions. The Japanese would appear to use this type of system; however, as we will show later in this chapter, that may not be the case.

In a sponsored mobility system, decisions are made as early as possible. The advantage of this process comes from the efficiencies of specialized socialization, training, and development. Turner (1960) used the British educational system as an example of the application of this norm. Of course, the testing and separation of students into various tracks also occurs in this country. In addition, our business firms, especially those with the most sophisticated human resource management systems, such as AT&T and the Bell operating companies, have relied heavily on this model. Howard and Bray (1988) have shown how assessment center scores and predictions have held up over 20 years of management careers.

It is interesting to note that the purpose of the assessment center is to create a more open contest—at least prior to the assessment. Consistent with their policy of promoting from within, AT&T needed a method to accurately predict management potential among craftsmen and technical personnel whose current jobs did not allow them opportunities to display supervisory or managerial skills. The assessment center gives these employees a chance to demonstrate such abilities under controlled conditions with objective evaluation. Without this their talents might never be noticed.

However, following the assessment, the norms of sponsored mobility appear to hold. The employees who do well in the assessment center will be provided with opportunities and experiences that are designed to develop their potential. While not officially out of the running, the others will not have comparable attention paid to their careers. In addition, the rating from the assessment sends a strong and clear signal to higher level decision makers about who should be promoted.

In the tournament system, a similar early decision is made. Here it is based on an evaluation of early performance as indicated by promotion to a higher level job. The model proposes that business firms initially allow all their members to compete in an open tournament. However, those who lose in the first round (by not being promoted) are eliminated from further competition. Furthermore, the remaining contestants must continue to win each successive contest or they too will be eliminated. Rosenbaum's research, which will be described in more detail below, strongly demonstrated the existence of such a system.

Another closely related issue addressed by Rosenbaum was whether "historical" or "ahistorical" models best describe career paths and chances for further mobility. Ahistorical models assume that an individual's chances of moving to a new position are a function of his or her current state or position; earlier, historical career information does not matter. Kelley (1973), in a study of occupational attainment, found that status at various points in life depended mainly on occupational status in the preceding period. Earlier positions only indirectly affected current status: "past failures are forgiven, and past successes are forgotten" (Kelley, 1973, p. 492). These are also known as "path independent" models because it does not matter how you reached your current position. The tournament model and the studies of early job challenge do stress the importance of early positions, and thus are historical or path dependent models.

Rosenbaum obtained data supporting the tournament concept from an "old, well established, autonomous, investor-owned firm, having offices in many cities and towns across a large geographic region" (1984, p. 4). The firm employed between 10,000 and 15,000 persons during the period studied, 1962–75. The firm was not identified further.

Focusing on movement through the five lowest levels in the firm, Rosenbaum (1979) analyzed personnel data for 671 employees who entered the firm between 1960 and 1962 and who remained through 1975. The results indicated that those promoted in the first period (the first three years) were much more likely to receive further promotions and reach higher levels than those who were not promoted early. In fact, only those promoted in the earliest period were able to reach middle management within the 13 year span of the study.

In a later analysis of the same group, Rosenbaum (1984) used a different measure of career attainment. Job status (a measure that reflected the demands and requirements of each job) was predicted both by individual attributes and by early job status. In addition, job status in 1962 had an effect on status attained by 1975 that was independent of intermediate job status (in 1965). This supported the lasting effects of early position.

Signaling Theory

Rosenbaum (1984) suggested signaling theory (Spence, 1973) as an explanation of the tournament pattern of mobility. This theory says that early movement is important as a criterion for later promotion because more objective standards are not available. Decision makers rely on the rate of upward mobility in relation to age or tenure as a signal of the individual's ability.

We agree with this explanation. Despite models prescribing how to improve the process (Stumpf & London, 1981), those who make decisions about promotions often work with very subjective information and operate under conditions of bounded rationality (March & Simon, 1958). Modern human resource information systems and skills inventories will never replace personal contacts as a key factor in decisions concerning selection or promotion. Decision makers often conduct a limited sequential search for acceptable candidates for a position. They will first consider familiar candidates and those who have had experience similar to that required in the open position (Campbell, Dunnette, Lawler, & Weick, 1970). A high level in the organization and an impressive track record contribute to an employee's familiarity to decision makers, increase the individual's managerial experience, and promote an image of high potential. In her case study of mobility in one large corporation, Kanter (1977) discussed the importance of such visibility.

Another recent study (Sheridan, Slocum, Buda, & Thompson, 1990) has investigated the importance of early signals of employee ability and the generalizability of the tournament model. Also investigated were the effects of the "power" of the department in which the new employee started his or her career.

According to strategic contingency theory (Salancik & Pfeffer, 1974, 1977), the departments within an organization may acquire differing amounts of power as a result of differences in their ability to deal with critical environmental exigencies. For example, in a consumer products company, the marketing department may have a great deal of power; while in a high tech company, the power may lie in the engineering or research and development department. Pfeffer (1981) has noted how the organization will benefit by allowing power differences to influence the executive succession process—those who reach the top should be the ones who have the most critical skills. Sheridan et al. (1990) hypothesized that power differences would effect early career mobility as well. Those who start in powerful departments have the advantage of mentors who may intercede favorably on their behalf, assist them in gaining visibility to the top managers, and provide them with important information earlier than others. Increased visibility, networking, and resources will provide the new recruit with a lasting boost for his or her career.

Sheridan et al. (1990) studied all employees who started a management career with a large public utility during a ten year period from 1977 to 1987. The researchers believed that a strong signal about an employee's ability would be transmitted by entrance into their first management position through the company's management trainee program. Management trainees were carefully screened college graduates who were introduced to the company's officers and department heads as the future leaders of the firm. They completed a two month orientation program in which they rotated through various departments. There were special dinners with officers of the company and group meetings with the vice president of human resources. Each trainee's progress was carefully watched and they were given feedback on job-related as well as personal issues. After the orientation, they worked as trainees in one department for 12 months; and then upon successful completion of the trainee year, they received their first management position.

Other managers were hired from outside without a training program or were promoted into management from non-management jobs. These employees received none of the special attention described above.

Departmental power, defined as "the ability of a department to influence other departments to bring about its desired outcomes" (Daft, 1986, p. 385), was rated by 23 senior executives of the firm. Six departments were classified as having a high level of power in this firm; ten fell into the medium power category; and another six were low power departments. The high power functions were customer service, distribution, operations, engineering, marketing, and the executive offices. It was felt that the members of these departments dealt with the most critical organizational contingencies.

The trainees generally showed faster career mobility than the other groups; that is, they changed jobs more frequently. Salary increases were greater for those in the trainee program, but this was mainly a catch-up effect since they started lower than the other new managers.

Department power affected career progress in a number of ways. Internal movements tended to be to new departments with the same level of power. Those who started in high power departments moved more quickly and experienced greater increases in salary than those who started in the low power functions. This effect diminished as the employees changed jobs, however.

The number of different jobs held was strongly related to salary increment. This led the researchers to suggest that successful new managers in this firm may be those who "churn" through the largest number of jobs.

It should be noted that the effects described in this study were not of large magnitude. The differences in job tenure that were attributed to career start or to department power were measured in months. Salary gaps and differences in job level were relatively small.

The tournament mobility concept received mixed support in this study. Tenure half-lives were determined for trainees, direct hires, and internal promotions. This is a measure of the point in time at which 50 percent of the managers have left a position. "Fast starters" were those who left their first job in less time than the half-life. Those who stayed longer than the half-life were classified as "slow starters." Fast starters continued to move more quickly. They had an average of 4.3 months less time in each job held after their first management position. However, 40 percent of the moves in this study were lateral transfers. The fast starters attained only slightly higher levels than the slow starters. Overall, the differences were not statistically significant.

The authors point out that the career management practices of this firm are consistent with their corporate strategy. This is a "steady state" firm (Kerr & Slocum, 1987) which is committed to its current business. Such firms invest heavily in management development in order to help employees understand the entire business and to create a cohesive corporate culture through extensive socialization.

The Japanese Approach

Japanese management development techniques are believed to be quite different from those found in most American firms. Ouchi (1981) compared the management styles in typical Japanese firms (Type J) with those of typical American firms (Type A), and then described the Type Z American firm which exhibits many practices similar to the Japanese. One characteristic of the Japanese firm is "slow evaluation and promotion." Ouchi describes a fictitious young man—Sagao, who enters a major bank after graduation from the University of Tokyo.

For ten years, Sagao will receive exactly the same increases in pay and exactly the same promotions as the 15 other young men who have entered with him. Only after ten years will anyone make a formal evaluation of Sagao and his peers; not until then will one person receive a larger promotion than another. (p. 22)

This system encourages cooperative behavior oriented toward long-term results. It should also ensure that Sagao and his peers will continue to be highly motivated during this ten year period of evaluation and that the best promotion decisions will ultimately be made. This process is very close to the contest mobility norm described earlier—everyone is in the contest for as long as possible.

Recent research, however, indicates that even in Japan open contests may not be reality. Wakabayashi, Graen, and associates (1988) have followed a group of 71 Japanese managers through their first 13 years of job tenure with "one of the leading corporations in Japan." This group of male college graduates joined the company in 1972, having passed an assessment center administered in 1971. The career paths of these young men appear to have been determined very early.

Measures of career attainment in 1985 such as bonus, salary, speed of promotion (from 1978 to 1985), and a promotability index (based on 1980–1985 evaluations) were predicted by ratings obtained during the first three years of employment (1972–1974). The predictors were job performance, the 1974 promotability index, and a measure of the quality of "vertical exchange" over the first three years. This last variable was measured by having the new recruits respond to a questionnaire which assesses the leader-member relationship (Graen & Cashman, 1975). A ranking of the prestige of their university predicted speed of promotion, promotability, and salary; while a measure of potential from the assessment center also predicted speed of promotion.

It was hypothesized that later measures of performance and promotability would improve upon the prediction based on the early indicators. This was not the case. Evaluations during the seventh year did not predict thirteenth year performance any better than the third year measures.

Although the final outcomes seem to have been determined in three years, no one was actually promoted for seven years. All of the managers were promoted in the first round, although the promotions came at three different times over a one year period. About three years later a second round of promotions occurred, again at three different times. In another three years, promotions came again, but this time to only 32 of the 71 managers. The small differences in the timing of the earlier promotions proved to be significant. Of the 32 who received the final promotions, 28 had been promoted in the first group six years earlier, and were also in the first group for the second promotion. The other four had been in the second group for the first promotion but in the first group for the second round of promotions.

This study clearly contradicts our earlier beliefs about Japanese promotion systems. Rather than having a relatively open contest, this company at least used a strong tournament model with some features of the sponsored mobility approach. The timing of the first promotion (after seven years) strongly predicted the third promotion (after 13 years). However, the information available after seven years did not predict any better than that which had been gathered in the first three years. This is consistent with the findings of Rosenbaum (1979). The winners are determined in the first three years of the competition. The fast tracks are partially set even before the contest begins, as evidenced by the impact of university ratings and assessment center potential ratings.

The authors of the study believe that those young managers who developed high quality relations with their superiors became part of an "in group" who began to move upward and inward toward the core of the career cone as proposed by Schein (1978). Those who were not able to do this found themselves on an "out group" track which leads laterally around the outside of the cone.

This very structured career system is administered by a highly respected management development section that has tremendous power. Their recommendations were almost always followed—top management approval would be required to change a decision made by this group. In this company, it was felt that such critical, long-term management development issues should be handled by a specialized staff, not entirely by line management.

CONCLUSIONS

There is much to be accomplished during the first few years of a career. The new employee must learn his or her job; must learn to work with peers, superiors, and possibly subordinates; must learn all the written and unwritten rules of the game; and must learn all about the corporate culture in order to be able to function competently. In addition, studies cited here indicate that the new employees must also prove their ability to perform at a high level and start to move very early—at least by the third year of employment.

Let us briefly review the evidence. The Bell System studies showed that those who received challenging first year assignments were more successful later on. Rosenbaum found that only those who were promoted within the first three years of their career made it to middle management within 13 years. Sheridan et al. found that entering the firm through a trainee program and starting in a powerful department enhanced one's career mobility. Finally, we saw that even in Japan career track decisions are made very early. The data reviewed so far seem to clearly describe sponsored and tournament models. You must prove yourself to be a winner very early or else you are out of the race.

What are the implications of such practices? We feel that there are generally negative consequences, both for the individual and for the organization. The individual may be still adjusting to an intense socialization experience—still "learning the ropes." The fast starter is likely to be the person whose anticipatory socialization was particularly effective or whose personality and family and school background prepared them well for this particular firm. But what about the person who does not "hit the ground running"? What about the "late bloomer"? There is little or no opportunity for this person in many firms. Often they do not know how limited their chances for upward mobility are, and they continue to work hard for many years, always expecting that maybe the next time they will get that ever elusive promotion. When they do realize that they are out of the competition, it may be too late for a change. The firm and the society are left with many frustrated employees with very negative attitudes toward their work and their employer.

Why do business firms make such decisions so early? The organization may feel that the development of top management skills takes many years and therefore early identification of management potential is necessary. But how accurate can such early evaluations be? We know that the necessary mix of technical, human, and conceptual skills changes as one rises in an organization. Can performance on an entry-level job predict performance as a top executive 20 years later? Can the problem be solved by using well designed assessment centers?

The 20 year longitudinal study by Howard and Bray (1988) provides us with the best data on this question, both because of the length of the study and because the initial assessments were never used in making the later promotion decisions. There were statistically significant correlations between the level reached within the organization and certain measures taken 20 years earlier. The best predictor was education—was the man a college graduate or not? Other predictors, such as personality and motivation, ability, and performance on managerial simulations (in-basket, competitive group discussion, business game, and interview) were more effective in forecasting which of the non-college men would be successful than they were with the college group. For the college men there were fewer significant predictors and the strength of the correlations was in the .20 to .30 range. This indicates that less than ten percent of the variance in career attainment can be explained by these factors. Predictions were made of those who would "succeed" (reach middle management or above). For the college group, almost 45 percent of those predicted to move up did reach level four or higher. Of those predicted to not be successful, slightly over 20 percent reached the same levels.

From an academic or scientific point of view, this is very impressive. However, let us consider the practical implications. If this information had been used, a strong signal would have been given to immediate supervisors and to higher level management that one group had potential and should be moved up, while the others could not and should not make it. Without this signal to help them, over 55 percent of the "high potential" group did not move up, while over 20 percent of those who might have been ruled out of further consideration for upward movement actually did make it.

The figures from the Howard and Bray (1988) research indicate the difficulty of predicting at the middle management level. Prediction at higher levels is much less accurate. Therefore, managed career systems—sponsored or tournament mobility systems which create separate and usually irreversible tracks for employees based upon early assessment or early performance—are less efficient from the firm's point of view than are more open competitions. Management development is an expensive investment on the part of the firm. However, managed career systems often cause the firm to invest heavily in the wrong people and to miss many other attractive candidates for promotion. Therefore we recommend that business firms try to delay such decisions as long as possible—at least five to ten years, if not indefinitely. Create truly open contests in which everyone, at every point in their career, still has a shot at a step up. Employees will be more motivated and productive and the task of finding talented candidates for upper management positions will be made much easier since there will be so many more people to choose from.

In the next chapter we will see that early identification and development is only one of a number of options for career systems and that career systems should be related to corporate strategy. We will further discuss the advantages and disadvantages, both to the firm and to the individual, of the various alternatives.

3

The Early Competition: Tournament or Horse Race?

In the last chapter we reviewed the well accepted notion that early promotions are necessary in order for a career to progress—the tournament mobility model (Rosenbaum, 1979, 1984). We also discussed the drawbacks of such career systems. In this chapter we will show that other career mobility systems do exist and show the importance of other early "signals," such as lateral mobility and the early functional area. We will also describe the relationship between career systems and corporate strategy and discuss further the advantages and disadvantages of emphasizing high rates of mobility (both horizontal and vertical) within the career system.

QUESTIONS ABOUT THE EARLY SIGNALS

Only two empirical studies have clearly demonstrated the existence of tournament mobility (Rosenbaum, 1979; Wakabayashi et al., 1988) and only one of these was conducted in an American firm (see Chapter 2). One other study described in Chapter 2 (Sheridan et al., 1990) found only mixed support for this model: "fast starters" did not reach higher levels in the firm but did have significantly shorter time in later jobs as compared to "slow starters." However, in this analysis, no distinction was made between promotions and lateral job movement. The fast starters did not necessarily move upward, they just moved sooner, and they continued to move more quickly; but many of the moves were just transfers. More moves did lead to greater salary increments. Career mobility was also enhanced by starting in the company's trainee program and by starting in a powerful department.

Other investigators have noted similar problems in measuring career progression. Many "promotions" and interorganizational moves do not necessarily represent upward mobility for they may actually be lateral moves (Cawsey, Nicholson, & Alban-Metcalfe, 1985; Stewart & Gudy-kunst, 1982). Veiga (1983) found time spent in a first position within a firm to be strongly related to average time per position later in a career. This again seems to imply that early movement leads to later success. However, he also showed that a very rapid rate of movement was associated with lateral moves and transfers and that managers from different functional areas move at different rates (Veiga, 1985). Managers on a "slow track" moved less frequently, but they reached the same level as those on the "fast track" by taking larger steps.

The motivational effects of the challenging first job have also been challenged. Taylor (1981) conducted a laboratory study in which subjects performed a variety of tasks, such as puzzles and memory exercises. The challenge of their first task assignment had less effect on performance standards, attitudes, and perceptions of competence than did the challenge of later tasks. A large survey by Williams and Van Sell (1985) sampled over 2,000 employees of hundreds of business, nonprofit, and educational organizations. In this study, good, challenging first jobs were negatively associated with self-reports of career advancement. Advancement was measured by numbers of promotions, jobs, functional areas, and organizations, all statistically controlled for numbers of years worked.

We believe that lateral mobility should not be confused with upward mobility but that it is probably a signal that higher level decision makers use when deciding who to promote. Kanter (1977) has described this as a factor which predicts chances of promotion in a large industrial firm. This may be because those who make such decisions see breadth of knowledge of different areas as a prerequisite for higher levels of responsibility (Kotter, 1982); or it may be that having held multiple jobs merely increases an individual's visibility within the firm.

Another variable that may act as a signal affecting chances for promotion is the functional background of the employee. Several studies have noted that firms in certain industries tend to choose their chief executives from particular functional areas (Piercy & Forbes, 1981—see also Chapter 7). Pfeffer (1981) developed a model of executive succession in which different functional areas gain power as a result of their abilities to deal with critical environmental issues.

At a lower level, Vardi and Hammer (1977) showed that the type of job technology—long-linked, mediating, or intensive—used by rank and file workers within a plant affected their chances for mobility. In a comparison of managers drawn from three similar major manufacturing firms, Veiga (1985) found that career patterns were related to functional area. The fast track managers, who moved frequently but often laterally, were likely to be from areas representing mediating technologies like marketing and personnel, and the slow track managers, who moved less frequently but more often vertically, were likely to be from intensive technologies like research and development and engineering.

The effect of business strategy on opportunities for promotion in different functions was studied by Slocum, Cron, Hansen, and Rawlings (1985). They found that in a defender firm, in which financial and production issues were more critical than growth and new products, there were more plateaued sales people than in an analyzer firm, which would be seeking new products and markets. The ability of different functions to contribute to the critical business issues seems to affect career paths.

In the next section we will present a study conducted by one of this book's coauthors (Forbes, 1987) which tested the tournament mobility model and also investigated two other promotion signals: number of different jobs held and early functional area.

TESTING THE TOURNAMENT MOBILITY MODEL

The strict tournament model implies that employees place out of major organizational tournaments when they fail in very early contests, and consequently they have little or no chance to be as successful as those who win the early contests. No data will fit this ideal model perfectly. However, modified models of sports competition may better fit the organizational promotion process. I considered three different sets of rules, varying with respect to the effects of early success:

1. Single elimination tournament—only those who win early contests are eligible to compete for the highest positions.
2. Round robin tournament—an early record of winning counts, but the major predictor of success is later competition—one loss does not necessarily mean elimination.
3. Horse race—early success may give a candidate a head start, but there are no extra points for an early lead. Later position is the best predictor of success.

Three hypotheses corresponded to these rules:

Hypothesis 1: All those who reach the highest levels in a tournament will have won in the early contest.

Hypothesis 2: Recent position will best predict final attainment, but early position will add significantly to the variance accounted for.

Hypothesis 3: Later position will best predict final attainment and early position will not add to the variance accounted for.

The first of these three hypotheses concerning the effects of prior promotions states the theory of the tournament mobility model, the second proposes a less strict form of path dependence, and the third implies path independence in the employee's careers.

In framing hypotheses concerning the two other types of signals that may affect decisions on promotions—functional area background and the number of jobs held—I paid close attention to the research setting, because the role and nature of the signals will vary with organizational characteristics. The data for this study were gathered from a firm in the oil and gas industry. Any firm competing in this industry in the 1970s was very much dependent on its technical experts. Critical competitive issues included the highly uncertain activity of exploration for new resources as well as complex problems of production, transportation, and processing. In addition, on the assumption that oil prices would remain high, this firm and many others were experimenting in areas such as the production of synthetic fuels and engaging in much basic research and development. Therefore, I hypothesized that a technical background would be valued by this firm and therefore related to greater career attainment during this period.

> Hypothesis 4: Final level of career attainment will be positively related to having initially held a position within a technical area.

I felt that the ideal candidate for promotion would have a technical background, but would also have experience in other functional areas.

> Hypothesis 5: Final level of career attainment will be positively related to the number of different jobs held.

Finally, I believed that each of these signals provides unique information. Therefore,

> Hypothesis 6: Early career attainment, initial technical function, and the number of different jobs held will each contribute significantly to the prediction of final career attainment.

RESEARCH METHODS

Setting

A large domestic oil company with personnel widely dispersed across the United States served as the research setting. The economic conditions within this industry and the financial position of this particular firm improved dramatically during the 1970s, the period of the study. During this period, the firm also underwent a major transition in business strategy. An earlier emphasis on the processing and regional marketing of petroleum products gave way to a new emphasis on producing, transporting, and distributing crude oil. The firm was also actively exploring alternative energy sources. The number of employees remained relatively constant—about 22,000—during this period, and there were no major changes in human resource management policies.

Data Collection and Population

The data were obtained from the firm's computerized records. Since the study focused on early upward movement into managerial positions, I conducted a search for all exempt, or salaried, employees still with the firm in 1981 who had been hired into entry-level, non-management positions in 1968, 1969, or 1970. Some typical entry-level jobs were accounting analyst, field auditor, sales trainee, junior engineer, junior chemist, programmer, and staff assistant. One hundred and eighty cases were found that met these criteria. Demographic data such as age, gender, and education were not available.

Measures

The company's detailed systems for job classification and salary grades were the primary data. Classification codes fell into three general categories, which I used to identify initial job functions: (1) technical/professional—engineers and scientists; (2) administrative—administrators, accountants, sales/marketing personnel, computer specialists; and (3) other—laboratory technicians, clerks, administrative assistants, customer representatives, draftsmen, and so forth.

Examination of the list of each employee's job codes provided the number of different jobs each had held. I counted only a change in functional area or level of responsibility as a different job. For example, moving from chemist to senior chemist was not counted as a job change, although it would result in a higher salary grade; moving from chemist to personnel specialist or to manager—chemical analysis was counted as a job change.

The actual salary grades served as one measure of career attainment. Company job analysts determined these grades, which were similar to Hay system grades and also similar to the measure of job status used in the Rosenbaum (1984) study. These grades reflected the worth of the employee's contribution to the company. As in many technically oriented firms, there were some technical specialists with high salary grades who did not manage large groups of people. However, their grades did reflect their status, salary, and career attainment. I measured career attainment yearly, using the highest grade attained during the calendar year.

Rosenbaum's early report (1979) used only broad management level to measure career attainment. To facilitate comparisons with that study, I created a second measure, grouping the salary grades into five divisions corresponding to levels in the organization. These ranged from non-management to upper-middle management, immediately below the vice presidential level. Promotions were defined as movements from a lower level to a higher one.

Two other differences existed between the measures used in Rosenbaum's 1979 study and the present one. Data were available for every year in this study, not merely for three to four year intervals as in the earlier research. Also, Rosenbaum identified movements by calendar year. However, since his group included employees hired in 1960, 1961, and 1962, those promoted in a given calendar year—1965, for example—may have had from three to five years tenure with the firm. In this study, I identified movements according to how long each individual had been with the firm, not by calendar year.

RESULTS

Analysis by Level

Comparing this study's data on movement through the general levels of the organizational hierarchy and Rosenbaum's 1979 data required that competition periods be defined. Because such a division is somewhat arbitrary, I followed his choice of three to four year periods, which allowed the time span to be divided into three portions.

Examining the actual pattern of promotions confirmed that natural breakpoints occurred at three to four year intervals. Inspection of a career tree for the cohort indicated that the firm promoted seven employees one level (into lower management) within their first four years. No one received another promotion until year 5. Furthermore, in years 5, 6, and 7, six employees were promoted to the second level of management, then none were promoted farther until year 8. Therefore, I defined years 1 through 4 as the first competition period and years 5 through 7 as the second competition period.

Comparing the progress of the seven employees who won (i.e., were promoted) the earliest competition with those who lost (were not promoted) shows that the early move increased the chances for further movement. However, many of those who did not move in the first period also moved up later. Of the seven early winners, three were still in lower management at the end of the 11 year study, two were in lower-middle management, one was in middle management, and one had reached

Table 3.1
Initial Job Category by Final Levels

	Final Levels – Year 11					
Job Category	Non-Management	Lower Management	Lower-Middle Management	Middle Management	Upper-Middle Management	Total
Adminis-trative	37	17	6	3	0	63
Technical	13	26	12	4	4	59
Other	46	5	5	2	0	58
Totals	96	48	23	9	4	180

upper-middle management. Looking at the "losers" showed that over half were still in non-management positions at the end of the study. Slightly over one-quarter had reached lower management; however, 21 of these employees had been promoted to lower-middle management, eight to middle management, and three made it all the way to upper-middle management.

Attainment by the end of the second competition was more strongly related to position at the end of the study; however, there was again evidence of later initial movement. Of the four employees who made upper-middle management, one had not yet received his first promotion at the end of the seventh year. Three of the nine who attained the next highest level, middle management, had received no promotions by the end of year seven. Therefore, the results did not support Hypothesis 1—the strict tournament model. It was not necessary to receive a promotion in the first competition or even in the second competition in order to move up later.

The relationship between advancement in the firm and initial job classification was examined. Table 3.1 shows that those who entered the firm in technical positions were very highly represented in management by year 11 and constituted the highest proportions of managers at all levels. In fact, by year 11, 78 percent of the technical entrants were in management positions, in comparison to 41 percent of those who started in administrative positions and 21 percent of those from other entry points. These results strongly supported Hypothesis 4.

An interesting interaction was discovered between entry position and movement during the various competition periods. In the first competition period, six of the seven early promotions to lower management were from administrative positions. By the end of the second competition period, there was no significant relationship between entry position and level attained. However, as seen in Table 3.1, by year 11 technical employees were way ahead. It seems that the timing of promotions was related to functional background and that initial functional area was more important than early promotion in determining who reached the higher levels.

More detailed analyses were possible by using salary grades instead of general management level. I looked at the intercorrelations among salary grade level each year, type of entry position, and number of different jobs held. These statistics may be found in Forbes (1987). Salary grades in the early years were related to grades in the later years but the correlations were relatively weak. The highest correlations were found between adjacent years. In addition, correlations among later years were consistently stronger than those among the earlier years, a pattern likely in any contest where all start in approximately the same position and spread out over time. Later grade levels clearly predicted final success in terms of salary grade much better than early grade levels.

The correlations also confirmed the interactions between type of entry position and time on the job. Having an administrative entry position was related to higher salary grade in years 1 through 5, but not in years 6 through 11. A technical entry position correlated positively with salary grade in years 1 and 2, not in years 3, 4, and 5, but again in years 6 through 11. This indicates that either of these entry points provided an initial advantage. Furthermore, administrative employees maintained their advantage through year 5 but then lost it. Technical employees temporarily lost their advantage following the second year but regained it again from year 6 on. This pattern again suggests that different career patterns exist for administrative versus technical managers.

The data described the careers of only those who stayed with the firm through the entire period studied. Different patterns of retention might also explain the advantage of a technical background. Perhaps superior technical personnel stayed with the firm while superior administrative personnel left. Such movement, which would contribute to different patterns of promotion for the two functions, could result from employees' awareness of differences between internal and external opportunities. However, the data were not available to test these possibilities.

Finally, the number of different jobs held did not make any difference in salary grade in the early years but was related to attainment in years 5 through 11. The number of jobs was not related to entry position. The correlational analysis supported Hypotheses 4 and 5.

Multivariate Analyses

We earlier decided that a strict single elimination tournament (Hypothesis 1) was not descriptive of the career patterns in this company.

Many of those who were passed over the first time were later successful. In addition, later positions and salary grades were better predictors of final positions and salary grades than were the early standings. Hypotheses 2 and 3 dealt with the issue of whether an early record of winning would help one's standing at the end of the contest. That is, are we looking at a round robin tournament—where losses count against you but do not eliminate you—or at a horse race—in which early position may have little or no effect on the final winner.

Hypotheses 2 and 3 were tested using hierarchical regression analysis. This statistical technique allows us to determine whether early progress in the promotion tournament actually adds anything to our ability to predict career attainment. Numerous combinations of early and later years were possible; however, to be consistent with the conventions adopted initially, I chose year 7, the end of the second competition period, as the later year and year 4, the end of the first competition period, as the early year. Year 4 did not add significantly to the variance accounted for. In fact, no earlier year added significantly to predictions based on attainment by year 7. The data were consistent with Hypothesis 3, which supports the ahistorical model of path independence. That means that past history is essentially forgotten and that later, more recent attainments are the best predictors of success.

Finally, I had hypothesized that early career attainment, early position, and the number of different jobs would all make independent contributions to the prediction of later success (Hypothesis 6). Since year 7 was a better predictor of final career attainment than year 4, I decided to investigate whether entry in a technical function and job mobility would add significantly to the already appreciable relationship between years 7 and 11.

By year 7, the end of the second competition period, 38 employees had received at least one promotion, but none had yet moved above lower-middle management. After year 7, small numbers of managers started to reach the highest levels attained during the study. Therefore, year 7 appears to be the year before the final competition begins. I computed a forward stepwise regression, entering year 7 first and entering the two other variables in the order of their contributions to additional predictability. The statistics indicated that all three variables—past attainment, initial function, and number of different jobs—contributed uniquely to the prediction of final career attainment. Early promotions (by year 4) had little impact in comparison to later progress (year 7), functional background, and breadth of experience.

DISCUSSION OF RESEARCH RESULTS

The results of this study offered only weak support for the tournament model of career mobility. Although early promotions were related to later attainment, strict tournament rules were not in force, because the losers—those passed over in the early periods—were later able to move up quickly. In addition, the data did not support the concept of path dependence in which the entire career path is critical. When attainment at the end of the second period of competition was used as the basis for the prediction of final career attainment, attainment after the first stage of competition added nothing to predictions. The results were more closely analogous to a horse race than to a tournament: position out of the gate had relatively little effect in comparison to position entering the home stretch.

Different mobility patterns for administrative and technical personnel may explain in part why the pattern of the early years did not always persist. Those who started in administrative positions began to move up early, but their progress seemed to level off quickly. A technical background meant a longer wait before upward movement; however, for some this was followed by rapid promotion.

The number of different jobs, which in this study meant different functional areas or different levels of managerial responsibility, also predicted higher career attainment. This was previously noted by Kanter (1977) and, since more jobs implies less time in any one position, this finding is also consistent with the research of Sheridan and his colleagues (1990) and Veiga (1983).

Three different types of information: past position, functional background, and the number of different jobs all seemed to act as signals to those making decisions about promotions. These signals were all strongly related to career attainment and together they accounted for 60 percent of the variance in level achieved after 11 years in the firm.

CAREER PATHS FIT CORPORATE NEEDS

The research that has been reviewed here shows that more than one type of career pattern exists. Is there a way to explain the differences? It appears that there is. If we accept the premise that human resource management practices evolve in order to help the organization accomplish its strategic goals, and that successful strategies are those that help the firm to deal with its specific environmental threats and opportunities, then there should be a relationship between human resource practices such as career paths and the organizational setting. Let us review the settings in which different career systems were found.

The AT&T studies showed the importance of successful performance on a challenging first job and the importance of successful performance in an assessment center evaluation (Berlew & Hall, 1966; Bray, Campbell, & Grant, 1974; Howard & Bray, 1988). This indicates that the Bell operating companies emphasized the early identification of management potential and that subsequent promotion opportunities were determined at a very early point in the career. This could be described as sponsored or tournament mobility. The setting was one in which there was a very stable and benevolent environment. At the time, the Bell operating companies were part of a regulated monopoly delivering a service that was based on well established technology. Success was a result of satisfying the customer and the state public utility commissions. Rather tall, centralized, bureaucratic organizations evolved in which everything was done according to Bell System standard operating procedures. Promotion within these firms was a carefully planned process.

The firm studied by Rosenbaum (1979, 1984) was described as an old, well established firm. Examination of the distribution of personnel across hierarchical levels shows that this firm had a rather tall organization chart with narrow spans of control. There were seven levels of management and over 9,365 nonmanagement employees in 1975 (Rosenbaum, 1984: Appendix 2.A). Of course, in this firm there was the clearest evidence of the tournament model of mobility. Other factors also influenced career attainment in this most comprehensive study including education, college selectivity, gender, and race (Rosenbaum, 1984)—indicating the possible sponsoring of certain groups.

The research recently reported by Sheridan et al. (1990) also seems to support a tournament model, although the findings are not that clear due to the fact that "mobility" includes both horizontal and vertical movements. However, the importance of entering the company trainee program and having an early assignment within a powerful department are evidence of a sponsored mobility career system. This company was also a public utility and thus in a regulated, relatively stable environment.

The Japanese study (Wakabayashi et al., 1988) indicated that although promotions are delayed in comparison to American firms, early decisions are made about who will be promoted. Here a relatively strong tournament appeared to be in effect. There were also indications of sponsored mobility, as evidenced by the effects of university ranking and assessment center potential measures. This firm is described only as "one of the leading corporations in Japan." It is a firm in which a desirable starting position is a sales job in a large branch store. This firm was clearly concerned about stability, as shown by the fact that "executives repeatedly emphasized that the future competitive position of their corporation depended critically on their ability to reproduce themselves" (Wakabayashi et al., 1988, p. 226).

Finally, a clearly different career pattern was found in our study of a large natural resource company. Here there were delayed patterns of promotion; early movement was not terribly important. However, early assignment and experience in the technical area was influential, as was the number of different jobs held. The most obvious difference between this firm and all the others was change. This firm was undergoing a major change in business strategy and beginning to experience rapid growth in earnings toward the end of the period studied. As a result, the company was also beginning to recruit and hire more managers and technical personnel from the outside. Internal promotions were not sufficient to satisfy the demand for talented personnel. In addition, it may not have been clear what type of personnel would be needed in the future—thus hindering long-term career planning and management. Highly structured, tournament-based career systems seem to evolve in the more stable or more regulated settings.

CAREER SYSTEMS AND CORPORATE STRATEGY

A number of models exist which may help us to understand the relationship between corporate strategy and career systems. Slocum and Cron (1988) have focused on the two types of business strategies known as defenders and analyzers (Miles & Snow, 1978). Defenders protect their niche in relatively stable environments. They rely on internal efficiency to competitively price their existing products or services. They generally utilize formalized, centralized control systems. There is often functional organization and managers are specialists who are promoted within their specialized areas. Because of the strategic orientation toward low cost, efficient production or operations, the powerful functions in such firms are the financial, accounting, and production areas.

Analyzers operate like defenders in some product markets but also are poised to move quickly to take advantage of new opportunities. There is a greater need for marketing expertise and scanning of the external environment. The firm must be organized to allow for flexibility as well as efficiency.

In the defender firm there is more stability and an emphasis on carefully developing those who are in the critical areas of production and accounting/finance. These firms use extensive on-the-job training and detailed succession planning programs. They typically hire into lower level positions and promote from within. They are likely to rely on early predictors of management potential. Although most managers move up within their functional areas, those who have been identified as high potential employees may have the opportunity to learn various functions.

Because the analyzers are looking for new opportunities as well as trying to protect established areas, the human resource practices and career patterns are different. Some individuals are brought in at entry level and trained within specific functions, but others are recruited from outside to provide immediate expertise. The areas of marketing, engineering, and production are all important. There is more of an emphasis on movement across functions and products as a means of learning about the various departments.

The opportunities for upward mobility varied in relation to strategy within a sample of seven mature industrial products manufacturers studied by Slocum and Cron (1988). The career phenomenon of plateauing occurs when the probability of further promotion in a company becomes very low. By considering both the perceived likelihood of future promotion and the current level of performance, we may classify employees into four categories. "Stars" are employees who are doing well and who are expected to continue to move up in the organization. "Comers" have been identified as having the potential to move up but are currently performing below their potential. "Solid citizens" are performing well but are unlikely to move any farther. And finally, "deadwood" are employees who are performing below standard and have little chance of moving up. Both solid citizens and deadwood are considered plateaued employees. In the defender firms, 66 percent of the employees were plateaued as compared to 27 percent in the analyzer firms. Fifty percent of the employees in the analyzers were considered comers compared to 19 percent in the defender firms, and 23 percent were seen as stars in an analyzer situation in contrast to 15 percent in the defender scenario.

Despite the plateauing, defender employees were less likely to leave the firm but more willing to relocate for another job in the company. They were more concerned about immediate promotions than were the employees of the analyzer firms. Employees in the defender firms also reported less challenge and involvement with their work, less satisfaction, and less visibility and influence to senior managers. In analyzer firms, employees are generally more motivated both by the challenge of their work and by the greater opportunities for advancement.

In the studies that we have reviewed earlier, the firms in which sponsored or tournament mobility systems were the norm appear to be those with a defender strategy: the Bell System companies before deregulation, the established firm studied by Rosenbaum, and the public utility in the Sheridan study. The study in which a horse race was found to describe the promotion pattern was in an analyzer mode. This company's business was changing; it was looking for new opportunities to supplement its traditional strengths; it was looking outside for new managerial and professional talent. The very early identification and development of higher level management candidates was not consistent with the strategy being adapted at this point in time.

The nature of career opportunities can be thought of as part of the organization's reward system. The relationships among business strategy, reward systems, and corporate culture have been studied recently by Kerr and Slocum (1987). This in-depth study of 14 companies focused on their corporate growth strategies. The authors used the steady state versus evolutionary dichotomy (Leontiades, 1980). Steady state firms are primarily internally focused. They may grow as the result of internally developed new products or through increased penetration of existing markets. On the other hand, evolutionary firms actively pursue new products and markets through mergers and acquisitions. Kerr and Slocum found that all but one firm with a steady state strategy had adapted what they called a hierarchy-based reward system. All of the firms with an evolutionary strategy used a performance-based reward system.

In a hierarchy-based reward system, performance evaluation is subtle and subjective. Performance is defined qualitatively as well as quantitatively. Superiors have a great deal of control over evaluation and, consequently, mobility within the firm. A close relationship with superiors and other mentors is essential in order to be successful. Parenthetically, this type of vertical exchange was found to be very important in the study of upward mobility in the Japanese firm discussed earlier (Wakabayashi et al., 1988). The reward system motivates more cooperative effort and long-term commitment. Managers are promoted from within and promotions are often given to an employee more for developmental reasons than for business reasons. There are many lateral and diagonal moves designed to help the employee understand the whole company and build stronger internal relationships. The system performs the function of completely socializing the younger manager into a strong corporate culture. As Kerr and Slocum point out, this type of system has been described by Ouchi as a "clan culture." A clan culture fosters long-term loyalty and commitment through this lengthy, sometimes arbitrary, socialization process.

The performance-based system is more objective. Rewards are based upon clearly defined expectations. The employee is much less dependent on the superior for evaluation or development. In fact, there is generally little concern with employee development. Socialization is not a primary purpose of the performance-based reward system. Neither cooperation with others nor learning the whole system were emphasized. Promotions were not necessarily from within—many top managers were brought in from outside. Kerr and Slocum describe the situation as a "mutually exploitive relationship." This is consistent with a "market culture" in which relationships are clearly spelled out and there is little need for loyalty or long-term commitments. There is an emphasis on individual initiative and accomplishment, however.

Each reward system seems to fit the needs of the firms in which they were found. The steady state firms were mature capital-intensive operations such as aluminum, forest products, power generation, pharmaceuticals, and machine tools. It was felt that successful managers would have a long-term commitment to the firm and be able to function well in a highly integrated organization. The hierarchy-based reward system develops such managers. The firms with an evolutionary strategy were generally conglomerates whose success depends on the management of a portfolio of businesses. In this situation, commitment to a particular business is of less value (and some might argue is actually a liability). Such firms are successful when the various businesses or divisions are given a high level of autonomy and are evaluated as objectively as possible. Loyalty and commitment are not a concern in a system where the possibility of divestment of businesses is a part of the corporate strategy. Again, the reward system promotes the type of behavior that is most compatible with the corporate strategy.

Returning again to our studies of career mobility, those firms with sponsored or tournament mobility appear to have been following a steady state strategy and therefore used these promotion systems to ensure an adequate supply of well trained, well socialized managers who understood the entire system and appreciated the subtleties of getting things done in a clan culture. This was the case in the utilities, Rosenbaum's firm, and of course in the Japanese firm. A more open system of competition was found in the oil and gas firm, which in fact was attempting to diversify and acquire new products and markets through acquisition. Here there was a great deal of emphasis on individual entrepreneurial ability and relatively little concern for loyalty or cooperation. The firm was looking for the most capable managers and was not terribly concerned about their earlier socialization, their networks, or even their early record of promotions.

At this point, we will discuss one more system for classifying career systems. While similar to those described above, this model introduces additional categories and further refinements that may prove helpful for our understanding of managerial careers. This model of career systems, developed by Sonnenfeld and Peiperl (1988), is based on two dimensions: supply flow and assignment flow. Supply flow refers to the degree to which personnel may easily move into and out of the firm. An internal supply flow implies promotion from within. External supply means that the firm actively recruits managerial and professional personnel from external sources. Assignment flow describes the bases for making job assignment and promotion decisions. These are seen within this model as being based primarily on either individual performance or on the degree of contribution to the group effort. Combining these two career properties results in four cells, some of which are very similar to the categories discussed previously. When an internal supply flow is combined with assignment based on contribution to the group, we have the career system that Sonnenfeld and Peiperl call the "club." Internal supply combined with assignment based on individual contribution is referred to as the "academy." External supply plus individual assignment criteria results in the "baseball team" and external supply with a group assignment basis is known as the "fortress."

The club recruits new employees primarily at the entry level and develops them slowly and carefully. The socialization of those selected into the trainee program in the public utility described by Sheridan et al. would be typical of club practice. There is an emphasis on fair treatment of members and loyalty to the organization is expected. Assignments and promotions are based on contribution to the group, not just individual performance. Members see their firm as providing important services—as having an important mission. An employee's perceived value (and consequently his opportunity for advancement) is influenced by status attainment prior to joining the firm. Those who have the right background or schooling may enjoy what we have called sponsored mobility. Strategically, clubs are likely to be "defenders," trying to perform efficiently and effectively within a limited domain. They are often monopolies or in regulated industries. Examples given by Sonnenfeld and Peiperl include utilities, airlines, banks, surface common carriers, as well as the military and government agencies.

Firms where internal supply flow is combined with assignment based on individual contribution are the "academies." Here the emphasis is on recruiting employees early in their career and developing them in-house. There is more emphasis on differentiating among employees based on their individual contributions according to Sonnenfeld and Peiperl (1988). Large, well established firms such as IBM, Kodak, and Exxon are typical examples of academies. The authors note how sharply career paths differ across different types of firms:

At IBM, point of entry is restricted to early career positions. An employee entering any given management group has an 80 percent chance of staying with IBM through to retirement. At a major New York City bank that same individual would have an 80 percent chance of quitting by the end of his or her first decade of employment (p. 593).

Within the academy there are often sophisticated career development practices: assessment centers, management development programs, career tracking and sponsorship of high potential employees, and dual career ladders. The system is designed to develop and retain in-house talent. As a result, employees are oriented toward personal growth and career development.

Strategically, firms using the academy career system are likely to be analyzers. They are protecting established core businesses but are also constantly looking for new products and services. They try to combine stability and innovation. They need employees who are motivated to learn new things and take moderate risks while remaining loyal to the firm. Sonnenfeld and Peiperl state that the following types of firms use the academy system: office products, pharmaceuticals, electronics, automobiles, and consumer products. The concept of tournament mobility fits nicely in this type of setting. There is an orientation toward long-term development of talented personnel; however, advancement is a function of individual performance which is evaluated on a regular basis. There are, in fact, likely to be multiple tournaments ongoing in various functions and divisions. A number of forces dictate against the adherence to a strict tournament in which only early winners succeed. These include the nature of the business—multiple existing products or services plus the constant search for new opportunities—and the nature of the career system—long-term commitment plus lots of lateral movement. Where more uncertainty exists early predictions are much tougher to make with any accuracy. Future needs are unknown. It is better to delay selection and develop many people and give them opportunities to prove themselves in many different settings.

The third type of career system described by Sonnenfeld and Peiperl is the "baseball team." As the name suggests, the orientation here is toward obtaining the best available talent in the labor market. These firms are looking for proven individual performers and are open to external labor markets at all levels. There is little concern with employee training and development. High turnover is expected and therefore there is no point in succession planning. The firm is often looking for high levels of creativity and innovation, and would be categorized as a "prospector." Successful employees are highly motivated people who see themselves as minor celebrities. Examples here include broadcasting, advertising, law firms, consulting firms, investment banks, and software development. The competition is very open, with employers continually searching for new talent and at the same time discarding those who are no longer that useful.

The last category is the "fortress" or the "institution under siege." This organization is struggling to survive and its needs take precedence over any individual concerns. They are hiring and firing in reaction to immediate market conditions. They may be in highly competitive businesses or in a crisis or turnaround scenario. The firm may be reacting to a change in the external business environment and/or may have changed its business strategy. Such "reactor" firms are often out of control as a result of poor management or due to the nature of their business. Examples given by Sonnenfeld and Peiperl are hotels, retailing, publishing, textiles, and natural resources. Unsuccessful baseball teams become fortresses very quickly. Here neither the firm nor the individual are concerned about career paths, immediate survival is the only issue.

As we have noted above, the career paths adapted by a firm seem to be a means for dealing with its particular business environment. The club, in a stable and often regulated environment, attempts to identify top management talent very early. Therefore, we see evidence of sponsored or strict tournament mobility. To get ahead, you need the appropriate background and education and/or you need to prove your ability very early through outstanding performance. As we saw, this pattern existed in the Bell operating companies as well as another public utility. It was also seen in a Japanese firm and was originally identified in the well established firm studied by Rosenbaum.

Our research study (described earlier in this chapter), which did not find strong tournaments in effect, was done in an oil and gas company undergoing a change in business strategy. The firm was becoming a major producer of crude oil, having previously been a regional refiner and marketer. It was moving from a defender strategy toward an analyzer strategy and also from a steady state position with respect to growth towards an evolutionary strategy. Developing and selecting people according to the rules of clubs or clans would no longer serve all of its needs. During this transition period, the firm was operating in many respects like a baseball team—seeking new talent in the external labor market and sending some existing players down to the farm. There was also evidence of a market culture with respect to the treatment of the new stars who were brought aboard and with respect to decisions concerning acquisitions and divestments. However, within the core business of this firm there were strong traditions, and loyalty and acceptance of corporate values were rewarded. Strategically, acquisitions were considered only if related to the core business. The career system would best be described as an academy which had entered the external labor market in order to cope with change.

Other factors affecting career paths were also operating in this case. The delayed promotion patterns found in this firm were at least partially due to changes in the profitability and size of the company. During the early portion of this longitudinal study, the company invested heavily in a very risky joint venture. The venture proved to be very successful with the payoffs coming toward the end of the period studied. Therefore, more opportunities for upward mobility were created in the later years. Different career patterns were found for those entering into different functional areas. This can be explained by again considering the firm's ability to deal with its external environment. Particular functional areas gain in power, influence, and upward mobility if they possess the skills needed to deal with critical environmental demands. In this firm, technical expertise was certainly related to the most critical tasks: exploration, production, processing, distribution, and research and development. Nontechnical administrative skills seem to have been less important. This is similar to the finding of Slocum and his colleagues (1985). Sales personnel were more likely to be plateaued when they worked in a defender firm in which financial and production issues were more critical than were marketing issues such as growth and new products.

The pattern of slower promotion for technical personnel may apply beyond this firm and industry. Veiga's (1985) data on managers in manufacturing firms showed slower rates of movement were associated with what he called intensive technology—activities like research and development and engineering. Perhaps it takes longer to evaluate the managerial potential of technical personnel, or perhaps their skills are too valuable to lose by early promotion into managerial positions. Our study spanned 11 years and we concluded that a strict tournament was not in effect because early promotions did not make that much difference. However, perhaps in this case the "early" contests take longer—possibly up to seven years. If this were the case, then a tournament may have been in effect, but employees, especially technical employees, were given longer to prove themselves.

The corporate strategy approach described above is useful in understanding how career patterns evolve or are developed in order to help the organization achieve its objectives. This does not just happen as if by magic, although it may appear that way to many people within the firm as well as to the more distant observer. A firm's success depends on the availability of competent human resources. Without the correct career system in place, the firm will not be able to accomplish its strategic objectives. Therefore it is essential that top managers and human resource professionals be aware of the strong connection between strategic planning and human resource planning—especially with regard to the design of the entire career system.

A key issue here is the promotion decision—what criteria are being used to choose those who move up and into contention for top executive positions? Following Rosenbaum's lead, we believe that human decision makers often rely on a small number of simple cues or in this case "signals." Academicians may infer the existence of different career systems by identifying the signals used in making promotion decisions. Practitioners may change existing career systems or develop new ones by influencing the choice of these signals. For example, if decision makers, consciously or unconsciously, look for signals such as socioeconomic background or the right education, then sponsored mobility will occur. If they believe that early performance and promotion are important indicators of ability, then we will see tournament mobility. Other signals that we have seen in the studies discussed here have included university status, assessment center evaluation, entry into a special trainee program, entry into a powerful department, early functional area, and a high level of lateral intrafirm mobility. Many of these signals serve a useful purpose in the organization. However, often career paths become institutionalized. That is, the use of a signal that seemed to make sense in the past leads to many powerful decision makers with similar backgrounds. These high level managers assume that the firm needs more of the same type of person and therefore select people just like themselves for promotion. Of course in a changing environment this practice can be disastrous.

THE FAST TRACK: ADVANTAGES AND DISADVANTAGES

So far we have discussed different career paths primarily from the organization's point of view. We have seen that many firms use early upward mobility as a signal indicative of management potential. Other firms that do not seem to emphasize early upward movement, such as the oil and gas company that we studied, still prefer those employees who have held a larger number of different jobs when making promotion decisions. At this point we will take a closer look at the advantages and disadvantages of such fast tracks—both for the organization and for the individual.

Advantages

In addition to being a step in an individual's career, job changes, both promotions and transfers, serve many other organizational purposes. Open positions are constantly being created in any organization. They are created by normal attrition and by growth and change in the organizational structure. Of course, someone must be found to fill these positions and the most obvious choices are people close to the open position—that is, those in the same function and at the same level or slightly below. Often, however, the firm will choose to move employees across functions or divisions. This strategy allows cross-fertilization. The person being moved has a chance to learn much more about the range of activities and opportunities within the organization. This is, of course, valuable experience for the employee who aspires to further upward mobility. The practice also may enrich those who have the opportunity to interact with the person from a different area. They may learn to appreciate the problems and issues faced by other functions and divisions by communicating with outsiders.

Frequent movement may also be an organizational tactic that helps create and maintain a strong corporate culture. Those who make frequent geographic moves come to identify more with the organization than with any particular community. Those who frequently change functional area will also identify more strongly with the company than with any specific professional groups. This is seen clearly in the military and in companies like IBM, where many employees believe the firm's initials stand for "I've been moved."

For the individual, job change is generally an opportunity for new learning and growth. Even lateral moves expose the employee to new challenges and allow them to develop new skills. Promotions are a natural progression as the employee gains experience and acceptance within the organization. People expect that they will be given more authority and responsibility as they mature in the job. They also expect that their status and financial position in life will improve with time on the job. The firm that does not satisfy these expectations will lose valued employees (Feldman, 1988).

Disadvantages

From the organization's perspective, moving employees is very costly. There are the obvious costs of physically relocating the employee plus the somewhat hidden costs of reduced productivity both before and after the move (Feldman & Brett, 1983, 1985). There is also a domino effect in which the first move creates another vacancy that must be filled, which creates another, and so on, thus multiplying the costs. Training costs must also be considered, as well as the possibility that the employee will refuse the move and may even leave the company (Feldman, 1988).

Because fast track employees realize that they will be moved within a year or two, and that short-term performance is essential for their career progress, they tend to focus on immediate results. They may abandon useful programs initiated by predecessors and replace them with their own inventions in order to gain more visibility and credibility. They may not support long-term efforts involving needed organizational change and development because they will not pay off quickly enough (Thompson, Kirkham, & Dixon, 1985).

Frequent job change can be a frustrating and stressful experience for the individual. Feldman (1988) has listed the many costs to the individual. These include increased demands for high performance with little training. They are expected to "hit the floor running" with a minimum of assistance from anyone else. Sometimes employees are moved so rapidly that they never learn the job. Feldman (1988) reports that:

One employee in production management had been promoted from plant manager to director of national operations to vice president, international operations in 18 months. At first, such quick promotions leave managers feeling exhilarated. Later, though, these managers feel frightened and out of control as they realize they are responsible for products or services about which they know virtually nothing. (p. 110)

The fast track manager may be learning to adapt strategies that will hurt both them and their companies in the long run. They may never be satisfied with any job because all they care about is the next position and getting to it as quickly as possible. They may never master the technical aspects of any function. They may ignore their families and never develop any interests outside of work. Finally, they may burn out at a relatively early age as a result of the stress of this type of career (Thompson, Kirkham, & Dixon, 1985).

Geographical relocation brings with it additional problems. Many employees do not want to move but are afraid of the possible negative impact of refusing. Economic hardship may accompany a move. This may come about as the result of higher costs of living or the difficulty of the spouse finding employment in the new location. Social relationships, both at work and outside, tend to suffer. Finally, there is the disruption of the lives of the spouse and children; however, recent research indicates that most families adapt rather well to moving (Feldman, 1988).

POLICY IMPLICATIONS OF TOURNAMENT MOBILITY

James Rosenbaum, who first proposed the concept of tournament mobility, has also been the most articulate critic of this system. In this section we will review policy implications of tournament mobility as discussed by Rosenbaum in his 1984 book.

Social scientists have often defended early career selection systems on the grounds that they allow efficient use of the organization's investment in its human resources. They minimize the number of employees in whom the firm must invest and they maximize the amortization time for the investment. This efficiency, however, assumes three preconditions according to Rosenbaum: "(1) they must use appropriate selection criteria, (2) they must increase amortization time, and (3) they must not reduce productivity by their selections" (p. 287).

With regard to the first point, the tournament model makes selections based upon short-term performance. Employees who demonstrate successful short-term results, perhaps even at the cost of long-term performance, will be promoted. As we noted above, the employees within such systems quickly learn the rules of the game and attend only to outcomes that will help them in the short run.

The system seems to be well designed to catch and correct errors of inclusion. If an individual with little true managerial ability wins the early contest, this may be discovered in the next competition (Rosenbaum, 1984). Ideally this would be the case. However, we feel that given the emphasis on short-term performance evaluations and the strong signals sent by early promotion, the lack of ability may not be detected until late in the career. Errors of exclusion are virtually undetectable. There are no second chances. Those who are not selected early are out of the running. This is an even more serious problem in sponsored systems. In these programs, identification of talented people occurs before any real performance evaluation can occur. Once the selection is made, many forces come into play to reinforce and validate the decision. Those selected receive special socialization and developmental experiences, often promotion opportunities are created for these "high potential" employees, and before too long, everyone, including the top management candidate, begins to believe in their ability. This may have worked effectively in many situations in the past and may still work well enough in stable regulated industries (which, in fact, was where we saw the strongest evidence of this practice); however, in the fiercely competitive world of the 1990s and beyond we should be trying harder to make the very best selections.

Rosenbaum's second criterion for efficient selection was that amortization time will be increased. It seems obvious that earlier decisions would allow this to occur. However, that assumes that everyone stays with the organization. In fact, selection of an employee for a fast track management development program may increase the chances that he or she will leave the firm. Younger people in general are more likely to change employers, and when they have been through some early managerial development their value in the external labor market increases. Investing in older employees may actually result in a greater return to the firm.

Lastly, Rosenbaum proposed that tournaments must not reduce productivity. On this point he argues persuasively that a tournament system is a major contributor to the mid-career crises experienced by many employees:

The career system may be instrumental in building up the skills, status, and expectations of high-potential people, and it may be powerful in its destructive force in lowering the skills, status, and expectations of employees who have been eliminated from further competition. It withholds further investments from them, it attributes low-ability status to them, and it creates the expectation that these individuals are not going any further in their careers. (p. 293)

In addition to contributing to mid-career crises, Rosenbaum expresses concern over the level of early career stress generated by the tournament system. The timing of this pressure is also unfortunate because it forces many young employees to choose between their careers and the high demands of a young family. This is particularly troublesome for women in the workplace and is often used as justification for discrimination against young women. Rosenbaum concludes that the "economic justifications of early selections require rethinking" (p. 299) and recommends that tournament mobility systems be replaced by more open systems that allow for delayed selections. This should result in more accurate selection decisions and eliminate many of the negative consequences of the tournament model. We agree and feel that changes in the business environment, in organizational structures, and in demographics are combining to make this a feasible and practical alternative. Our specific recommendations will be presented in the last chapter of this book after we have examined research on the later stages of the executive career.

4

Mid-Career Issues

This chapter will describe two related studies. One represents an extension of the research from Chapter 3 up to the general management level. The other is an extension of research on the careers of top executives—down to the general management and functional vice president level. As we will show later in the book, achieving this level is a major step on the path to the top.

In the previous chapter we reported on three career history variables that were related to promotion chances early in the career. These were early upward mobility, initial functional area, and breadth of functional experience. The longitudinal studies that focused on these factors only examined the first 12 or 13 years of an individual's career. We were interested in whether the influence of these "signals" extended beyond that early period. Also, although we described these as signals used by promotion decision makers in lieu of better information on a candidate's ability, we did not actually observe the decision process. It was merely inferred from statistical relationships. For these reasons, we designed a study in which top executives were asked to evaluate fictitious candidates for a general management position. The candidates' career histories varied along these three dimensions.

General management has been defined as " . . . positions with some multifunctional responsibility for a business (or businesses)" (Kotter, 1982, p. 2). Achieving a general management position is an important mid-career achievement in many executives' careers. It has been described as a critical threshold to senior management (Sorcher, 1985).

John Kotter (1988) has made the case that in today's complex business environment, we need leaders who possess not only motivation, ability, and integrity but also three other characteristics that are primarily developed as the result of career experiences. These are relatively broad knowledge of their industry, their firm, and of different functions; a relatively broad set of good working relationships within the firm and industry; and a good track record and reputation in a broad set of activities. This breadth might be enhanced by a number of different career experiences. The most relevant, however, would be actual responsibility for a wide variety of functions or products. This might come as the result of frequent job changes (transfers and promotions) or it might come as the result of early attainment of a general management position.

The nature of the general management position has been studied by Kotter (1982) in his in-depth analysis of the work of 15 general managers. These managers all had multifunctional responsibilities and most of them were responsible for sizable corporate divisions or regions. Even at this level, one common characteristic of all the managers studied was broad knowledge of their firm and industry. Kotter describes the typical general manager as an "expert" in his business.

There were commonalities in the backgrounds of the 15 general managers as well. Their family environment was one in which they had a close relationship with one or both parents. The parents were upwardly mobile and at least one had a two or four year college degree. The fathers were in business or managed a non-business activity. None of the general managers were only children. They were all leaders in school and all possessed at least undergraduate degrees in business-related areas.

They all seemed to have equally successful early careers. They quickly settled into a firm that matched their interests and values. They spent the large majority of their careers within one industry and with one firm. They experienced early success and were rapidly promoted into positions with more responsibility and challenge. Most of them rose within only one functional area. None had experience in more than two different functions. Most reached the general management level between the ages of 34 and 40. All of these experiences helped prepare them for the complexities of the general management position (Kotter, 1982).

A STUDY OF THE GENERAL MANAGEMENT PROMOTION DECISION

We will briefly review the literature on early career mobility which points to the existence of three types of signals that might be used by promotion decision makers at the general management level (see Chapters 2 and 3 for a more detailed discussion).

Many authors have emphasized the importance of early upward movement (Rosenbaum, 1979) and the establishment of a reinforcing "success cycle" as prerequisites for a successful management career (Berlew & Hall, 1966; Bray, Campbell, & Grant, 1974). The early research on the topic implied that unless an individual has a good, challenging first job and receives quick, early promotions, the entire career will suffer.

The strongest evidence for the effects of early promotions came from the research of Rosenbaum (1979) and his tournament model of mobility. He found that those who were promoted early rose to higher levels than those who were not. The first group remained in the tournament, but those not promoted in the early rounds were effectively eliminated from later competition. Other research has questioned the generalizability of this finding. Forbes (1987—also in Chapter 3 of this book) found that those who remain in non-management positions for as long as seven years may still move quickly and be in contention for the same promotions as those who were promoted early. The relationship between these systems and corporate strategy as well as policy implications of the different systems were discussed in the previous chapter.

Another career factor that seems to predict upward mobility is breadth of experience (Forbes, 1987—also Chapter 3; Kanter, 1977; Sorcher, 1985). In addition, Kotter (1987) has recently proposed a list of attributes required for effective leadership in senior management positions. The list includes broad industry and organizational knowledge, broad relationships in the firm and in the industry, and a broad track record. However, in Kotter's (1982) study of general managers, he found that their early career had been spent in only one or two functional areas.

A third factor which may affect promotion chances within organizations is the functional background of the candidate. Our research has shown that firms in certain industries tend to choose their chief executives from particular functional areas (see Chapter 7). Pfeffer (1981) has developed a model of executive succession in which different functional areas gain power as the result of their ability to deal with critical environmental contingencies. Other studies have shown that the career paths for different functional areas are related to business strategy (e.g., Slocum, Cron, Hansen, & Rawlings, 1985).

Although academic research has shown that these relationships exist, we wondered whether top managers were aware of them and whether they consciously used these criteria when making promotion decisions. It is possible that those who have moved more quickly or have broader experience are simply more visible and better known to the top management decision makers. In addition, organizational power and politics or a bias in favor of those with similar backgrounds may account for preferences for particular functional expertise.

There have been only a few controlled studies of the promotion decision process. In one study, 75 line managers were asked to rate the importance of various types of information for making a promotion decision (Taylor, 1975). They were later observed using the same types of data in a personnel decision simulation. Interestingly, there was little correspondence between the ratings and the actual usage. In the ratings they said that they preferred more objective and seemingly more relevant sources of information such as job performance appraisals and psychological test results. They actually used more of the data from other sources such as the application form (which gave general background such as education, employment history, etc.) and interview data (impressions of the candidate and quotes from the interview). Job performance data was used the least—even less than a source called "grapevine" which contained rumors about the subject from his boss, secretary, salesmen, and customers. It would seem that decision makers are seeking a personal feel for the candidate and do not get that type of information from more objective sources. In order to gain more understanding of the promotion decision process, we conducted a controlled study using policy capturing methodology.

Policy Capturing Methodology

The policy capturing technique allows a researcher to determine a decision maker's "policy," that is, how the decision maker used or weighted the available information in making a judgement. The approach requires each decision maker to evaluate a number of individuals or items which vary on several potential decision criteria. The method has been used to study such decisions as organizational and job choice (Feldman & Arnold, 1978), labor arbitration decisions (Cain & Stahl, 1983), assessment center ratings (Russell, 1985), performance appraisal (see Hobson & Gibson, 1983, for a review), and promotion decisions (London & Stumpf, 1983; Stumpf & London, 1981).

The policy capturing studies of promotion decisions involved middle levels of management and used a variety of career signals. In the Stumpf and London (1981) study, candidates for a promotion to a third level management position within a bank were evaluated by a group of managers and by a group of business students. Five attributes were manipulated: managerial potential ratings, political recommendations, position proximity to the vacancy, candidate weakness, and sex. The potential ratings were similar to those that might be generated by an assessment center evaluation. Political influence was manipulated by having half the candidates identified as "interesting" by the rater's immediate superior. Other research had suggested that one's closeness to a vacancy might be a criterion for promotion. Candidates who work close to the opening would have the most immediately available knowledge about the job. This variable was manipulated by describing some candidates as branch managers in the district with the vacancy (high job knowledge), some as branch managers in other districts (moderate job knowledge), and others as bank officers at the same level who worked in different areas such as commercial banking or bank operations (low job knowledge). Each candidate was also described as having one weakness, either in administrative or in interpersonal skill areas.

On the average, all of the signals except sex were used by both managers and students. Interactions among the variables were also important. For example, the combination of a high potential rating and political support from above had a strong influence on the promotion decision. Another interesting finding was that six distinct policy clusters were found. This means that the decision makers combined the information in six different ways. Many focused on just one variable, for example, potential or position, while others combined multiple sources of data.

In a similar study, a group of managers evaluated 20 candidates for a third level bank management position and later for a telephone company management position (London & Stumpf, 1983). The decision variables here were managerial potential ratings (from their supervisor), having been assessed at an assessment center, the closeness of their position to the vacancy, and sex. The assessment center manipulation was whether they had been to an assessment center or not; the assessment results always paralleled the supervisor's potential rating. All candidates had "outstanding" performance ratings. In general, all of this data had some impact on the decisions that were made, with the exception of sex. There were two significant interactions. One showed that position proximity was not that important for those with the highest potential ratings and the other indicated that preference might be given to females who were close to the vacancy.

Of course these were only simulated decisions, but they show that promotion decisions are strongly influenced by the immediate supervisor's rating of the candidate's "potential"; that political considerations may play a role; that assessment centers are believed to provide useful information; and that managers believe that, in general, those closest to an opening should be chosen to fill it.

In our research, a different set of variables was used. We were primarily interested in testing whether the career history variables identified in our earlier study would be used by top executives when making a general management promotion decision. Also of interest was the question of whether lower level managers and professionals would perceive that these variables are used in the same way as top executives report. Many employees of business organizations are unaware of the actual mobility patterns that affect their careers (Rosenbaum, 1984).

We manipulated the following variables:

1. Early functional background (sales and marketing or technical and operations or accounting and finance),

2. Breadth of experience (specialized in one functional area or experienced in all three),

3. Upward mobility curve (steady movement with an early career start or later more rapidly accelerated movement).

We were also interested in the relative importance of each factor and in the preferences of each rater. The same hypotheses were tested with a group of young managers and professionals. In addition, for this group a fourth variable, type of management education, was added. This signal consisted of an MBA degree versus in-house training.

Research Method

Subjects. The executive decision makers were past and present members of the board of trustees of a medium-sized midwestern university. Thirty-two members were contacted by mail and 15 (47 percent) completed and returned the promotion decision exercise. The following industries were represented: manufacturing (4), banking (3), transportation (2), oil and gas (2), utilities (1), retailing (1), public accounting (1), and venture capital (1). Five of the respondents were present or past chairmen and chief executives; five held the title of president; and five were vice presidents or regional managers.

The young managers and professionals were students in a part-time Masters of Business Administration program at the same university. Members of two classes were asked to participate and completed exercises were received from 22 individuals. All participants had at least two years of full-time work experience. Nine were in professional or technical positions, while 13 were managers. The highest ranking managers were department heads. They were employed in a variety of industries.

Experimental Manipulation. The participants were instructed to evaluate candidates for a general management position using criteria which would be relevant in their particular organizations. The task was described as follows:

This is a study of the factors which influence managerial promotion decisions. Your task is to rank in order a group of potential candidates for a general management position.

There is an opening for the position of president and general manager of a growing division of your firm. The company is committed to filling the position from within. All candidates are in vice president positions but in other divisions of the firm. Also, all candidates are in the age range of 38 to 42; having been with this firm for 15 to 20 years; and in their current position for 2 to 4 years.

Twelve potential candidates have been tentatively identified. Your specific task is to choose the most promising three candidates for further interviewing.

The next best three should also be identified as a back-up group. In addition, it is desirable to have an overall ranking of all 12 from number 1, the most qualified, to 12, the least qualified.

The MBA students received the same instructions, but the words "a large *Fortune 500* firm" were substituted for "your firm" and there were 24 candidates to be ranked. The raters were given a ranking sheet and 12 or 24 one page "Corporate Executive Succession Planning Candidate Career Summary" sheets. Each page described one candidate.

Career path was described as either having involved early identification as an effective manager followed by promotion every 3 to 4 years, or as one where 7 years were spent as an individual contributor followed by rapid promotion (every other year on the average). Early experience was described as having been in one of the following functional areas: 1) technical and operations, 2) sales and marketing, 3) accounting and finance. Breadth of experience was manipulated by stating that the candidate's career had either been focused in the area of his early experience or that he also had experience in the other two functional areas.

Analyses. The data in a policy capturing study are initially analyzed for each rater. This may be done using either regression or analysis of variance techniques (Cohen & Cohen, 1975). The individual regression beta weights or ANOVA (analysis of variance) effect sizes may then be grouped, averaged, and compared as new data (Stumpf & London, 1981). Analysis of variance and multiple regression analyses were performed for each ranking. Only variables that exhibited statistically significant effects were considered to be part of the decision policy.

Results

The most important variable used by our sample of top executives was breadth of experience. On the average, it accounted for 69 percent of the variance in the promotion rankings. All the executives used this criterion and for all but one it was the most heavily weighted variable. Early versus late movement and functional area were used less frequently and weighted less heavily. On the average, movement accounted for about 12 percent of the variance in ranking and functional area accounted for another seven percent.

For the younger managers and professionals, both breadth of experience and the MBA degree were heavily weighted. Every member of this group used both variables. Again, not all subjects used movement or function.

Four different decision policies were identified. Five top executives used only breadth of experience to make their rankings. One used breadth of experience plus early versus late movement; one used breadth plus functional area; and eight used all three criteria.

The younger managers and professionals were more inclined to use all the information given to them. They all made use of the education variable. Thirteen of the 22 also used breadth of experience, movement, and function. Four used breadth plus movement; four others used breadth and function; one was influenced only by breadth of experience.

When we examined the direction of the relationships from the individual regression equations, some interesting patterns emerged. First, all raters preferred the candidates with greater breadth of experience. With respect to career movement, more raters favored the early movers. However, three of the nine executives who used movement preferred the candidate who moved later in the career; as did seven of the 17 young managers and professionals. Functional preferences were evenly distributed across the three areas in both groups. All but one of the manager/professionals preferred the MBA degree over in-house training.

Discussion

The results indicate that career history parameters are important factors that influence the decision to promote a candidate to the general management level. These are not the only factors considered and several executives commented on the various personal factors that they use in making such decisions. Lower level managerial and professional personnel also seem to be aware of the importance of these variables.

Everyone in the study recognized the importance of breadth of experience as a requirement for a general management position. This is logical given that general management implies multi-functional responsibility and it supports the previous findings and opinions on this topic (Forbes, 1987; Kanter, 1977; Kotter, 1988; Sorcher, 1985). One chairman and CEO (the head of a $2 billion manufacturing firm) commented on the need for the "three legs of the stool," meaning that general managers need experience in operations, marketing, and financial areas. The importance of this factor was consistent across all industry groups represented and also recognized by the younger employees.

Preference for a particular functional background seemed to depend on the needs of the firm or of the division to be headed. The chairman and CEO of a large transportation company reported favoring a sales and marketing background since the division to be headed was described as "growing." The president of a commercial bank preferred sales and marketing since he saw his firm as "market driven." Those with technical and operations backgrounds were preferred by a top executive of a diversified manufacturing firm which was moving more into electronics and aerospace. The principle that career opportunities for different areas are related to business strategy comes through very clearly in these decisions.

With respect to career movement, two banking executives and one transportation executive preferred the late bloomer; however, six other executives favored those who moved early. This indicates that there is not universal agreement that early movement is a relevant signal of higher level ability. In addition 40 percent of the manager/professional group preferred the late bloomer.

It is important to note that one-third of the top executives chose to ignore both early functional area and early movement as promotion criteria. Two others ignored one of those factors. This suggests that the importance of these early signals may fade. Perhaps later promotions (at the general management level) are more of an open contest and not as influenced by the early history of the candidate. This was the area of greatest difference between the executives and the younger personnel. The lower level employees were more likely to believe that all the variables should be used.

The one criterion that everyone agreed upon was breadth of experience. It is preferable that the person chosen for a general management position already be familiar with a variety of functional areas. If he or she is to manage these functions, then he or she should understand them. This finding supports Kotter's (1988) emphasis on broad knowledge and experience as essential for successful leadership at higher levels of management. Organizations that wish to develop successful general managers should provide more opportunities for cross-functional movement. Likewise, managers should actively seek out such opportunities if they aspire to general management positions.

The preference for functional area seems to depend on the needs or strategy of the organization or division at a particular point in time. This supports the strategic contingency approach to executive succession (Pfeffer, 1981). These needs may be rather stable and predictable or may change rapidly over time. For example, in power generating utilities many managers have the engineering backgrounds needed to deal with operating problems; however, at the highest levels we often see the legal backgrounds needed to handle regulatory problems. In the telephone industry, the strategically critical skills have changed as a result of deregulation. The earlier preference for those with experience in operations or manufacturing seems to be giving way to recognition of the need for a marketing orientation. As the environment changes business strategies must change and so do human resource requirements.

The importance of early upward movement also seems to depend on the situation. Six executives preferred early movement; however, six did not use this variable at all, and three others preferred the late mover. The executive preferences probably reflect the culture or the strategies of their firms as discussed in Chapter 3.

This policy capturing study provided us with data on the career history variables that are used as signals by top executives when choosing a general manager. The study was useful as an extension of our research on early careers. Although factors had been identified which were related to more successful careers, we did not know whether top executives would actually base promotion decisions on those variables. We were also interested in whether the same factors studied in the previous research would be used when making a higher level promotion. As discussed above, breadth of experience was universally desirable at the general management level, while the preferred functional background and the timing of upward mobility depended upon the situation.

The policy capturing study gave us more information about career experiences that are seen as necessary to get to the general management level. We will now move on to a study in which we analyzed movement from the general management and senior functional management level on up to top corporate management.

A STUDY OF ALTERNATE ROUTES TO THE TOP

In his recent book on corporate leadership, John Kotter (1988) emphasized the point that the successful executive should have a broad, general background in his or her firm and industry. This is consistent with our findings above on the importance of breadth of experience in promotion decisions. Many studies of the backgrounds of top executives find that a majority report experience in general management or general administration (e.g., Bonfield, 1980; Dommermuth, 1966).

We also know that business firms tend to prefer leaders with the expertise to deal with critical strategic problems (Pfeffer, 1981). In Chapter 7 we will provide evidence of how the functional backgrounds of CEOs have changed over the past three decades and how different industries prefer particular functional backgrounds for their CEOs. For example, technical and operations backgrounds have been increasing while marketing has generally declined. However, marketing is the predominant background in consumer goods industries such as household products, while production is emphasized in basic industries such as steel.

Another issue that we have not yet addressed in this book is the question of whether it is wise to change employers frequently in order to attain upward mobility. Although movement early in the career is normal and expected, it appears that the successful top executive quickly settles into one firm or at least into one industry. In fact, one study found that 54 percent of CEOs worked for only one employer (Tuckel & Siegel, 1983). This might seem like excessive inbreeding if, in fact, top management skills were universal and easily transferable across firms and industries. Technical skills and general management skills may be applicable in a variety of settings, but as Kotter (1982) has noted, "the general manager is not a generalist," he or she is instead an expert in a particular firm and industry. Others have argued the similar point that executives must possess "institutional" skills—e.g., a detailed working knowledge of the entire organization and the industry that comes only with years of experience (Shetty & Peery, 1976). These same authors found that 89 percent of CEO appointments came from within the firm. Furthermore, 92 percent came from within the firm or from within the same industry; and 95 percent came from inside the firm, from the same industry, or from a related industry. Outside appointments are relatively rare and usually associated with performance problems within the firm (Helmich, 1977).

We felt that full understanding of the route to the executive suite must simultaneously involve data on inside versus outside promotions, promotions to and from general management positions, and promotions to and from functional areas. Too many previous studies had focused only on the top positions and where the new executives came from. This may be misleading since an "insider" may have only been with the firm a few years, or a "general manager" may have recently been moved from a functional specialty. To see the entire picture required a study of promotion patterns and key lateral moves within the top management team from the chairman of the board down to the functional vice presidents.

Data Source

The data for this study were obtained from leadership position changes announced in the "Who's News" section of *The Wall Street Journal* from January through September of 1985. Entries were recorded only when there was a clear indication of both previous and newly assigned positions. This study included only promotions within large firms, with the 1985 listing of *Forbes 500* used to define the large firms.

Positions were recorded as "top management," "general management other than top management," and "functional management." Positions carrying the title of chairman, vice chairman, president, CEO, chief operating officer, and chief administrative officer, or any combination of these were classified as top management. Executive vice presidents and senior vice presidents whose titles clearly indicated responsibilities in more than one functional area were classified as general management other than top management. Functional area managers were corporate

Table 4.1
Classification of Managerial Appointments

New Position	Organizational Level		Total
	Corporate	Division	
Top Management	211	275	486
General Management	52	31	83
Functional Management	89	32	121
Totals	352	338	690

vice presidents of a particular function, e.g., finance or operations. These same categories were used at the corporate and at the division level, giving us six different types of positions.

Managerial changes where the description of the scope of responsibilities did not clearly fall into one of these categories were excluded from analysis. Moreover, only initial movements into each of the categories were included. For example, a president and CEO who was named to the additional position of chairman, or the upgrading of an incumbent vice president of finance to senior vice president—finance were not included.

Analysis

A total of 690 appointments was recorded. A breakdown by position and organizational location is shown in Table 4.1. Our analysis consisted of identifying the source of appointments to these key positions—starting with corporate top management and then moving down.

Appointments to Corporate Top Management. As shown in Table 4.2, there are many different routes to corporate top management; however, the most well worn path is through a corporate general management position. Twice as many appointments were made from this type of position as from the next most popular—division top management (68 versus 34). Corporate functional managers and outside top managers (from the same industry) were also strong contenders (28 and 27 appointments, respectively). These four categories accounted for 78 percent of the appointments to top corporate management.

The total number of outside appointments (29 percent) was higher than in previous studies that focused on only chief executives as opposed to the entire top management team. Outsiders were likely to come from

Table 4.2
Sources of Appointments to Corporate Top Management

Previous Location	Previous Position			Totals	
	Top Mgmt.	General Mgmt.	Functional Mgmt.	Number	Percentage
Corporate Headquarters	0	68	28	96	47.5
Division	34	11	2	47	23.3
Outside (Same Industry)	27	15	5	47	23.3
Outside (Different Industry)	6	1	5	12	5.9
Totals					
Number	67	95	40	202	
Percentage	33.2	47.0	19.8		100.0

top management and were more likely to be chosen from the same industry by a ratio of about four to one.

About 20 percent of the appointments were from functional areas. Nearly three-quarters of these appointees were from corporate headquarters while one-quarter were outsiders. A majority of these corporate functional moves were from the financial area (53 percent). Although not included in the table, nine directors moved into corporate top management. In seven of these, the previous incumbent had resigned, been fired, or died. In other words, these appointments were largely due to unexpected events and indicate that the company was not prepared for a succession event at that point in time.

Appointments to Corporate General Management. Since corporate general managers were the strong favorites for promotion into top management, we next examined promotions into this position. Top corporate functional positions were the primary feeders into corporate general management, providing about 40 percent of the appointees (see Table 4.3). These were followed by appointees from divisional top management with 23 percent (12/52). Outsiders comprised one-quarter of the appointees and 73 percent of these (8/13) were serving in top or general management positions within the same industry. Only four of the 52 appointees were from a different industry and all four moved from functional positions.

Table 4.3
Sources of Appointments to Corporate General Management

Previous Location	Previous Position			Totals	
	Top Mgmt.	General Mgmt.	Functional Mgmt.	Number	Percentage
Corporate Headquarters	0	0	21	21	40.4
Division	12	3	3	18	34.6
Outside (Same Industry)	3	5	1	9	17.3
Outside (Different Industry)	0	0	4	4	7.7
Totals					
Number	15	8	29	52	
Percentage	28.8	15.4	55.8		100.0

Appointments to Divisional Top Management. We next analyzed the promotions into divisional top management positions. Most appointments were from general management positions (43 percent). Division general management was the single largest source, providing one-quarter (69/275) of all the appointments (see Table 4.4). There was also considerable interdivisional mobility, with 16 percent (45/275) of the selections coming from top managers of other divisions. Overall, 38 percent of the appointments were from the same division and 30 percent were from other divisions of the same firm.

Twenty-two percent of the moves were from outside the firm. Fifty of the 61 outside appointees were serving in top or general management positions. As with corporate top management, about four times as many outsiders were from the same industry.

When functional managers were selected to fill top division management positions, they usually came from the same division (44 percent). However, 22 percent were from other divisions and 20 percent moved from corporate headquarters.

Appointments to Senior Corporate Functional Positions. As shown in Table 4.5, we recorded 89 appointments to senior functional management positions at the corporate headquarters. Approximately one-third of these came from the divisions. Most of these appointments involved moves from the same functional area at the division level but 11 out of 30 were

Table 4.4
Sources of Appointments to Divisional Top Management

Previous Location	Previous Position			Totals	
	Top Mgmt.	General Mgmt.	Functional Mgmt.	Number	Percentage
Corporate Headquarters	0	10	16	26	9.5
Division (Same)	0	69	36	105	38.2
Division (Different)	45	20	18	83	30.2
Outside (Same Industry)	24	17	8	49	17.8
Outside (Different Industry)	6	3	3	12	4.4
Totals					
Number	75	119	81	275	
Percentage	27.3	43.3	29.5		100.0

from top or general division management. There were 13 cross functional moves within corporate headquarters.

In contrast to the other positions we studied, more than half of the corporate senior functional positions were filled from outside the firm and about one-third (29/89) were from a different industry. Selections from outside the industry were likely to involve certain functions. More of the appointments to chief financial officer came from outside the industry than from any other source. Furthermore, six of the seven top legal positions were filled from outside the industry. In contrast, only six of 30 top marketing people came from a different industry and all of the top operations appointments were made from within the firm.

Other Appointments. There were two main sources for filling the 31 division general management openings. More than half of these were interdivisional moves and most of them came from either a top or general management position. About one-quarter came from functional area positions in the same division. Fewer than 20 percent were outsiders.

Over 60 percent of the functional positions at the division level were filled from other divisions, with most having served in the same function before the transfer. About one-third were outsiders and all of these were

Table 4.5
Sources of Appointments to Senior Corporate Functional Positions

Previous Location	Functional Area				Totals	
	Fin.	Opns.	Mktg.	Legal	Number	Percentage
Corporate Headquarters[a]	8	1	4	0	13	14.6
Division[b]	12	7	11	0	30	33.7
Outside (Same Industry)	7	0	9	1	17	19.1
Outside (Different Industry)	17	0	6	6	29	32.6
Totals						
Number	44	8	30	7	89	
Percentage	49.4	9.0	33.7	7.9		100.0

[a] These appointments represent cross-functional moves within the corporate headquarters.

[b] Eleven (11) of these appointments were from top or general management of a division.

in the same functional area before the move. Over 20 percent were outsiders from different industries.

Discussion

We will consider the findings from the top down. The data seem to indicate rather well structured, well planned succession patterns. The range of positions from which top managers are chosen seems to be most restricted at the highest levels. A wider search for candidates, a more open contest, exists at the lower levels. Many top managers are chosen from the general management (executive and senior vice president) positions immediately below. Secondary sources are positions close to or similar to top management. These include division top management, corporate level functional management, and top managers from other firms in the same industry. Many of those who move from corporate functional management into top positions have had previous experience as top managers or general managers at the division level. At this level, very few appointments come from more distant, more dissimilar positions such as non-corporate functional positions or positions within other industries.

Corporate general management is the primary feeder into the top and is, in turn, fed from two primary sources. These are corporate functional management and top division management. The paths into corporate level functional management and into top division management are quite different, however.

As was the case with top corporate management, top division managers are chosen most frequently from division general management. Here, however, a wider range of other sources seems to exist. These include: division functional management, management from other divisions, and management from other companies within the same industry. Very few division managers are chosen from outside the industry.

In contrast to the pattern described above, slightly more than 50 percent of the corporate level functional managers in our study were chosen from outside the firm, with almost one-third coming from different industries. Although most functional promotions come from lower level functional positions, about 12 percent of the senior corporate functional positions were filled by division top or general managers.

This analysis indicates that there are two primary paths to top corporate management positions. These paths tend to converge near the top, however, they originate from different areas. One path is through the generalist position of division top management, while the other goes through the specialist area of corporate functional management.

Those who come from division top management are generalists with previous responsibility for an entire business or division of the company. Before this, many had been functional managers and many came from other divisions. These are the general managers, who, as noted by Kotter (1982), do not specialize in a functional area but do specialize in a firm or industry. Relatively few top divisional managers came from a different industry. Here it appears that knowledge of the firm or at least of the industry is essential for success. On the other hand, the functional managers do specialize in one professional area and their skills seem to be more easily transferred across companies and even across industries. There is some movement across these two paths at lower levels, but there seems to be a major convergence at the corporate general management level. In this position, the functional specialists must finally learn more general skills before making the last step to the top.

Our findings indicate that the candidate for top management need not have general management experience during the mid-career phase—it can come later. A functional specialist path exists which allows for more inter-firm and inter-industry mobility. While it is true that most CEOs are promoted from within and that they need general management experience, functional specialists often come into the firm as corporate vice presidents of functions such as finance or the legal area. These newcomers may then move into other functional areas and/or into corporate general management and eventually into corporate top management.

While in-depth knowledge of the firm and industry are certainly needed at the top, it appears that many firms are willing to go outside the firm and even outside the industry for certain types of functional expertise. These managers may later receive general management training (and testing) at the corporate general management level. The existence of such career paths allows the firm to obtain critically needed specialists and new blood at a high level in the firm, and then, if their skills are needed at the top, broaden their experience as senior vice presidents or executive vice presidents.

These high level promotion patterns that we have tried to describe are very complex. They reflect the effects of a number of simultaneous forces. Strategic contingencies are such that at different times, different specialized functional expertise is needed at the top. For example, an oil and gas company or an electric utility may normally rely heavily on technical expertise. However, when faced with serious regulatory problems, they may replace the technical specialists with legal experts. Even firms that normally promote from within may go outside for such talent. However, as we have seen, the functional specialist may not move directly into a top management position but instead be given some general management experience first.

Normally, the same firm may emphasize general management experience and in-depth knowledge of the firm. Candidates for the top positions may be moved into general management at the division level at an early age; given experience in other divisions in order to learn more about the entire company; and then moved into general management at the corporate level. In some companies, those with general management experience take a brief detour into critical functional areas such as finance before continuing on to the top. This has been a traditional pattern at General Motors.

The preferred pattern also depends upon business strategy and related career systems such as those discussed in the previous chapter. As Kerr and Slocum (1987) have noted, steady state firms, that rely on internally generated growth, tend to develop career systems that move people around internally in order to learn the whole system and in order to develop strong internal relationships. Here we are most likely to see the general management pattern leading to the top of the organization. On the other hand, the evolutionary firms that grow through outside acquisitions are generally not that well integrated and therefore do not emphasize cross-functional or cross-divisional movement. They are more likely to go outside the firm for managerial talent, while the steady state firm will typically grow its own top managers. The more specialized functional path, with more inter-firm and even inter-industry movement, is likely to be common in the conglomerates that result from an evolutionary strategy for growth.

We also previously noted the differences between firms that tend to hire at the entry level and promote from within (clubs and academies) and those that actively recruit in the external labor market (baseball teams and fortresses) (Sonnenfeld & Peiperl, 1988). The former tend to be defenders or analyzers, with a more stable strategy of protecting their existing niche. They can plan for human resource needs more accurately because of relative stability over time and therefore are more likely to try to develop the managerial expertise that they anticipate needing in the future. The latter firms are likely to be prospectors or reactors, who are either continually searching for new opportunities or who are merely trying to survive in an uncontrollable and unpredictable environment. Neither firm has the luxury of being able to plan its long-range human resource needs, and therefore neither firm tries to develop managerial talent internally. The more stable and more internally oriented clubs and academies are where the general managers would be carefully groomed for the top positions. On the other hand, the functional specialist might be called in from outside to help the prospector exploit a new opportunity or to aid the reactor in surviving unanticipated threats.

TOP EXECUTIVE PROFILES

The General Management Path: John A. Young, Hewlett-Packard Company

The only son of an electrician and housewife, Young was born in Numpa, Idaho, in 1932, and grew up in Klamath Falls, Oregon. He graduated from Oregon State University in 1953 with a B.S. in electrical engineering and from 1954 to 1956 served with the U.S. Air Force in its Research and Development Command. On release from the military, Young earned an MBA from Stanford and in 1958 joined Hewlett-Packard as a marketing planner.

After serving in various marketing and finance positions for five years, he was promoted to general manager, microwave division in 1963. He became vice president, electronic products group in 1968, and in 1974 was appointed executive vice president and elected a company director. Promotion to president came in 1977, followed by CEO in 1978. At age 46, he became the first non-founder to lead Hewlett-Packard.

This career path shows very rapid advancement within one company. Young entered industry late, at age 26, but with a technical degree, research and development experience from the military, and a Stanford MBA. These credentials, combined with further breadth of experience in the marketing and financial areas, helped him to become a general manager in only five years. From there, he steadily achieved broader general management responsibilities until he reached the top.

The Functional Specialist Path: Robert L. Crandall, AMR Corporation

Crandall's career is marked by frequent movement—a pattern that he apparently became accustomed to at a young age. His father, an insurance salesman, moved frequently and Crandall attended 16 schools in 12 years. He graduated from the University of Rhode Island in 1957 with a B.S. in business administration. After a short stint with John Hancock as an office supervisor, he earned an MBA from Wharton in 1960, and joined Eastman Kodak as a credit supervisor. Two years later he left to become customer financial service director for Hallmark Cards.

In 1966, Crandall moved to TWA as assistant treasurer. He was promoted to vice president, systems and data services in 1970; and a year later became vice president, controller. He then left TWA in 1972 to become vice president, finance at Bloomingdales. The following year he joined American Airlines as senior vice president, finance. Crandall moved to senior vice president, marketing in 1974; and was promoted to president in 1980. In 1985, he was named chairman and CEO of American and its parent company, AMR.

This career history shows how the functional specialist can pursue a successful, high mobility career. Financial experts are typically called in when tough cost cutting measures are needed and Crandall entered American Airlines at the functional vice president level. His strategy for dealing with deregulation in the airline industry has been to reduce fares and win huge wage concessions from union workers. Even with his financial expertise, he spent a good number of years later in his career broadening his background and learning about the company: first as the head of the marketing function for six years, and then as president for five more years.

Aided by MBAs from prestigious schools, both men started moving up the ladder early in their careers. Both careers demonstrate the importance of the appropriate functional backgrounds for the particular organization, and the importance of breadth of experience—which may come either early, as in the generalist career (Young), or later, as in the functional specialist career (Crandall).

5

Paths to the Top for Women

Although we are now in the last decade of the twentieth century, there are still only a very small number of women in the upper management levels of American business corporations. In this chapter we will examine, in some detail, the backgrounds and positions of those women and also look at their progress during the 1980s. Our analyses show that fewer than three percent of all high level corporate executives are women. Even when we examined the number of newly appointed managers at the highest levels, we found women to be less than six percent of the total.

Why are the numbers so low? There are a variety of suggested explanations. Perhaps they have chosen not to be business executives either by entering other occupations or by not being willing to make the commitment to the organization that is needed to rise to the top. Perhaps women are just not as well qualified; or perhaps there are even basic gender differences that prevent women from being as effective as men in the role of business executive. Perhaps they are just as capable but they have been discriminated against by the men in their "old boy" networks who have created a "glass ceiling" to keep women out of top management positions. Or perhaps they do want those positions, can handle them very well, and today's business organizations are trying to move women into higher level executive positions, but—this is a long, tedious process and perhaps some of the strategies for accomplishing this goal have been of limited effectiveness.

WHAT IS KEEPING WOMEN FROM REACHING THE TOP?

Career Choices

There are a variety of social and biological forces that influence the occupational choices and aspirations of women. Many women choose not to enter the business world or, once there, choose not to compete as fully for upward mobility as men. For some, the decision is made because of faulty perceptions and bad advice; for others, it is made because of the existence of alternatives that are generally unavailable to men.

There is clear sex stereotyping of many occupations—including business executive. Because of this, women have historically considered a smaller range of alternative occupations than men, usually focusing on the female-dominated fields. In the past, women have tended to choose lower level and less prestigious occupations than men. And, within their chosen occupation, the career aspirations of women often tend to be lower than those of men (Greenhaus, 1987).

Why do women make such choices? There are three general explanations (Greenhaus, 1987). First, women are more aware of and concerned about family responsibilities. Because they have traditionally assumed the primary responsibility for child-rearing, they are very conscious of this role when they make occupational decisions. In fact, women often make plans about marriage and family before they make their career decisions (Nieva & Gutek, 1981). They may then choose lower level or less prestigious occupations that fit into the broader plans for their lives. A second explanation is that women have lower perceptions of their own competence in many occupations and therefore shy away from these areas. This may be due, at least in part, to the lack of female role models in male-dominated professions such as business management. The third factor contributing to such choices for women is the lack of social support for entering or competing in male-dominated occupations. Career choices are influenced by family members (parents, siblings, spouses, and even children), by friends, by teachers and counselors. The advice and support from such sources often leads women away from highly competitive, male-dominated professions.

In this section, and throughout this book, we may be implying that "higher level" or "more prestigious" occupations are better. This is a value judgement that is widely held in our society—particularly in the business community. We do not subscribe to that position. Instead, we believe that everyone should be free to choose an occupation where they can best use their natural abilities, where they will find satisfaction, and where they can best contribute to the welfare of their families and societies. We do believe that women represent a valuable resource that has not been fully utilized by business organizations. However, we have the greatest respect for those women who choose to go against a growing social expectation that they do enter the business world and compete as aggressively as men. Women should not be ashamed to choose to spend part or all of the career portion of their lives working in the home and raising their children. The skills, the responsibilities, and surely the working hours of that position equal or exceed those of a top business executive.

A controversy concerning careers for women in business was ignited recently by an article in the *Harvard Business Review* by Felice Schwartz (1989). Schwartz is the president and founder of Catalyst, a non-profit organization that has worked for years to foster women's careers in the business world. Many have attacked the article as hurting the advancement of women because it advocated what some called a "mommy track." In fact, the author was arguing that business firms must provide viable career alternatives to women if they are going to attract and retain the women that they will need to fill middle and upper level management positions in the coming decades.

According to Schwartz: "The gender differences relevant to business fall into two categories: those related to maternity and those related to the differing traditions and expectations of the sexes. Maternity is biological rather than cultural. We can't alter it, but we can dramatically reduce its impact on the workplace and in many cases eliminate its negative effect on employee development" (p. 66). She suggests that businesses must recognize the reality of the "career-and-family women" who want a serious career and also want to participate actively in raising their children. Such women should be offered more than a six-to-eight-week maternity leave. They should have the option of leaving for six months, a year, or even five years.

The controversy arises because these women will be either temporarily or permanently out of the competition for the highest level positions. As we have shown in Chapters 2 and 3, in those organizations where careers progress according to tournament rules, this so-called "mommy track" will probably lead to an early plateau. However, if, as we have suggested, business firms adapt more open contest rules for upward mobility, then these women can more readily reenter the competition. In fact, reducing the strictness of the timing of career competitions and providing more opportunities for leaves would allow businesses to attract and retain more capable men as well as women.

Managerial Ability

There is no scientific evidence to support the contention that women do not have the capability to be outstanding executives. Comprehensive reviews of the thousands of studies on male-female differences conclude that although there are some differences, the strongest finding is that men and women are very similar in their abilities (Deaux, 1984). A review of studies on gender differences in leadership styles and effectiveness concludes that although there were some differences in effectiveness, these were found only in laboratory studies, not in real world settings (Dobbins & Platz, 1986). Other differences in how women behave in the workplace may be due to differences in personality traits (which in turn may be genetically determined or due to early socialization) or may be caused by the differing opportunities for women in the workplace (Downey & Lahey, 1988).

A thorough comparison of males and females is reported by Howard and Bray (1988) as part of their study of telephone company managers. There were some differences, but nothing to indicate that the women would not be effective; in fact, perhaps they would make better managers than the men. For example, the women were better students through high school, college, and graduate school. As might be expected, the men scored higher on an occupational commitment scale. The women seemed more ambivalent when interviewed about the importance of their jobs and careers. Personality tests showed that the women were higher than the men on scales measuring positiveness, affability, poise, and flexibility. There were statistically significant differences between the sexes on only one ability measure: Administrative Ability; and the difference was due to the fact that women scored higher than men on the creativity dimension.

On the overall assessment, differences appeared on seven of the ten dimensions. Females were higher on Administrative Skills, Interpersonal Skills, Work Involvement, and Social Liberalism; while men scored higher on Advancement Motivation, Independence, and External Self-Development. In weighing all these factors to make predictions about their management potential, the assessors apparently saw many trade-offs between the different strengths. Just as many women as men were predicted to move up in their companies. While there are differences between women and men in work-related abilities, type of motivation, and expectations, and while there may be situations in which men are more effective managers, there are certainly just as many situations in which women will be more effective.

Barriers to Progress for Women

Although the extent of intentional discrimination against women is impossible to assess, the data on the number of women in managerial positions (even in organizations that employ large numbers of females)

would suggest that it does exist. Many women report that they have
been discriminated against. In a survey of 110 male and female professionals from *Fortune 500* firms, 46 percent of the women but only 14
percent of the men reported being discriminated against (Trost, 1990).

It is, perhaps, the more subtle, unintentional discrimination against
women that is the more damaging. For example, exclusion from the
informal organization is a commonly reported problem. It may just happen because men (and women) often are more comfortable interacting
with those of the same gender. Traditional norms may exist within the
informal organization regarding gatherings for lunch, or breaks, or other
social activities such as golf or drinks after work. The female manager
may find herself interacting more with lower level women such as secretaries than with her male peers. By not being "one of the boys," she
may miss out with respect to critical informal information and with
regard to the ever important activity of network building. Her visibility
to the higher level male executives will be greatly reduced.

Stereotypes imposed by the male managerial majority may lead to
further isolation. Kanter (1977) notes that women may often be assigned
informal roles such as nurturant "mother" or tempting "seductress." If
they accept the role they may feel exploited; if they reject it they may
be even further ostracized from the informal organization. Our stereotypes of feminine versus masculine behavior also put many women into
a no-win situation. Some men feel that women will not make good
managers because they are too emotional and not tough enough. However, the woman who tries to behave in a more masculine manner is
often seen as too pushy or belligerent. A utility company vice president
has reported: "A man who's aggressive is considered assertive; when a
woman is, she's considered a bitch. It takes a lot of patience" (Rogan,
1984, p. 35).

Some of the problems faced by women are actually the result of men
trying to protect the "weaker" sex. Often women are given less challenging assignments than men (Mai-Dalton & Sullivan, 1981; Taylor &
Ilgen, 1981). This results in their building a less impressive track record
than men with comparable abilities. Since in many firms an early record
of success is a crucial signal that promotion decision makers look for
(see Chapters 2 and 3), the woman's entire career trajectory may be
lowered.

Many top managers report that their careers were helped by the existence of a mentor (Roche, 1979), but women may find it more difficult
to find suitable mentors in male-dominated fields such as management
(Hunt & Michael, 1983). The mentor provides the protege with coaching,
social support, sponsorship, exposure to top management, and identification with a successful role model (Greenhaus, 1987). These are all

important activities that will help the young manager develop important skills and become known to the higher level executives whose opinions will make or break his or her career.

Management is a high-pressure, stressful occupation for anyone and many people experience burnout of one form or another. It is particularly stressful for women. It is a brave woman indeed who enters this strange culture in which she may not know all the important rules of survival and where there may be no one to teach her how to play the game. As noted above, she is likely to be harassed, stereotyped, isolated, and victimized by overt or covert discrimination. She may receive inadequate support from either within the organization or from her family and friends. On top of all this, there is the reality of family responsibilities. Although in the modern two-career family there is more sharing of responsibility for the home and for the children, the heaviest burden still typically falls on the woman.

Three of the most common causes of stress in organizations are role conflict, role ambiguity, and role overload (Katz & Kahn, 1978). Furthermore, the process of job burnout is believed to occur when highly motivated individuals find themselves in organizations that simultaneously frustrate their aspirations while pressuring them to meet the needs of the organization (Moorhead & Griffin, 1989). Clearly, the path to the top of a business organization is a particularly difficult and stressful one for a woman. Successfully dealing with these challenges can be rewarding, however. Seventy-five percent of female vice presidents reported that they sometimes feel exhilarated by job-related stress, and one-third frequently felt that sensation (Rogan, 1984).

Misdirected Efforts

We feel that at this point in time there is a general consensus that more women should be in upper level management positions within major business corporations. However, progress has been very slow. We further believe that there are a number of other factors, in addition to those already discussed, that may help explain the apparent resistance to women at the top. These factors fall into three categories: actions by business firms, actions by women in business, and the basic nature of organizational structure and career patterns.

During the 1970s and early 1980s, business firms were under great pressure both from public opinion and from the courts to put women in more responsible positions. To some extent the response was one of tokenism and cooptation. Women were selected to serve on the boards of directors, women were appointed as corporate officers, and women were promoted into management positions in greater numbers. However, these women typically had little power. As we will document further below: the women on boards often did not have the expertise to participate in discussions of critical business issues; and the women who were made corporate officers were usually given the positions of secretary or treasurer; furthermore they were often older and less well educated women. We also suspect that early promotions of women into managerial level positions were often based on seniority, not necessarily managerial potential. While these moves allowed business firms to cite numbers which indicated progress for women, the figures were largely "window dressing." They did not represent real change in the roles of women in the power structure.

Real change is coming, but it requires that women prove themselves according to the same criteria used to evaluate male candidates for executive positions. This means that the entire career path is important: that candidates for executive positions often must start proving themselves very early, that early experience in critical functional areas matters, and that breadth of experience is required. This implies that only those women who started their careers after the company became serious about women executives may have a real shot at the top.

As we will show in the following chapters, there are certain functional areas that are more likely to lead to the top. The "right" area depends upon a number of factors; however, it is likely to be a function that contributes to what are believed to be the critical tasks facing the organization. It is likely to be a "line" function such as marketing or production or a critical control function such as accounting or finance. It is not likely to be a supporting "staff" function such as personnel/human resource management or public relations/communications, although this may be changing (Solomon, 1990). The latter areas are where many women choose to work or where they are assigned due to stereotypical thinking. While women (and men) may have very rewarding careers in these functions, they may not be on the right track if they aspire to the very highest positions in the firm.

Finally, let's consider the time that it takes to develop a top female executive (much more will be said about top executives in general in the following chapters). The following may be a typical scenario. Assume that in Year 0, a firm makes a strong commitment to developing and promoting women all the way to the top. The top executives look around and find that there are very few women even in middle management positions. Because of discrimination (intentional or unintentional), those who have moved up are older than their male peers. In addition, they are in what are believed to be noncritical staff functions. So as a result very few of these women are identified as serious contenders for top management. Therefore, the focus is on younger, newly hired women. Of course, the company cannot immediately promote these women into top executive positions. However, five years later, some of these women are promoted into lower level management positions at the same rate as men who were hired at the same time. Ten years later, they are promoted into general management or functional vice president positions at the same rate as the men. And finally, ten years after that, they enter top management in the same proportions as men.

Assuming the ideal conditions of 1) hiring of equal numbers of high potential young women and men (the Bell System study indicates that this is realistic—Howard & Bray, 1988), 2) equal retention of the same people (this may not yet be realistic), and 3) equal promotion rates for men and women, it would still take 25 years before women and men enter top management in equal numbers. Assuming, further, that for some enlightened companies, Year 0 was 1975, the women hired in that year will not make top management until the turn of the century. In some companies, Year 0 may have been earlier, in others, it may not have occurred yet.

Conditions 2 and 3 above appear to be related. Recent surveys of both male and female professionals have shown that women are much less likely to remain with their present employer than men. Furthermore, the reasons that are given for leaving are enlightening. Men were actually more likely to consider a job change for personal reasons than were women. The women plan to leave because their career progression has been blocked (Trost, 1990). Business firms must do more than just promote a token few women or else they will lose the best of the future female executives to the competition.

THE EXECUTIVE WOMAN: WHO IS SHE AND WHERE IS SHE?

Our first study of women who were corporate officers was conducted in the early 1980s (see Forbes & Piercy, 1983 for more details). At this time, women had only begun to make very slow progress into the highest levels of American corporations. The futurist Herman Kahn was asked how long it would be before 25 percent of the chief executives of *Fortune 500* companies were women. Kahn replied: "About 2,000 years, but make it 10 percent and I'll say within 20 years" (Robertson, 1978). Even this prognostication may have been overly optimistic. At the time, female representation in the highest executive positions was very low. A survey by *Fortune* of the top officers and directors of their 1,300 company population found just 10 women among the 6,400 officers and directors (0.16 percent), and this number had not increased from 1973 to 1978 (Robertson, 1978).

Even when listed as corporate directors, women were often not in positions of great influence. The directors on whom the chairmen relied most heavily were the outside CEOs or other persons with CEO-level experience, which few women possessed (Schwartz, 1980). Women were being chosen to bring to the board the "outsider's" point of view. They usually represented academia, the public sector, the media, the consumer, or minorities, as well as other women. Joan Ganz Cooney, who had served on several boards, said that corporations like to get "twofers" or "threefers," people with backgrounds in more than one outside area (Cooney, 1978). As more women move up into higher level management, it seems that concern with having women on the board may be waning. A survey by the executive search firm of Korn/Ferry found that the percentage of billion dollar companies with women on the board had leveled off at about 50 percent. However, among banks and financial institutions the percentage had dropped to about 60 percent—down from about 75 percent a few years earlier (Bennett, 1987).

Women officers, too, were often in positions of lesser influence. A survey of corporate-level women by Heidrick and Struggles, the executive search firm, reported that although 28 percent were at least vice presidents, 51 percent were secretaries or assistant secretaries. More than half of these women entered the organization in a clerical position and may not have the training or experience to influence top level decision making (Heidrick & Struggles, 1980).

It was clear at the time that women had very little power at the top levels of U.S. corporations. This was, in part, because relatively few women had the managerial, professional, or technical skills to contribute at the highest levels. Change was occurring, however. Women were obtaining more technical training and more business education, especially at the MBA level. These well educated women were moving into middle and upper-middle management positions at fairly young ages ("What's needed," 1980).

The trends seemed to indicate that we would see many more women in positions of executive responsibility in the future. Therefore we undertook a study to learn more about female executives (officers and upper level managers). We examined their backgrounds (age, education, place of birth, and mobility) and their current positions (titles, industries, size of companies). We examined in detail issues such as how the younger women executives differed from the older in terms of education and position, and whether the opportunities for women are greater in certain industries, or in firms of a certain size, or in particular geographical regions. It was anticipated that this study, which described the female executive of 1982, would serve as a benchmark against which the future progress of women managers could be measured. One follow-up study, conducted five years later, has already been completed and the results will be presented later in this chapter.

Data Source

The data for this initial study were obtained from Volumes 1, 2, and 3 of *Standard and Poor's Register of Corporations, Directors, and Executives* for 1982. Volume 2 contained a listing of approximately 70,000 directors and executives. This listing was reviewed and approximately 1,300 names (1.9 percent) were identified as those of females. Those who were serving only as directors were removed from the list, resulting in a sample of 1,262. Names, titles, dates and places of birth, education, and organizational affiliations were recorded. Volume 1 was the source of information about the individual firms in which the women were serving. Here we obtained information on the firm size, location, and industry. Volume 3 was the source for the number of women added between 1970 and 1981. Although not all female corporate executives are listed in this register, we were confident that the sample was representative in terms of both numbers and positions within the firms' hierarchies.

Results

New Entrants. In 1970, females represented two percent of the new additions to this register. They remained at or below that level for the next four years, and then the percentages started to rise. There was a particularly significant rise from 1977 to 1981, at which time the proportion of new entrants reached just over four percent. The placement of these new entrants was also changing. We looked at the percentage of newly listed female executives who were in positions of vice president or higher. This figure was at about 40 percent in 1970. There was a gradual decline in new additions to higher level positions from 1971–1973, a general leveling through 1977, and then a 57 percent increase from that time through 1981. In 1981, almost 60 percent of the newly listed female executives were going into upper level positions. These figures indicated that women were not only making more progress into the executive ranks, but were also attaining more responsible positions.

Background. The women who had risen to the top had certain background characteristics in common. They tended to be middle-aged or older. Ages ranged from 25 to 92, with a mean of 52.8 and a median of 55. Only about one out of six was under 40, while more than two-thirds were over 50, and one of eight was 70 or older.

About 96 percent of the female executives were born in the United States, the remainder being foreign-born. Large urban areas were the birthplace for a disproportionate number of female executives. While only 29.6 percent of the 1930 population (year of birth of the average female executive at the time of the study) lived in cities with populations of 100,000 or more, 47.3 percent of the female executives were born in such cities. Moreover, 72.6 percent of female executives were born in cities of 25,000 or larger, while only 40.1 percent of the population lived in such cities at the time.

The Northeast region of the country was the birthplace for nearly four out of ten of the female executives (38.9 percent). This region was followed by the North Central (Midwest) (32 percent), the South (20.9 percent), and the West (8.2 percent). We compared the percentages of female executives born in each area with the proportion working in each region and with the percent of the 1930 population in each area. The percentage working in the Northeast almost equaled the percentage born in the area (36.8 percent), and both percentages exceeded the proportion of the population living in the area at the time of birth (28 percent). This indicated a high level of opportunity for women in this region.

The percentage of women executives born in the North Central region was approximately equal to the proportion of the population from that area (31.3 percent). However, the percentage working in the area was lower (27.5 percent), indicating that this region had been feeding executive talent to the other areas. The percentage of executive women working in the South (22.3 percent) slightly exceeded the percentage born there, but both proportions were significantly lower than the population percentage for that region (30.7 percent). This indicated that there was relatively less opportunity for women in this area. Finally, in the West the opportunities (as measured by the percentage working there) were good. The proportion of executive women working there (13.4 percent) exceeded both percentage of women executives born there and the 1930 population percentage (10 percent). Thus the West has been a region of promise for talented businesswomen.

In another analysis of female executive mobility, we compared the number of women born in each region with the number of those who had stayed and with the total number working in the area. There were 470 women executives born in the Northeast, and of these, 381 had stayed in the area. This was the highest percentage for any region (81.1 percent). There were only 444 women in the group employed in this area, however—a net loss of 5.5 percent. Most of those who left the Northeast went to the South (46 out of 89).

The North Central was the region of birth for 386 executives. Of these, approximately 72 percent had stayed in this region (279) and only a total of 332 were working there. This represented a net loss of 14 percent. The North Central area fed all the other regions with slightly more emigration to the West.

The South experienced a net gain of 6.7 percent of executive women working there in comparison to the number born in the region. Of the 253 women born in the South, 183 (72.3 percent) stayed, but the total working there was 270. Most of this immigration came from the North-east. The women who left the South were most likely to head west.

There were only 99 executive women born in the West. Seventy-three stayed in that region, however, there were 162 working there. This was a net gain of 63.6 percent. As our general population and our industries have moved south and west so have upwardly mobile executive women.

As a group, these women were not that highly educated. Nearly half (48.1 percent) did not have four year undergraduate degrees. About one-third had undergraduate degrees and about one in five possessed a graduate degree. However, those with no degrees were concentrated in the over–50 age group. The younger executives tended to be more highly educated. Of those under 40, better than three out of four (78 percent) had at least an undergraduate degree and more than one-third (35 percent) had a graduate degree.

Female executives employed in the Northeast were more highly ed-ucated than those in the other geographical regions. In the Northeast, almost three out of five had an undergraduate degree and slightly less than one out of four had a graduate degree. In the other regions slightly less than half had undergraduate degrees, and in the South and West only one out of eight had a graduate degree.

Summarizing her background, we found that the typical female ex-ecutive was in her mid–50s and was born in a large city in the Northeast or North Central regions of the country. Although there has been move-ment to the South and West, she probably still works in the same region where she was born. Her level of education depends on her age and region of employment. Although about half of these female executives did not possess a college degree, most of the younger women did. In the under–40 age group more than one-third also had graduate training. The level of education was greatest in the Northeast.

Business Positions. We examined the positions in which the women executives were working as well as the relationships between the po-sition and the executive's age, and education. Also investigated were the industries and the sizes of the firms and the relationships between these variables and age, education, and positions of the female execu-tives.

Approximately 15 percent of the executives in this study were the heads of firms (president, chairman, or CEO). However, these were for the most part smaller firms. The sample was fairly evenly divided between those serving in positions titled vice president and higher (49.2 percent) and those serving in what are apparently lower level positions (manager, counsel, secretary/treasurer, secretary, and trea-surer).

Several background factors were found to be related to the positions held by the female executives. The average age of those who headed firms was 63, well above the mean age of 57 for chief executives of the 800 largest firms at the time. In addition, almost 60 percent were 60 years of age or older. The average ages for vice presidents, managers, and counsels were 51, 47, and 48, respectively. For those in secretary and treasurer positions the ages were in the 56 to 58 range. The age distributions suggest that most of these women were already at the peak of their careers. The large majority (more than 70 percent) of those in secretary and treasurer positions were over 50. However, at the executive vice president, vice president, and manager levels, more than 40 percent of the women were under 50. Since it is from these three levels that upward movement is most likely to occur and since the average chief executive is appointed at the age of 49, many in this group may have still been in the running for further promotion. Because of the existence of age norms for promotions in industry (Lawrence, 1988), however, the majority of these women would not be serious candidates for higher positions.

Another factor working against the upward movement of these women is the lack of education. For those in positions of manager, vice president, and executive vice president, approximately one-third to one-half did not have a college degree. In the secretary and treasurer positions, 57 to 66 percent did not possess a degree.

Where were these women employed? This sample represented a wide range of industries although almost half (48 percent) were employed in various manufacturing firms. The next largest group was in banking (12.3 percent), followed by business services and retail trades. Also represented were insurance, wholesale trades, financial services, construction, transportation, and utilities.

A younger female executive was found in certain industries. The highest percentage of women under 50 were in the financial services, transportation, utilities, and banking industries. Although only 32 percent of the female executives in this study were under 50, in these industries about 50 percent or more were under this age. In the wholesale trades, retail trades, and manufacturing industries, we found the highest percentages of women over 60 years of age.

Education seemed to be more important in certain industries. Female executives in the utilities, business services, and banking industries were more highly educated, with more than 60 percent having at least an undergraduate degree. The highest percentage of graduate degrees were found in the utilities, banking, and financial services industries. Those with the least amount of formal education were in construction and wholesaling.

Because of the large number of female executives in manufacturing, this classification was examined in more detail. Within this group, 20 percent were in the printing industry, followed by fabricated metal prod-

ucts and machinery with approximately 15 percent in each. The remaining 50 percent were fairly evenly distributed among the nine other
groups. Female executives in these first three industries tended to be
both younger and more highly educated. The printing industry in particular seemed to provide outstanding opportunity for women. Here,
more than three out of four occupied positions of manager or higher;
and one out of four served as CEO. More than 60 percent had at least
an undergraduate degree, and more than 20 percent had graduate degrees.

Banking and financial services had the highest percentage of
women in upper management positions, with three out of four at the
level of vice president or higher. These were followed by business
services and insurance where more than half of the female executives
were in upper management positions. The construction industry
ranked lowest with only about one out of five women in upper management positions. Next lowest were utilities and transportation with
about one out of three in higher level spots. In these last two industries, the female executives were concentrated in the secretary and
treasurer roles.

Female executive age, education, and positions were all related to the
size of the firm. As firm size increased, the proportion of women aged
60 and above decreased, while the percentages in their 30s and 40s
increased. For example, in firms with $5 to $10 million in sales, about
18 percent of the women executives were less than 50; while in the firms
with over $1 billion in sales, over 54 percent were under 50 years of age.

Education was also strongly related to the size of the firm. While an
older woman with little formal education could make it to the top in the
smaller firms, higher education became almost mandatory in the largest
firms. In firms in the $5 to $10 million sales category, 70 percent of the
women had no undergraduate degree. In the billion dollar firms, 89
percent had at least an undergraduate degree, and 44.5 percent had
graduate degrees.

Positions held were also related to firm size. The percentage of
women heading firms decreased as the size of the firm increased.
Although one out of five of the female executives serving in firms
with sales of less than $5 million was the chief executive, there were
none occupying this position in the firms with sales in excess of $1
billion. In these large firms there were, however, significantly greater
percentages of women in the positions of vice president and executive vice president than in any other size firms. In the firms with
sales ranging from $5 to $500 million, the greatest percentage of the
women executives were corporate secretaries. Thus it appears that
the greatest opportunities for women exist in the smallest and in the
largest of American firms.

Conclusions

The women in this study occupied three distinct types of positions. First, there were those in chairman/president/CEO positions. Next there were the executive vice presidents, vice presidents, and managers. Finally, there were the corporate secretaries and treasurers. A different type of women was found in each position, they served in different types of firms, and they surely had different chances for further upward mobility.

The chief executives (15 percent of the sample) tended to be located in the Northeast, were older, fairly well educated, and were likely to head smaller firms in the wholesale and retail trades, manufacturing, and business services. The vice presidents and managers (43 percent of the sample) were also likely to be located in the Northeast but were younger and more highly educated. They were most likely to be employed by the larger firms. A very high percentage of the women in banking, insurance, and financial services were in vice presidential level positions. Those in the secretary and treasurer positions were older and less well educated. They were distributed fairly evenly throughout the country and were likely to represent a high percentage of the women executives in the medium-sized firms.

At the time of this study, fewer than two percent of corporate executives were women. The proportion of newly appointed executives who were women had doubled over the preceding decade, from two to four percent. In addition, although many female officers were in the positions of secretary and treasurer (41 percent), the percentage of new appointees at the vice presidential level or higher had increased from less than 40 percent to 57 percent over the previous 11 years. Thus, it seemed that slow but sure progress was being made by women into the executive suites.

There seemed to be regional differences in opportunities and in the inclination of women to accept these opportunities. For example, more women executives were born in the Northeast than one would expect based on the population, while there were fewer from the South than expected. Regional differences in the socialization of young women as well as differences in the level of industrialization are two explanations for these results.

Many female corporate officers were not likely to experience any further upward mobility. They were older and in dead-end positions such as secretary or treasurer. Those women who had achieved chief executive status were also older and headed the smaller firms. However, a significant number of highly educated younger women had reached the vice presidential level in the larger firms and in the service-oriented firms. Breakthroughs of women into major chief executive positions are likely to be made by this group of women. Therefore, based on this study, we would predict that the first female chief executives of major firms would be highly educated, younger women, employed by the largest firms, in the service industries (banking, insurance, and financial services), and in the Northeast region of the country.

THE EXECUTIVE WOMAN: PROGRESS DURING THE 1980s

While our research seemed to indicate that women were making meaningful progress, not everyone was that optimistic. Morrison, White, and Van Velsor (1987) argued that although women had already broken through the "glass ceiling" by entering high level general management positions, they were facing an even more formidable "wall" that prevents entry into the top executive suite. Their research was based on in-depth interviews with 76 women in or near general management positions at 25 *Fortune 100* companies. They also talked with 25 "savvy insiders" about the special problems encountered by women in major corporations. While the study provides excellent insights into the problems, pitfalls, and politics of the big corporation, its assessment of the future may be too pessimistic (Fagenson, 1987).

Business Week provided a more upbeat analysis in a cover story with the headline: "They're About to Break Through to the Top." Here it was noted that 37 percent of corporate managers were women, up from 24 percent a decade earlier. The story provided profiles of five women positioned properly as candidates for chief executive positions; and also identified 50 more "women to watch" who may become future chief executives (Baum, 1987).

The *Business Week* article suggested that women managers were younger, better educated, and in higher level positions than ever before. However, only limited data were presented to support this argument. Our second study was designed to examine that proposition in more detail. We again looked at the placement of women with respect to position, industry, age, education, and geographical area. This analysis also allowed comparisons with the earlier data reported above (Forbes, Piercy, & Hayes, 1988).

Data Source

As in the first study, the source of our data was *Standard and Poor's Register*. We gathered data from the 1987 register to compare with the 1982 data previously used. Volume 2 was reviewed and 1,945 names were identified as female. This represented an approximately 50 percent increase in the number of females listed in the register. However, the number still only represented less than three percent of the over 70,000

Table 5.1
Female Executives by Title (Percentages)

TITLE	1982	1987	Change Increase (+) Decrease (−)
President	15.1	16.2	+ 7.3
Executive Vice-President	6.9	13.1	+89.9
Vice-President	27.2	37.5	+45.2
Manager	9.0	4.8	−46.7
Counsel	0.8	1.4	+75.0
Secretary & Treasurer	9.9	6.3	−36.4
Treasurer	6.2	4.1	−33.9
Secretary	24.9	16.5	−33.7

names listed. Names, titles, dates and place of birth, education, and organizational affiliation were recorded. Volume 1 was the source of information about the firms in which the women were serving. In addition, Volume 3 was reviewed in order to determine the number of women added to the list between 1982 and 1987.

Results and Discussion

New Entrants. Our previous analysis showed that in 1970 women represented about two percent of the new additions to the register. They remained at or slightly above two percent until 1978. The next four years showed a steady increase with the percentage doubling to 4.1 by 1981. Our later analysis indicated that in the 1982–1984 time period there was a decrease to the three- to three-and-a-half percent level. However, this was followed by significant increases in both 1985 and 1986. In the last year that we analyzed, the proportion of new entrants who were women was almost six percent. New entrants listed had increased by almost 50 percent in five years.

The Positions of Women Executives. As shown in Table 5.1, the number of females in more senior positions had increased sharply. While there was only a slight increase at the highest level, the proportion of women who were in the executive vice president and vice president levels increased substantially. This is important because it is from these positions that movement into the top level spots will occur. The proportion of females in the lower level corporate positions had decreased apprecia-bly—especially the percentage in the secretary role from which there is little upward mobility.

We also examined the functional areas in which women at the vice presidential level were working. Here we found that 22.3 percent were in staff functions, such as human resources, administration, and public affairs, that have traditionally been more open to women but which do not typically lead to the top. However, 24.6 percent of the female vice presidents were in production/operations, marketing, finance, or legal areas—the functional backgrounds of a majority of chief executives.

Age Shifts. The age of the female executive group dropped in five years. While in 1982, only 32 percent were under 50, this had increased to 49 percent by 1987. The proportion over 60 decreased from 37 percent to 25 percent during the same time period. A larger pool of younger high level women was being created from which selections might be made for top executive positions.

The female executives of 1987 were not only younger but they were also reaching higher positions at an earlier age. The average age de-creased in every position with the sharpest declines at the vice president (51 to 40) and at the counsel (48 to 40.5) positions. Substantial decreases were also seen in the ages of executive vice presidents (53 to 49) and managers (47 to 44).

Equally impressive was the sharp rise in the percentages of executives who were under 50 years of age. This figure rose substantially in all of the key promotable categories: executive vice president (37 to 57 per-cent), vice president (43 to 60 percent), manager (53 to 67 percent), and counsel (60 to 88 percent). This further extends the cadre of promotable female executives.

Industry Representation. Between 1982 and 1987 there was a significant shift in industry representation among the female executives. The largest change was a reduction in the proportion employed in the manufactur-ing sector. In 1982, 48 percent of the women listed were employed in manufacturing; but in 1987 this figure had dropped to 37 percent. Sizable increases were found in financial services (2.5 to 5.9 percent), banking (12.3 to 15.4 percent), insurance (4.6 to 7.1 percent), wholesale trades (3.7 to 6.0 percent), utilities (1.5 to 3.6 percent), and business services (8.9 to 10.8 percent). Smaller gains were made in retailing (5.5 to 6.4 percent) and transportation (2.1 to 2.6 percent), while the percentage in construction stayed about the same (2.5 to 2.6 percent). While structural changes in American industry may account for some of this change it is highly unlikely that this is the sole reason. It appears that women are moving to the service industries where they believe their best oppor-tunities for advancement lie.

The ages of the women executives decreased in all industries except construction and utilities, where there were slight increases. The sharpest decline was in manufacturing (56.8 to 51.3). However, this average age is still high from the point of view of opportunity for upward mobility. This is reinforced by the fact that only 36.2 percent of the women in manufacturing were under 50. The lowest average ages were in services such as banking, insurance, financial services, and business services and in transportation. The average age was 47 to 48 in all of these industries. In addition, these industries had the highest percentages of women under 50—ranging from 56 to 62 percent. These statistics further support our argument that the first breakthroughs to the top will occur in service industries.

Education. The level of education reported for female executives was much higher in 1987 than it was in 1982. In 1982, nearly half (48 percent) of the female executives lacked an undergraduate degree, while in 1987, this figure had dropped to only 18.7 percent. The percentage with only an undergraduate degree increased from about one-third (33.7 percent) to almost one-half (49 percent). The number with graduate degrees also increased quite substantially, from 18.2 percent in 1982 to 32.3 percent in 1987. The level of education was even higher in the younger age groups. More than half of those under 40 had completed graduate training.

Level of education was positively related to the size of the firms. For example, in manufacturing firms only about 16 percent of the women employed by small firms (less than $10 million in sales) had graduate degrees. This increased to over 40 percent when firm size exceeded $100 million in revenues and jumped to 60 percent in the billion dollar firms.

Geographical Location. In the 1982 study, we found that most of the executive women were employed in the Northeast region of the country. This was followed by the North Central, South, and West, in that order. The rank order had not changed by 1987, however, the percentage in the West was increasing while the proportion employed in the North Central region had declined. Regional economics and the shifting of industry from the "rust belt" to the "sun belt" probably can explain these trends in female employment.

The North Central region has been underrepresented by women executives in comparison to its population. It was even more poorly represented at the higher managerial levels (vice president and above). The Northeast had a higher percentage of upper level managers than its overall proportion of women managers. This may be due to the concentration of financial and service firms in that region.

Conclusions

Our analysis of the backgrounds and positions of almost 2,000 female executives indicated that significant shifts were occurring that should give hope to aspiring female executives.

First, a major shift was seen into the higher level positions of vice president and executive vice president, and away from secretary and treasurer positions. In addition, the women in these higher level positions were younger and much more highly educated than was the case five years earlier. The data indicate that the "glass ceiling" is being broken by larger numbers of younger, better educated women.

There also seemed to be movement away from the manufacturing industry and into services (banking, business and financial services, and insurance). Geographically, women were moving away from the North Central (Midwest) region of the country and into the West. In both cases, women appeared to be moving where the best opportunities lie.

While our research provided evidence of relative progress, the number of women in executive positions as a percentage of the whole is still unbelievably small. In 1987, fewer than three percent of all positions listed in the *Standard and Poor's Register* were held by women. Furthermore, the proportion of newly appointed executives who were women was only five to six percent. Our figures indicate that through the 1970s and 1980s this percentage was doubling every ten years. However, many of these women were not in contention for further promotion due to age, education, or placement in dead-end positions. Therefore, women probably make up not more than three percent of the candidates for CEO positions at the present time. If we assume that these women are equally qualified with male candidates, however, then they should start to move into top positions soon. If even one or two percent of the firms within the *Fortune 1000* were headed by women this would mean that there would be 10 to 20 female CEO of major firms. We predict that this breakthrough will begin to occur during the 1990s, and that by the year 2000 the "wall" between women and top management will look like the wall between East and West Berlin.

HOW WOMEN WILL REACH THE TOP IN THE 1990s AND BEYOND

The next decade or two will represent a time of unparalleled opportunity for women in the business world. There has been discrimination in the past and there still remains a great deal of bias and stereotyping, but this will change. Although many may wish it were different, the free enterprise system is not necessarily set up to do the right thing according to moral or ethical principles. Male business leaders cannot hire, develop, and promote women just because their consciences are bothering them. However, they can and will hire, develop, and promote women because it is necessary for the success and (for some) for the survival of their companies.

As we have indicated throughout this book, the world is changing very rapidly. Change simultaneously represents a threat, a problem, and an opportunity. At the current point in time, the "mega-forces" of economics, technology, and demographics are converging in such a way that women (and minority group members) will have to be moved into positions of increasing power and influence.

Economics and technology are causing our business organizations to move away from the traditional bureaucratic model in which all important (and many non-important) decisions are made at the top of a multilayered hierarchy; in which the work is done in rigidly defined, specialized, functional areas; and in which impersonal rules and procedures govern all activity. Such organizations work very well when you know exactly what you want to do and how to do it. Unfortunately, when things change, these systems are so closed that they do not see the change, and so rigid that they cannot adapt to it. Successful firms today are moving toward what Tom Peters has called "the flexible, porous, adaptive, fleet-of-foot organization of the future" (1987, p. 659). It will be very difficult indeed to build "walls" or "glass ceilings" within these new systems.

In the successful business organization of the twenty-first century, the key competitive capabilities will be creativity and innovation as opposed to efficient performance of routine operations. This capacity will be fostered by the unique combination of individualistic thinking and teamwork. The advice given to many women in many traditional organizations was to try to be "one of the boys." In the business firm of the future, a more "feminine leadership style" (Loden, 1985) may actually be more effective than the competitive, authoritarian, masculine style.

Furthermore, shifting demographics will dictate that these organizations must be staffed by more and more women. Between 1988 and the year 2000, white men will be leaving the work force in record numbers. They are being replaced by newly hired workers who are more likely to be women or minority group members. Eighty-eight percent of the growth in the work force from now until the end of the century will be from women, blacks, Hispanics, and Asians, including immigrants (De Venuta, 1990).

How should women prepare for this opportunity and how should they manage their careers? Our advice is based on the results of the studies described in this chapter on women, the previous chapters on early career issues, and also on the following chapters, which will describe top executive careers.

Education

Our research on the backgrounds of women executives clearly indicates that those who are the more recent arrivals in important high level positions (vice president and above) are very well educated. They possess master's degrees in many areas. Depending upon the nature of the business, specialized master's programs may be helpful, but in general the very popular Master of Business Administration (especially from a top school) provides increased credibility to the woman manager. We found that the position of legal counsel is being filled by women in many corporations. This is an area in which more specialized graduate training is required and an area from which many firms (especially those subject to heavy governmental regulation) choose their CEOs. Graduate work beyond the master's level is also helpful. A doctorate in an area related to the business of the organization provides tremendous credibility and often increased visibility. Advanced education serves at least two functions related to career mobility. First, it gives you knowledge and skills that make you more marketable, that help you perform your job more effectively, and that give you more influence within the organization. Second, a graduate degree is a "signal" that many top managers consider when making promotion decisions. It shows that you have the level of intellect and the motivation and perseverance needed to enter and complete a rigorous academic program. This may suggest to many that you also have the ability to function at the highest executive level.

Early Identification

Although we have argued that this is not necessarily the best system, many corporations are strongly influenced by early success and promotion as signals of ability. Many also rely on assessment center evaluations to identify those with managerial potential. Problems with both approaches have been discussed in the earlier chapters and alternatives will be offered later in this book. However, at the present point in time it is critical to realize that in many corporate career systems, unless you win the early competition and are promoted quickly, you may be out of the running for the higher positions in the organization (Rosenbaum, 1979, 1984; Chapters 2 & 3). Many firms believe that early identification is necessary in order to justify the heavy investment that they will make in managerial development. The investment must be amortized over a long period of time. In fact, this is a consideration that often works against the advancement of women, since they are believed to be more likely to leave the corporation, depriving the firm of any return on its stake in their development. It follows therefore that in order to be considered a candidate for top management a woman must send a strong signal of commitment to a career and of loyalty to the firm.

Functional Background

The quickest path to the top in any organization is through the functional areas that are most critical to the effective performance of critical tasks. For example, in a consumer products company, the most critical function is often marketing. In a utility, it might be the engineering or the legal function. The top executives in a computer company might have a background in design or system analysis.

Although the functional specialist may make it to the top if her skills are needed there, many firms prefer a person with broader experience. The recent study of executive women by Morrison, White, and Van Velsor (1987) confirms this point. Taking a new job in a different part of the company was described by one "savvy insider" as a critical turning point for highly promotable women. Not only does it broaden the base of experience but, for women particularly, it indicates appropriate risk-taking ability. For many women the move requires leaving a staff position in which she has technical expertise and experience and in which women are accepted and moving to an unfamiliar, male-dominated line spot. The move may appear to be a lateral transfer into a position where the chances of failure are high, and as a result many women may refuse such a job change. However, this is part of the development process and is also a crucial test that must be passed—for men as well as women.

Industry and Geographical Area

Our research has shown that while there are more women executives in manufacturing firms than in any other industry, the numbers are increasing more rapidly in the service sector—particularly, insurance, financial services, business services, and banking. In addition, the most women executives work in the Northeast and North Central sections of the country, but the most rapid increase in numbers is occurring in the West. Two factors seem to be responsible for these changes. The first is the relative growth and decline of the industries and geographical regions themselves. The other is the traditionally greater acceptance of women in the service industries than in manufacturing.

Before concluding that women should all move into service industries in the West, let's look at some other figures. Although the numbers are still low, the greatest relative increase in women executives between 1982 and 1987 occurred in the utility industry (140 percent). Impressive gains were also made in wholesale trades and in transportation. In addition, we are seeing turnarounds in many manufacturing concerns in the "rust-belt" regions of the country. These newly revitalized manufacturing firms are smaller, leaner, flatter, and less committed to the traditional ways of doing things (that's what got them in trouble in the first place). They are operating in a highly competitive world market and need people who can produce results—not people who fit an obsolete stereotype of what an effective manager should look or act like. We believe that women executives are needed in all industries, especially in the traditionally masculine areas. Aspiring women should also be reminded that top executives may change firms or industries early in their career but that they typically settle down to the task of learning all about a particular firm or industry where they stay put as they rise to the top.

TOP EXECUTIVE PROFILES

Profiles of high ranking women executives confirm our conclusions and recommendations (Baum, 1987). Based on a survey of their top 1000 companies, *Business Week* identified "Fifty Women to Watch" for movement into chief executive positions. Thirty-one of these successful executives had graduate degrees; there were 16 MBAs, eight with other master's degrees, five J.D.s, and two Ph.D.s. The careers of the most promising executives were described in more detail, and we will briefly summarize two very different career paths here. A profile of another successful woman, Karen Horn, President of Bank One, Cleveland, can be found at the end of Chapter 8.

Ellen Marram received an MBA from Harvard in 1970 and worked in marketing and product management for Lever Brothers, Johnson & Johnson, and Standard Brands. She was a group products manager at Standard Brands when it was acquired by Nabisco in 1981. In 1987, she was promoted to president of Nabisco's billion dollar grocery division where she now has responsibility for eight different functional areas: marketing, business development, finance, manufacturing, information systems, quality assurance, personnel, and research and development (Baum, 1987). The importance of education, the right functional background, developing within one industry, and finally, breadth of experience are clearly illustrated.

The opportunities that change in old line manufacturing firms can present are exemplified by the career of Roxanne Decyk. Also well educated, Decyk has a J.D. from Marquette. She joined International Harvester (now Navistar International) in 1981 as corporate secretary. Only three years later she was promoted to a senior vice president for administration with the mandate of developing a more participative culture in this traditionally autocratic firm which was undergoing major restructuring (Baum, 1987). The role of Roxanne Decyk in revitalizing Navistar has recently been described by Borucki and Barnett (1990). She played a key part in diagnosing the problems that were making the turn-around difficult and in developing the new culture, mission, and strategy.

The times they are a-changing and the composition of the executive suite will be changing with the times. This is a truly unique and exciting time for women in the business world.

6

The Origins and Formative Years of the Chief Executive Officer

In 1989, America's 800 highest paid business CEOs ran companies that employed 20 million workers and generated $3.2 trillion in revenues ("The power and the pay," 1989). What is known about these business leaders? How did they rise to such prestigious and powerful positions? Are people from particular backgrounds more likely to become top executives? Do today's CEOs differ in origins and background from their predecessors of previous generations?

Since the beginning of the large-scale business enterprise there has been interest in the backgrounds of the executives who direct and shape these organizations. Early researchers asked: Are there common threads in their origins and formative years that might prove to be indicators of future success? In this chapter we will ask and answer that question as well as the additional question: What long-term trends may have changed over time and what new trends, if any, may have arisen in recent years?

EARLIER STUDIES OF THE BACKGROUNDS OF CEOs

Gregory and Nau (1962) examined the social origins of 300 business leaders in the textile, steel, and railroad industries in the 1870–1879 decade. Miller (1962) analyzed similar data for 190 chairmen and presidents of leading industrial firms, public utilities, and financial institutions for the 1901–1910 time period. In her comprehensive study of 428 leading business executives, Newcomer (1955) chose three time periods: 1900, 1925, and 1950. Warner and Abegglen (1955) examined the backgrounds of more than 8,500 business leaders through questionnaires and personal interviews. We conducted a detailed study of the background of the 791 top CEOs in 1978 (Piercy & Forbes, 1981) and have also carried out a similar analysis on the *Forbes* listing of the 800 highest paid CEOs of 1989.

In November 1952, May 1976, and April 1986, *Fortune* published results of their surveys of CEOs which, among other things, provided characteristics and background information. Additionally, there have been several studies published in academic journals in recent years which provide further insight into various aspects of the early years of America's business leaders. Together these studies create a picture of the backgrounds of top corporate managers for well over a century. Significantly, where the time periods of these studies overlap, we will show that the findings are very consistent.

The data bases for the various studies differ both in sample sizes and composition; however, these differences are largely a reflection of the changes that have taken place in American industry over the years. Except for a few railroads, the names of companies headed by the business leaders of the 1870s are not recognizable today. Only a handful, such as General Electric, Westinghouse, and AT&T, are recognizable from Miller's study of top executives at the turn of the century. Nevertheless, these studies all had a common purpose; namely, to profile America's business leaders at a particular point in time. The differences in sample composition and size will not invalidate historical comparisons.

To the best of our knowledge, no other studies of CEOs have attempted to compare current data with such a wide array of earlier research. In this chapter, we will explore the early years of today's CEOs and make comparisons with those of previous generations. First, we will examine the CEOs' family backgrounds and places of birth. Following this, education and personal characteristics will be discussed. Finally, we will show how they entered the workplace.

SOCIAL STATUS

Historically, America's business leaders have come from upper- and middle-class families. Gregory and Nau, in their study of the industrial elite of the 1870s, estimated that about 90 percent were from this segment of the population (Gregory & Nau, 1962, p. 202). Miller's (1962) study of the first decade of the twentieth century arrived at similar findings. He concluded: "... poor immigrants and poor farm boys who become business leaders have always been more conspicuous in American history books than in American history" (p. 328).

Newcomer (1955), who studied the executive of 1925 and 1950, found little difference in the two periods but, in general, there was a decline in upper-class family backgrounds and an increased representation from the middle and lower classes in comparison with the 1900s. She did note, however, that the percentage of CEOs from poor families increased with the size of the firm (p. 64).

By 1976, the upper and lower middle classes provided more than four-fifths of the *Fortune 500* chief executives, leading Burck to conclude that "today's CEO is substantially a product of the middle class" (1976, p. 174). The number whose fathers were business executives had sharply shrunk, while those whose fathers were blue collar or clerical workers had increased from one in 20 in 1900 to nearly one in four by 1976.

While confirming the greater representation among those with middle-class backgrounds, Boone et al. disagree with Burck's conclusion. They found that the CEO of 1986 was four times more likely to have grown up in an upper- or upper-middle class household than the typical American of the same age (Boone, Kurtz, & Fleenor, 1988b, p. 37). While according to their classification, only 18 percent of the CEOs were from upper-lower and lower-lower class family backgrounds, this was the background for 54 percent of the population of the same age. They conclude that " . . . the majority of the nation's business leaders come from the relatively privileged class" (1988b, p. 37).

These studies appear contradictory and the most likely explanation is differences in defining different classes. What one researcher calls lower-middle class, another may consider upper-lower class. Our interpretation is that socioeconomic class does make a difference. Those from higher classes typically do have an advantage, but the advantage derives primarily from the things that a more privileged background has taught them, not from the social status itself. Higher social status brings with it better schooling, better networks developed through family and school contacts, and often more social poise and self-confidence. Later in this chapter we will examine the educational backgrounds of chief executives and note the tremendous concentration from a very small number of schools. To a large extent this effect may be overcome, however. Pfeffer (1977) found that the effects of social origin on salaries are less for those with a Master's degree in business administration (MBA); and are less in certain positions or organizations (specifically, less for those in line versus staff positions and for those in manufacturing and in larger organizations). Likewise, Useem and Karabel (1986) found that the mobility of senior managers was affected less by socioeconomic background for those with advanced business degrees.

FATHER'S OCCUPATION

Another factor, that reflects social status but also affects the type of early role models available to an individual, is the father's occupation. For the youth of the second half of the twentieth century, the mother's occupation may be equally important; but since the CEOs of the past

Table 6.1
The CEO's Father's Occupation (Percentages)

Occupation	Time Period				
	1870s[a]	1910[b]	1950[c]	1976[d]	1986[e]
Head of Same Corporation	N/S	N/S	12	9	8
Business Executive	51	55	44	38	49
Professional	13	22	17	25	19
Clerical Worker	N/S	N/S	6	6	3
Laborer	8	2	7	15	15
Farmer	25	14	13	7	6
Public Official	3	7	1	N/S	N/S
Totals	100	100	100	100	100

N/S Not separately identified.

[a] Francis W. Gregory and Irene D. Nau, "The American Industrial Elite in the 1870's," published in Men in Business, William Miller, Editor, Harper and Row, New York, 1962, p. 202.

[b] William Miller, "American Historians and the Business Elite," published in Men in Business, William Miller, Editor, Harper and Row, New York, 1962, p. 325.

[c] Adapted from Mabel Newcomer, The Big Business Executive, Columbia University Press, New York, 1955, pp. 53-54.

[d] Charles G. Burck, "A Group Profile of the Fortune 500 Chief Executive," Fortune, May 1976, p. 174. It was necessary to interpret figures from a graph so accuracy is probably + or - 10 percent.

[e] Maggie McComas, "Atop The Fortune 500: A Survey of the CEOs." Fortune, April 28, 1986, p. 30. It was necessary to interpret figures from a graph so accuracy is probably + or - 10 percent.

and present were born in an earlier time and were, and are, almost exclusively male, we will focus on the father's occupation.

Almost two-thirds of America's CEOs are the sons of business executives or professionals. Moreover, when the CEOs whose fathers headed the same firm are included, the figure increases to three-quarters (see Table 6.1).

Newcomer (1955) found that in 1950 the proportion of executives and professional men among the fathers of business leaders was six to seven times that of business executives and professionals in the general population. Conversely, the proportion of skilled and unskilled workers among the fathers of top executives was less than one-twentieth that of the male population.

The number whose fathers were farmers has steadily declined from one-quarter in the 1870s to six percent in 1986, a decline that has been offset by an increase in those whose fathers were skilled or unskilled laborers. In fact, since 1950 the percentage of CEOs whose fathers were either farmers or laborers has remained steady at about 20 percent.

In more detailed analysis of these occupational groups, Warner and Abegglen (1955) found that CEOs were more likely to be the sons of certain professionals than others. They compared the frequency of CEO's fathers' occupations with the proportion of the national population represented by that profession. For the professions of law, the ministry, engineering, and medicine, the ratios were 8 to 1, 5.5 to 1, 4.8 to 1, and 4.8 to 1, respectively. When examining the lower status groups, they found additional status distinctions. Most of the business leaders who came from farm backgrounds were the sons of owners and managers of large farms. Most of those who came from laborer families were the sons of skilled rather than unskilled workers.

Our discussion of both social status and father's occupations seems to indicate substantial social stratification within the business community in this country—not necessarily the Horatio Alger story we prefer to believe. The son or daughter of the unskilled laborer certainly has to work harder to reach the top than those whose parents are professionals or business executives, but the data indicate that it can be done.

RELIGIOUS AFFILIATION

At the turn of the century, over one-half (55 percent) of the top business executives were Episcopalians and Presbyterians. At that time, these two denominations accounted for less than one-fifth (19 percent) of the U.S. population of the same age (Miller, 1962). This over-representation has continued. In 1986, over one-third (35.2 percent) of the CEOs indicated one of these two as their religious preference, although they comprised less than one-twentieth of the national population (McComas, 1986). Over the entire period covered by these studies of CEOs, the Methodists and Baptists have been the most underrepresented groups, although substantial gains have been experienced by the Methodists.

The earliest, and the most recent studies, reveal an over-representation of Jewish business leaders in comparison with their proportion of the U.S. population. Newcomer (1955) found that the Jewish top executives were heavily concentrated in the merchandising, entertainment, and communications industries. McComas (1986) found that 7.6 percent of all CEOs were Jewish in contrast to about a two percent representation in the general population.

Catholic business leaders have increased substantially in number in the last 35 years, although they continue to be underrepresented in comparison to the percentage of Catholics in our total population. In 1950, less than one-tenth of the top business leaders were Catholic, in contrast to about one-third of the national population of the same age (Newcomer, 1955). By 1986, almost one-fifth (19.1 percent) of the top executives were Catholic, while Catholics made up a little more than one-quarter of the general population (McComas, 1986).

The finding that some religious groups are overrepresented, while others are underrepresented, among top business executives is most probably a reflection of the differences in socioeconomic status and father's occupational status. In many cases, these are differences that go back for generations. Religious groups whose members have been well established in business or the professions (in this country or elsewhere) tend to prepare their children to continue in such occupations. Those whose members have been small farmers or laborers may assume that their children will continue in that tradition. This is not to deny that religious intolerance may have played a part in establishing and maintaining these differences, but to assert that in recent years social status may be the more important factor and that the "handicap" of lower social origins can be overcome. As recently arrived Asian-Americans can attest, the single most powerful equalizer is education—a topic that we will examine later in this chapter.

BIRTHPLACE

What are the geographic origins of American business leaders? Have there been marked shifts in these origins over time or have they remained constant? Is Burck's assertion that "the Middle West has been the breeding ground of chief executives" (1976, p. 174) valid?

Region of Birth

The regional birthplace of native-born business leaders was compared to the regional population at the average time of birth for the four time periods: 1870s, 1900s, 1952, and 1989 (see Table 6.2). The Northeast has long been the region of birth for the largest number of America's chief executives; followed in order by the Midwest, South, and West. In the 1870s nine out of ten top business leaders were from the Northeast. By the turn of the century, the proportion from this region had declined to

Table 6.2
**Regional Birthplace of Native-Born CEOs and Regional Population in
Decade of Birth (Percentages)**

| | Time Period | | | | | | | |
| | 1870s[a] | | 1901–1910[b] | | 1952[c] | | 1989[d] | |
Regional Birthplace	CEOs	Pop.	CEOs	Pop.	CEOs	Pop.	CEOs	Pop.
Northeast	91.0	41.0	61.0	33.7	35.0	27.7	37.1	27.3
Midwest[e]	4.5	8.9	24.4	22.0	41.1	34.7	30.0	30.5
South	3.4	49.4	10.0	35.4	18.0	32.3	24.1	31.6
West[e]	1.1	0.7	4.6	8.9	5.9	5.4	8.8	10.5

[a] Adapted from Francis W. Gregory and Irene D. Nau, "The American Industrial Elite in the 1870's," published in Men in Business, William Miller, Editor, Harper and Row, New York, 1962, p. 197.

[b] Adapted from William Miller, "American Historians and the Business Elite," published in Men in Business, William Miller, Editor, Harper and Row, New York, 1962, p. 322.

[c] Adapted from "The Nine Hundred," Fortune, November, 1952, p. 132.

[d] Data compiled from "The Power and the Pay: The 800 Best Paid Executives in America," Forbes, May 29, 1989, pp. 159–245.

[e] For the 1870's and 1901–1910 studies business leaders born in the West North Central Region were included in the West rather than the Midwest. To make figures comparable, the West North Central population figures are also included with the West for these two periods.

less than two-thirds and by 1952 it was just over one-third, where it has remained.

Within the Northeast, the New England states had a five to three margin in numbers of CEOs over the Middle Atlantic states (New York, New Jersey, Pennsylvania) in the 1870s. However, by 1910 the Middle Atlantic area had gained the lead by two to one; and by 1989 this had increased to almost a four to one ratio.

Overall, the Midwest has been the second most productive region for CEOs. In the 1952 survey, it surpassed the Northeast; however, this was short-lived. By 1989, the Northeast regained the lead. Within the Midwest region, the East North Central states (Ohio, Indiana, Illinois, Michigan, and Wisconsin) have maintained about a two to one ratio over the West North Central states (the Dakotas, Minnesota, Iowa, Nebraska, Missouri, and Kansas).

The South and West have both shown a steady rise in number of

CEOs. The percentages increased three-fold from the 1870s to the turn of the century. During the first half of the twentieth century, the South increased another 80 percent while the West increased by slightly less than one-third. Between 1952 and 1989, the upward trends continued with the South increasing by about one-third and the West gaining another 50 percent.

A more detailed geographical breakdown was not available for the South and West for the earlier studies. However, by 1952, one-half of the Southern-born business leaders were born in the South Atlantic states, with one-quarter from the East South Central and one-quarter born in the West South Central regions. In the West, the Pacific states had a two to one margin over the Mountain states.

By 1989, there had been only slight changes in either region. In the South, the West South Central area increased to nearly one-third of the total at the expense of the South Atlantic region, while the East South Central states remained relatively unchanged. The Pacific states maintained their two to one advantage over the Mountain states in the West.

In summary, while still dominant, the Northeast's role as the leading birthplace for America's top business leaders declined steadily until the mid-twentieth century while the other regions all increased. Within the Northeast, a shift occurred from New England to the Middle Atlantic states. Over the last four decades, the Midwest has declined while both the South and the West have continued to increase.

Comparisons with Regional Populations

The comparison of the numbers of CEOs born in each region with the population at about the time of the birth of the CEOs provides a more accurate picture of the relative productivity of each region. Until the turn of the century, the Northeast maintained about a two to one ratio of CEO percentage to population percentage. By 1952, this ratio had declined to five to four and in 1989 was about four to three.

The Midwest, which included only the East North Central states in the earliest two studies, has shown considerable variation. From a one to two ratio of business leaders to population in the 1870s, there was an increase to a nearly proportional representation by 1910. By 1952, however, the proportion of top executives surpassed the population percentage (about a six to five ratio). The most recent data reveals that this over-representation had declined back to the point where CEO numbers and population were in proportion. Although the actual number of CEOs born in the Midwest exceeded the number from the Northeast in 1952, on a proportional basis, the Midwest was still slightly behind and has been throughout the 120 years covered by these studies. Thus the data do not bear out the belief that the Midwest is the breeding ground for top business leaders.

The South, while still underrepresented, has shown a steady gain throughout the entire time period. Despite having about half of the nation's population in 1820, only 3.4 percent of the business leaders in 1870 were southern-born. As the South's population has decreased, the percentage of southern-born CEOs has increased. In the 1901–1910 time period, the ratio of CEOs to population was two to seven. By 1952, it was about three to five; and by 1989, it was four to five.

The West, like the Midwest, has shown considerable variation. The proportion of CEOs from this region in the 1870s actually exceeded the population percentage at the time of their birth. By the early part of the twentieth century, the proportion of CEOs to population had fallen to slightly over one to two. In 1952, the percentages were in proportion, but by 1989 the West was underrepresented by about one-fifth.

Until recent times the top echelons of business have been the exclusive domain of white males. Blacks and white females have been virtually excluded. Additional analyses were carried out to determine whether the inclusion of only white males in the population figures would change the relationships between CEO percentages and population percentages. In 1952, the South's population percentage would be reduced by about one-quarter to 24.6 percent while the Northeast and Midwest increase to 30.8 and 38.5 percent, respectively, and the West increases by less than one percent. When these figures are compared to the percentage of CEOs born in each region, the Northeast's overrepresentation decreases to about one-seventh; while the South's underrepresentation is decreased to one-quarter. The Midwest and West are about proportional. By 1989, the Northeast's overrepresentation increased to about one-fifth, while the Midwest, South, and West were underrepresented by 2.4, 3.5, and 1.1 percent, respectively. This adjustment of the population figures appears to explain a large part of the South's underrepresentation at the top of America's business firms. However, it does not explain the over-representation of the Northeast.

Comparisons with State Populations

In a further effort to determine whether or not the geographical area of birth is a significant factor in reaching the top in the business world, a state-by-state comparison was made. Our study of 791 CEOs in 1978 (Piercy & Forbes, 1981) revealed that the native-born business leaders came from 47 of the 50 states, with only Nevada, New Hampshire, and Wyoming not represented. These three excluded states accounted for less than two percent of the 1920 population. A state-by-state comparison of the 1920 population and the percentage of CEOs born in each state revealed that the differences were less than one-half of one percent for 32 of the 50 states. Excluding the three states in which no CEOs were born, there were only six states in which the absolute differences in percentages were greater than one percent.

New York had 9.8 percent of the population but was the birthplace for 12.6 percent of the CEOs; and Illinois with 6.1 percent of the population was the birthplace for 8.5 percent of the top executives. States underrepresented by more than one percent were Pennsylvania (8.2 percent of the population versus 6.1 percent of the CEOs), South Carolina (1.5 percent of the population and 0.4 percent of the CEOs), Kentucky (2.3 percent of population and 1.1 percent of CEOs), and Alabama (2.2 percent of the population and 1.1 percent of the CEOs).

In 1989, there was an even closer relationship between CEO state of birth and state population. Forty-eight states and the District of Columbia were the birthplace for one or more of the CEOs. Only Wyoming and New Mexico, with less than one-half of one percent of the nation's population, were not represented. In 34 of the 50 states, the population percentage and the percentage of CEOs born in the state differed by one-half of one percent or less. The difference between population percentage and percentage of CEOs exceeded 1.5 percent in only one state. New York, with 10.2 percent of the population, was the birthplace for 14.9 percent of the CEOs.

Size of Birthplace

A disproportionate share of America's business leaders have been born in its major cities. Miller (1962) found that 41 percent of the business leaders at the turn of the century were born in cities of over 8,000 population. Yet, at the time of birth of these leaders, only one-eighth of the population lived in cities of this size. Conversely, while 40 percent of the leaders were born in rural areas (less than 2,500 population), these areas accounted for 83.2 percent of the population (Miller, 1962, p. 386).

This large city dominance has continued. In 1952, the percentage of CEOs born in cities with populations greater than 400,000 was almost two and one-half times that of the population percentage (Warner & Abegglen, 1955, p. 20). By 1989, cities with populations in excess of 100,000 accounted for 29 percent of the nation's population but were the birthplace for 53.5 percent of the CEOs. This large city over-representation is not even across geographic regions. On a per unit of population basis for cities with populations exceeding 100,000, the Northeast had a ratio of CEOs to population of 2.2 to 1. In the Midwest, it was 1.57 to 1; in the South, 1.55 to 1; and in the West, 1.64 to 1.

Perhaps most striking in these comparisons is the under-representation of rural areas. From the turn of the century until 1989, the percentage of CEOs born in rural areas was less than one-half that of the population percentage. In 1989, it was only about one-quarter.

Birthplace and the Location of Industry

The best explanation for the differences between population percentages and the percentage of business leaders born in the area is that top executives were born in areas where there was a greater concentration of industry. It is commonly thought that the attainment of high executive positions requires much geographic mobility. However, in our study of CEOs in 1978 (Piercy & Forbes, 1981), we found that 35 percent of the CEOs were headquartered in their state of birth. In nine industries, representing 36 percent of the sample, more than 50 percent of the CEOs had headquarters in the state where they were born.

The firms from which the business leaders were drawn for the 1870s and 1901–1910 studies were identified by the researchers. Where possible, we determined the location of these firms and compared the location with the birthplace of the executives. In the 1870s study, about four-fifths of the firms were in the Northeast, 15 percent in the Midwest, and five percent in the South and in the West. For the 1900s study, two-thirds were in the Northeast, almost one-quarter in the Midwest, and again about five percent in the South and West. These figures roughly approximate the percentages of business leaders born in each region (see Table 6.2). An even closer relationship exists for 1989 between the location of firms and the birthplaces of the CEOs. The Northeast was the location of 32.5 percent of the corporate headquarters and the birthplace for 37.1 percent of the CEOs. In the Midwest, the figures were 25.8 percent (headquarters) and 30.0 percent (CEOs). In the South: 24.5 and 24.1 percent; and in the West: 17.5 and 8.8 percent.

It appears that the labor market for executive talent is not as open as we might think. The decisions to first pursue a career in business and then to aspire to a top position, as well as the ability to succeed in this endeavor, are strongly influenced by social expectations and the availability of role models. Those who grow up in large cities and/or in more highly industrialized areas may see relatives, friends, and neighbors who are successful business leaders. The culture may encourage bright and capable young men and women to pursue careers in this area. Those whose early years are spent in smaller towns or rural areas do not have the real firsthand experience of knowing anyone in a managerial capacity in a large corporation. Of course, they know of large corporations and may even aspire to employment in such settings. However, they may be handicapped by a lack of knowledge of the culture of corporate America.

As industry has become more widely dispersed and the country has become more highly industrialized, individuals from more regions of the country have developed an awareness of the opportunities available to them and have sought careers in business. Today all parts of the country are well represented among the business elite. There is a relatively close correspondence between population percentages and the proportion of CEOs born in each region.

Foreign-Born CEOs

America has traditionally been known as the land of opportunity for newcomers from other lands. Does this opportunity extend into the halls of corporate America? In the 1870s, about 10 percent of the business leaders were foreign born (Gregory & Nau, 1962). Newcomer (1955, p. 43) found continuing decreases in this percentage with 8.8 percent in 1900, 6.6 percent in 1925, and 6.0 percent in 1950. We found that the proportion of foreign born stood at 4.2 percent in 1978 and 5.6 percent in 1989.

At the turn of the century, the majority of foreign-born business leaders were English speaking and were either Canadian or West European. By 1950, there were still only two foreign-born top executives from other than Canada or Europe. One was born in New Zealand and one in the Virgin Islands. Since that time, there has been a substantial widening of the geographical base. In 1989, foreign-born CEOs came from 23 countries. The largest number (6) were from England, followed by Canada and Germany (4 each), China and Australia (3 each), and Japan, South Africa, and Israel (2 each). Four were from Eastern European countries.

Foreign-born CEOs are found in all industries. About half head manufacturing firms, while one-quarter are in banking. Others are in wholesaling, retailing, communications, transportation, utilities, financial services, and leisure services.

When compared to the total foreign population, foreign-born business leaders were underrepresented by about one-third in the 1870s. That underrepresentation steadily decreased until 1950 when the percentage of foreign-born CEOs and the percentage of the foreign-born population became about the same. Since 1950 they have remained in proportion. There do not appear to be any significant barriers to the rise of foreign-born business leaders. As the business world becomes more internationalized, we would expect to see even more foreign-born CEOs.

THE EDUCATION OF AMERICA'S CEOs

How well educated are our business leaders? Where were they educated? What is the relationship between the choice of a college and area

Table 6.3
Educational Level Attained by CEOs

Highest Educational Level Attained	Time Period		
	1952[a]	1976[b]	1989[c]
High School	16	14	11
Undergraduate Degree	48	46	43
Master's Degree[d]	36[d]	24	30
Doctorate (Includes law degrees)	[d]	16	16

[a] "The Nine Hundred," Fortune, November, 1952, p. 135.

[b] "A Group Profile of the Fortune 500 Chief Executive," Fortune, May 1976, p. 173.

[c] Data taken from "The Power and the Pay: The 800 Best Paid Executives in America," Forbes, May 29, 1989, pp. 159–245.

[d] The percentage is for postgraduate study. All may not have had master's degrees while some may have attained doctorates.

of birth? Is education concentrated among a few select institutions and, if so, is the trend towards greater or less concentration? These questions will be addressed here.

Not surprisingly, the formal education of top business leaders has long surpassed that attained by the general population. Newcomer (1955) found that as early as 1900 the proportion of top executives who attended college was eight to ten times that of the male population of their generation. Moreover, the proportion of college-educated business leaders increased somewhat faster than that of the male population as a whole during the 1900–1950 time period.

The educational level of CEOs as reported in more recent studies is shown in Table 6.3. Over the last four decades, the number without at least an undergraduate degree has declined 37.5 percent, although one in ten is still not a college graduate. Those with graduate degrees have increased by 30.6 percent over the same period.

The level of formal education has shown a steady increase until recently. A detailed examination of the 1989 data reveals that the proportion of CEOs born after 1945 who have graduate degrees is more than double that of those born prior to 1926. While nearly one-third (31.4 percent) of the latter group had only a high school education, only about one in eight of the former group had attained only this level. Surprisingly, the educational level peaked with those who entered the work-force in the mid- to late-60s and has since declined.

CEOs without Undergraduate Degrees

CEOs lacking undergraduate degrees were born in 29 of the 50 states and, on a regional basis, were in about the same proportion as the regional population. The Northeast and South had slightly fewer CEOs without undergraduate degrees in relation to their population while the Midwest and West had slightly more without college degrees. A higher than proportionate share of the less well educated CEOs were born in cities with populations in excess of 100,000. While cities of this size were the birthplace for 54 percent of all CEOs, they were the place where 64 percent of the less educated CEOs were born. Cities with populations in the 25,000 to 100,000 range were the birthplace for fewer CEOs without college degrees than would be expected from their proportion of the total population.

Undergraduate Education

Recent data on the undergraduate education of CEOs indicate that such degrees were awarded by 237 schools in 44 of the 50 states and the District of Columbia. This figure represents 11.8 percent of the degree granting institutions during the period in which the degrees were typically awarded. A decade earlier, our analysis showed 204 institutions (11 percent of the total) awarding undergraduate degrees (Piercy & Forbes, 1981). Thus there appears to have been a very slight widening of the educational base within the past ten years.

Areas of Study. The primary areas of study at the undergraduate level are difficult to compare over time because of the different classifications used in the various studies. The more recent studies reveal that about one-half majored in business and economics, one-quarter in engineering, 12–15 percent in the liberal arts, and 6–7 percent in the physical sciences (Boone, Kurtz, & Fleenor, 1988a; McComas, 1986). Our analysis of *Forbes'* 1988 listing of the top paid CEOs reveals two important points relating to undergraduate studies. First, the major fields of study are not evenly distributed across industry groups. Those with engineering degrees are concentrated in the manufacturing and utilities industries. Nearly one-third of the CEOs in manufacturing and about one-half in utilities majored in engineering, while virtually none of the CEOs in such industries as banking, insurance, and transportation had engineering degrees. Second, the engineering degree has been decreasing in popularity while business and economics have been increasing. Comparing the proportions of CEOs with engineering degrees attained before and after 1951 we find a decrease of one-half; while at the same time the number with majors in business and economics has almost doubled.

Location of Undergraduate Studies. There has been a tendency to remain close to home when selecting a college for undergraduate studies. Over half (52 percent) of the CEOs completed their baccalaureate studies in their state of birth and four-fifths remained in the same geographical region.

Analysis of movement for undergraduate study indicates that the Northeast had the largest net gain with 30, while the Midwest lost the same number. The West had a net gain of 11 with the South losing 11. Two-thirds of the net gain for the Northeast came from the Midwest while one-sixth came from the South with the remaining one-sixth from the West. The fact that the Northeast provided undergraduate education for more than two of every five (41.4 percent) CEOs is partially explained by the popularity of a few prominent schools, most of which are located in that region.

Newcomer (1955) found that the most frequently attended schools by the business leaders of 1900 were, in order, Harvard, Yale, Columbia, MIT, and Michigan. These five universities were also among the most frequently attended by the CEOs of 1925 and 1950, although there were some changes in their relative positions. Princeton, which was not among the top five in 1900, replaced Michigan in 1925, and by 1950, was in third position. In their 1955 study, Warner and Abegglen found that 42.8 percent of the business leaders did their undergraduate work in only 14 colleges; while another 12.3 percent went to a second select group of 10 colleges. Among the first group were nine from the Northeast (the six mentioned above plus the University of Pennsylvania, New York University, and Williams), four from the Midwest (University of Illinois, University of Michigan, University of Chicago, and University of Minnesota), and one from the West (University of California at Berkeley).

Since the 1950s there has been some lessening of this concentration, although it still exists to a considerable degree as shown in Table 6.4. In 1978, ten schools representing only 4.7 percent of the degree awarding colleges in the study provided undergraduate education for 29.3 percent of the CEOs. The situation was very similar in 1989, when the top 11 schools accounted for 25.4 percent of the undergraduate degrees. Dartmouth, the University of Texas, and Williams were in the top group in 1978, but were replaced by MIT, North Carolina, Cornell, and New York University in 1989. The three schools that were replaced in the top grouping still ranked very high in 1989 with eight, nine, and four CEO graduates, respectively. Geographically, the dispersion of the top schools remained about the same from 1978 to 1989. In 1978, six of the ten were located in the Northeast, two were in the Midwest, and one each was in the South and West. In 1989, seven of the 11 were in the

Table 6.4
Universities Awarding Ten (10) or More Degrees and Total Degrees Earned

	Undergraduate		Graduate	
University	1978[a]	1989[b]	1978[a]	1989[b]
Yale	46	27	c	c
Princeton	24	26	c	c
Harvard	17	20	77	86
Dartmouth	16	c	c	c
Stanford	15	10	10	20
Northwestern	14	11	c	c
Univ. of Pennsylvania	13	20	12	19
Univ. of Texas	11	c	c	c
Williams	10	c	c	c
Univ. of Michigan	10	11	11	16
Mass. Inst. Technology	c	12	c	15
Univ. of North Carolina	c	12	c	c
Cornell	c	12	c	c
New York Univ.	c	11	12	15
Columbia Univ.	c	c	12	20
Totals	176	179	134	191
Total Degrees Earned	601	706	260	374
Percent Awarded By These Schools	29.3	25.4	51.5	51.1

[a]   James E. Piercy and J. Benjamin Forbes, "Industry Differences in Chief Executive Offices," MSU Business Topics, 1981, 29, 17-29.

[b]   Data compiled from "The Power and the Pay: The 800 Best Paid Executives in America," Forbes, May 29, 1989, pp. 159-245.

[c]   Less than 10 degrees awarded to CEO's included in sample.

Northeast, two in the Midwest, and again one each in the South and West. At both times, the top four schools were all in the Northeast.

Overall only 47 percent of the CEOs went out of their state of birth for undergraduate education. However, at the top 11 universities, nearly three-quarters (73 percent) of the CEOs were from out of state. Yale (which graduated the largest number of CEOs) also had the largest out-of-state percentage (96.3). Yale was followed by Princeton with 88.5 percent from out of state, and then Pennsylvania (80.0 percent), Michigan (76.5 percent), and Harvard (68.4 percent). Yale drew from all regions of the country, but the Northeast was the most heavily represented. Princeton had the most balanced geographical representation, with 39 percent of its out-of-state graduates from the Northeast, 30 percent from the Midwest, 22 percent from the South, and nine percent from the West. Interestingly, these figures closely approximate the percentage of CEOs born in each region. Harvard's out-of-state graduates were predominantly from the Northeast and Midwest. The other leading universities' out-of-state graduates were primarily from the same geographical region.

Graduate Education

There were 374 graduate degrees earned in 97 U.S. and nine foreign institutions by the 1989 top CEOs. The American schools were located in 36 of the 50 states and in the District of Columbia. The schools in the Northeast awarded more than half of the graduate degrees, followed by the Midwest, South, and West. Advanced degrees were earned from 34 northeastern institutions, 23 in the Midwest, 29 in the South, and 11 in the West.

The most popular graduate degree, the MBA, accounted for almost half of the total. Nearly one-quarter were law degrees, followed by masters of science with one-eighth, and Ph.D.s with one-tenth. Our study of 626 top CEOs in 1978 revealed that advanced degrees were earned by 260 of the top executives who attended 91 different institutions (Piercy & Forbes, 1981). Six of the schools awarded 51.5 percent of the total number of degrees (see Table 6.4). Harvard, with 77 degrees, clearly dominated the field. In 1989, the same six, plus MIT, accounted for 51.1 percent of the graduate degrees awarded. Harvard continued to lead the pack by a very wide margin. All except Michigan and Stanford are northeastern schools.

The dominant position of these schools was evident in all academic areas. They awarded almost two-thirds of the total MBAs, about two-thirds of the law degrees, masters of arts, and Ph.D.s, and also one-fifth of the masters of science degrees. Harvard alone accounted for over one-third of the MBAs and one-fifth of the law degrees. Six other schools whose numbers were not shown in the graduate columns of the table awarded five or more graduate degrees. Two of these were in the Northeast (Cornell with nine graduates and Princeton with five), one was in the South (Southern Methodist—six graduates), and one in the West (University of California—five).

The number of CEOs with graduate degrees increased by 44 percent from 1978 to 1989; however, the number of different schools awarding graduate degrees to these executives increased by only 6.6 percent. Apparently, the concentration of education within only a small number of schools has not weakened significantly.

Only one in seven CEOs completed both their undergraduate and graduate education at the same school; however, this differed greatly across disciplines. One-third of those who earned law degrees and master of science degrees did so at the same university where they completed their undergraduate degree. For the MBA, only 15 percent chose the same school, and for both the M.A. and Ph.D. the figures were only 11 percent.

The average time lapse between completion of the undergraduate degree and the MBA was 4.4 years. One-quarter of the CEOs, however, took six years or longer. Other master's degrees usually followed immediately after undergraduate work. Likewise, law school immediately followed undergraduate education for most of those who chose this degree. Sixty percent completed law school within three years after their undergraduate degree and only 12 percent took longer than five years. The average time between completion of undergraduate schooling and graduate work was longest for the Ph.D. (5.9 years). Of CEOs with this degree, only one-quarter completed this degree within three years and two took as long as 17 and 21 years.

Graduates of Advanced Management Programs

Another form of management education is the "advanced management program," designed for those who have already reached senior level management positions. Livingston (1971) cites evidence that the executives who attended these programs after about 15 years of business experience earn approximately one-third more than most MBAs from leading universities. The MBA median salaries tend to plateau about 15 years after entry into business. He suggests that the greater earning power of the advanced management program graduate is due to their development of leadership skills that are not taught in formal management education programs.

From our study of 509 of the highest paid CEOs, as listed in *Forbes* (1988), we identified 20 (3.9 percent) as having completed an advanced management program. Three-quarters of these were Harvard trained, with the remaining one-quarter graduating from five other programs. This management education came after about 16 years of experience and when all had reached the level of corporate vice president or higher. One of these CEOs was not a college graduate, three-quarters had undergraduate degrees only, and almost three quarters possessed graduate degrees.

The average length of time to reach the top was 25.6 years for the advanced management program graduates versus 26.6 years for all CEOs in the study. However, those with MBA degrees reached the position of CEO in 24.7 years; about one year sooner than the graduates of the advanced management programs. This leads us to conclude that there is little difference in the effectiveness of the two types of programs.

EDUCATION VERSUS SOCIAL STATUS

In a study of 2,729 senior managers and directors of 208 *Fortune 500* companies, Useem and Karabel (1986) assessed the relative impact of social status versus education in relation to reaching the position of CEO. Since this is an important study with respect to the issues raised in this chapter, we will discuss it in some detail.

The sample consisted of six to eight managers in the highest positions in each firm plus ten of the outside directors. With respect to education, distinctions were made between "top college" or "top program" and unranked college or program at the undergraduate level and with regard to MBA programs and law schools. The top undergraduate programs were identified as Columbia, Cornell, Dartmouth, Harvard, Johns Hopkins, MIT, Pennsylvania, Princeton, Stanford, Williams, and Yale. The authors considered the following to be the top MBA programs: Columbia, Dartmouth, Harvard, MIT, Northwestern, Stanford, California—Berkeley, California—Los Angeles, Chicago, Michigan, and Pennsylvania. They considered the top law schools to be: Columbia, Harvard, New York University, Stanford, California—Berkeley, Chicago, Michigan, Pennsylvania, and Yale. A manager or director was identified as having upper-class origins if he appeared in the *Social Register* or if he attended one of the nation's fourteen most exclusive preparatory schools. Using these measures, one in six (16.2 percent) of the senior managers in the study was classified as having a high social origin.

The percentages of senior managers who were CEOs were compared for different educational backgrounds. The group whose members were most likely to be chief executives consisted of those with only a B.A. from one of the top colleges. The next greatest proportion of CEOs was found among the graduates of the top MBA and top law programs. Next came those with B.A.s or MBAs from less prestigious institutions; and last were the managers with no college degrees. The data indicate that if one already has a B.A. from one of the 11 top colleges, chances of reaching the top of a *Fortune 500* firm are not enhanced by the graduate management education available at even the most highly ranked schools. In addition, earning an MBA from a lesser program was not found to increase one's chances beyond that of the holder of a B.A. from a lesser school. The manager with a B.A. from a lower ranking school does increase his chances of reaching the CEO level by attaining an MBA from a top school. The reader must keep in mind that this study included only senior managers. With a broader sample of managers, it is likely that an MBA from a lesser ranked program would increase one's chances of reaching the senior management level (but possibly not the very top position).

The influence of an undergraduate education seems to be largely due to upper-class status (or perhaps an image of such status). The percentage of senior managers with B.A.s from the top colleges who were also of upper-class origins was very high. In fact, among those from Harvard, Yale, and Princeton, the proportion is about 50 percent. Among the graduates of the top MBA programs, however, the proportion from the upper class drops to about 21 percent. Perhaps the most significant finding is that although social origin makes a great difference in reaching the top for those with undergraduate degrees from unranked colleges, for those with B.A.s from the top colleges or with MBAs from top programs, social origins make no difference whatsoever. Thus, the study clearly shows that the effects of social status are no more important than those of educational achievement. High levels of the latter can completely compensate for the former when predicting which senior managers are most likely to reach the top executive position in a large business corporation (Useem & Karabel, 1986).

Useem and Karabel (1986) feel that the effects of social status are due to greater access to elite business networks. This is supported by their finding that social status was a better predictor of multiple directorships and leadership of business associations than it was of CEO status. They further suggest that the effects of both social status and elite educational status are due to the tendency of those in the highest levels of corporate America to trust most fully those of similar social and educational background. This would explain why events that occurred long ago still have an effect on the career prospects of senior managers.

THE PERSONAL CHARACTERISTICS OF CEOs

Boone, Kurtz and Fleenor (1988a) provided some additional insight into the early years of today's CEOs. They found that 79 percent worked while attending high school; and more than half (56 percent) either received a scholarship or paid part or all of their college expense by working. Thirty percent paid their total college expense through self-funding. While two-thirds of the CEOs came from affluent backgrounds, less than one-third relied on parental funding for their college education.

Many authors have reported a low correlation between grades and later achievement; however, Boone et al. (1988a) found that 91 percent of the CEOs achieved overall college grade point averages of A or B. They also found that about three-eighths of today's CEOs participated in at least one intercollegiate sport. In general, only about two percent of all college students participate in varsity sports. Furthermore, three-quarters of the CEOs held at least one office in a fraternity, club, or other campus organization during their college years. Thus it appears that CEOs exhibit high levels of independence and responsibility and set high standards of achievement for themselves early in adulthood.

COMPANY FOUNDERS

Are there differences in the backgrounds of the entrepreneur in comparison to the professional manager? Fifty company founders were identified among the 1989 *Forbes* listing of the highest paid CEOs. There were few significant background characteristics which would distinguish the founders from the other CEOs. Six percent were foreign born—about the same as for all CEOs. The ratio of founders to all CEOs was slightly higher in the West; while the Midwest was slightly underrepresented. This ratio was comparable to the national norm in the Northeast and the South. One distinguishing feature was the fact that 61.7 percent of the founders were born in cities with populations in excess of 100,000, in contrast to 54 percent of all CEOs. Founders also had slightly less formal education than the typical CEO. Sixteen percent only graduated from high school, in comparison with 10 percent for all CEOs. Eighty-four percent of the founders had a baccalaureate degree (versus 90 percent overall) and only 40 percent had graduate degrees (versus 47 percent overall).

Founders cover the spectrum of American industry, although one-half are concentrated in retailing, and computer hardware and software. These industries are followed by manufacturing (20 percent of the founders), banking (10 percent), and insurance (10 percent). Others are found in wholesaling, health care, communications, and broadcasting.

ENTRY INTO THE WORKFORCE

As a consequence of longer periods of education and military service, the age of entering the full-time workforce has been steadily increasing. In the 1870s, about one in five of the business leaders had their first full-time job before the age of 16, and over one-half entered the workforce before age 19. These ages remained largely unchanged over the next three decades; however, by 1950 only one of each 20 CEOs had started full-time work before age 16 and 85 percent were 19 or older. Our study of America's top CEOs in 1989 reveals that none entered the workforce before age 16 and 97 percent were 19 or older. The average age of entry into the workforce was a surprising 24 years.

The reasons for this late entry age are evident if we examine the paths from high school into the workforce. This group reached their late teens from the latter part of World War II through the Korean conflict. Upon graduation from high school, only 3.1 percent went directly into the workforce. Slightly over one-quarter (27.2 percent) either chose or were drafted into military service, while 69.7 percent entered college.

After undergraduate studies, slightly more than one-quarter (28 percent) of those who went to college first entered the workforce, while one-third continued with graduate schooling, and 39 percent went into military service. One in every nine who entered college from high school acquired both military service and graduate training before entering the workforce.

Only 7.7 percent of those who entered military service from high school went directly into the workforce upon completion of that service. Ninety-two percent went from the service into college. One-third of this group continued on to graduate studies before entering the workforce.

CEOs in the 1986 study served in the military forces at a 50 percent higher rate than the male population of similar age. While 64.2 percent of the chief executives had military service, only 42.1 percent of the total male population of the same age group served in the military. This experience may have provided an advantage with respect to maturity, self confidence, and leadership ability.

CONCLUSIONS: DO THE EARLY YEARS MAKE A DIFFERENCE?

There are three things that an individual must do to reach the top of a major American business corporation. First, he or she must choose to enter the business world and make a commitment to devote a tremendous amount of time and energy to the task. Second, the aspiring top executive must develop the knowledge and ability to do the job. Third, the candidate must convince others that they can handle the responsibility of stewardship over a major business enterprise. The conditions of one's early background have a strong and lasting impact on all three of these requirements.

We feel that the regional area of birth primarily affects the first two requirements. Growing up in an area where there is a concentration of industry influences the decision to enter the business world and also affects the early socialization experiences which in turn partially determine one's ability to function in this world. Our data show that the typical CEO was born in a large metropolitan area. In addition, the Northeast region of the country has produced business leaders beyond its proportion of population for well over a century. There is a correlation between the location of the largest number of business firms and the birthplace of the largest number of CEOs.

There are signs that the Northeast's long-term lead as the birthplace of chief executives may soon fade. This position has been maintained primarily at the expense of the South, which is the region where the greatest gains in industrialization have been occurring. Moreover, the continuing rise of minorities and females into the upper echelons of management will result in a widening of the pool of potential candidates for top executive positions and this may also increase the numbers from the South. The growing concentration of trade and industry in the Pacific is causing many American businesses to move West which should further weaken the geographical trends of the past. In the future we would expect to see more CEOs coming from the larger metropolitan areas of the South and West.

The foreign born continue to be represented among CEOs in about the same proportion as in the general population. There has, however, been a considerable widening of the geographical base from which the foreign-born CEOs come. Until the turn of the century, foreign-born business leaders came mainly from Canada and Western Europe. Today we find most regions of the world represented. By this criterion, opportunity in American business is greater today than it ever has been.

The proportion of CEOs coming from different social classes has changed very little over the years. Therefore, we have little reason to believe that America's top business leaders will not continue to come primarily from the middle and upper-middle classes. Social status plus the occupation of the father influence all three of the requirements for ascension to the top in business. Throughout the twentieth century, most top executives have had fathers who were also business executives. It is not unusual for children to follow their father's occupation. Thus more people from these classes will choose to pursue a high level business position and they are likely to be better prepared to succeed in such an endeavor (at least early in their career). In addition, if the candidate for a top position comes from the highest social status group this further boosts chances for late career upward mobility. At the highest levels, the ability to gain acceptance within the elite business networks outside the company becomes very important.

Education can compensate for a disadvantage in social status. An especially strong boost seems to be provided by an undergraduate or graduate degree from one of a few prominent schools. We feel that the effect here is due to perception not ability. A degree from an elite undergraduate institution or from a high ranking business or law school implies that the holder has either a great deal of ability and motivation or comes from a high social status family (or both). Thus this credential sends a signal to high level decision makers that this candidate poses less of a risk than someone without such a background.

Higher levels of education are becoming prerequisites for upward mobility within major business firms. Today's business leaders, like those of the past, are much better educated than the general population. The level of education has continued to rise. Nine out of ten CEOs have an undergraduate degree and nearly half have earned at least one graduate degree. In general, more education increases both the ability to perform at the highest levels and the perception that one has that capability.

At the undergraduate level, business and economics continue to increase as the major areas of study of top executives. Almost half majored in these topics. The same is true at the graduate level where the MBA accounts for about half of the degrees held by CEOs. This is followed by the law degree with nearly one-quarter. Over the last four decades, the popularity of the engineering degree as the undergraduate major of top executives has declined.

The motivation for achievement and leadership seems to have developed early among top executives. Leadership skills, as reflected in athletics and other extracurricular activities, as well as good academic records and a sense of independence and responsibility were present during their college years.

The age at which CEOs entered the full-time workforce has steadily increased over the last 120 years, reflecting the national trend. By 1988, the average age had reached 24. This late entry is attributable to prolonged education and military service. It is unlikely that this age will decrease significantly. While future CEOs may be less likely to have military service, the educational process will continue to lengthen.

The entrepreneur is found in most segments of American industry, although about one-half are concentrated in the retailing and computer industries. Company founders and the professional managers who run most of our large firms are similar in most respects. However, the founders have less formal education and are more likely to have been raised in major cities. They also tend to be concentrated in the higher and lower age groups. About one-quarter (24.1 percent) are over 65 (in comparison to only 8.6 percent of all CEOs), while 13.0 percent are under 45 (in comparison with 6.4 percent for all CEOs).

The company founders who are included in the data analyzed here have proven that they are effective, successful top executives—they have built large money-making firms. Not everyone chosen as a chief executive officer of a major business firm will be a winner. Therefore comparing founders with CEOs of other firms may help us determine which factors reflect performance-related ability or motivation and which are selection criteria which may not be so directly related to performance. This argument would lead us to the conclusion that entrepreneurial ability and motivation does not depend on formal education. In addition, age does not seem to be as important among the founders as it is for CEOs in other firms. Our larger, more mature firms seem to rely more on standard, objective (but perhaps irrelevant) criteria such as age and education when choosing top executives. It can be argued that the characteristics that predict success as an entrepreneur are different from those that predict success in large bureaucratic firms. In fact, some research would support this argument. However, most of today's large business firms are trying to become more entrepreneurial and therefore should reconsider some of these "objective" selection criteria.

When compared to the general population, today's CEO is much like his counterpart of a century ago. He is a white male, most likely born in a large metropolitan area in the Northeast. His family were upper or upper-middle class and his father was a professional manager or other professional. He is much better educated than the general population. His undergraduate degree was earned in his home state or from a prominent northeastern university. College education came either before or immediately after military service. He is likely to also have a graduate degree, probably in business or law. If so, this degree was likely to have been obtained from one of ten to 12 prominent universities, most of which are also located in the Northeast. He paid some or all of his educational expenses and while on campus was active in athletics and other extracurricular activities. Because of advanced schooling and military service, he did not enter the full-time workforce until age 24.

This describes the typical CEO of a major American business firm as we enter the last decade of the twentieth century. However, the variation around this profile is tremendous. There are many CEOs whose fathers were laborers (15 percent). There are CEOs who have only a high school diploma (11 percent). Hundreds of different universities are represented in the ranks of today's CEO. There are CEOs who were born in all parts of this country and in many other countries. In many respects, this profession has been much more open than most high paying professions. We believe that in the future it will be forced to become more open to previously excluded groups such as women and minorities. The door is open for those with intelligence, determination, leadership ability, and perhaps some luck, to reach the pinnacle of American business.

TOP EXECUTIVE PROFILES

A Contrast of Backgrounds

We will compare the backgrounds of two CEOs born at about the same time, in different parts of the country, and in very different socioeconomic circumstances. At the end of Chapter 4, we profiled John A. Young, CEO of Hewlett-Packard. His early background is of interest here. He was born in 1932, to a working-class family in a small town in Idaho, and grew up in a small town in Oregon. Young earned an engineering degree from Oregon State University, served in the military, and then went back to school for an MBA from Stanford. He went to work for Hewlett-Packard in 1958 and 20 years later became CEO.

In 1935, James D. Robinson III was born into a wealthy banking family in Atlanta, Georgia. Robinson graduated from Georgia Tech in 1957 with a B.S. degree. After serving two years as a lieutenant in the Naval Reserves, he also went back to school for an MBA from Harvard in 1961.

Robinson joined Morgan Guaranty Trust Company in New York, and from 1961 until 1966 he worked in various departments before being appointed assistant vice president and staff assistant to the chairman and president.

In 1968, he left Morgan to join White, Weld and Company as a general partner in the corporate finance department. Robinson left White, Weld in 1970 to become executive vice president at American Express. He was promoted to president in 1975, and in 1977 was appointed chairman and CEO.

These profiles illustrate the diversity of opportunity available in American business. Both men were born and raised in regions of the country that have been underrepresented in the CEO population. One was born to a family of modest means in a small town, one to a wealthy family in a large metropolitan area. Both attended undergraduate colleges near their homes, served in the military, and then received MBAs from elite universities. Most importantly, both men entered firms and industries that valued their particular strengths. At Hewlett-Packard, Young could use his technical and business skills and, given his Stanford MBA, not be handicapped by his social origins. Robinson, on the other hand, could take full advantage of his business skills and his access to the elite social network by working in banking and financial services. With the deregulation of financial services and the diversification of American Express, one of Robinson's critical roles has been personal involvement in shaping government policy (Bateman & Zeithaml, 1990).

7

Industry Differences and Changes over Time in the Career Paths of Chief Executives

In this chapter we will return to some of the issues first raised in earlier chapters. These include the basic proposition that firms in different environments adapt different strategies and structures, different cultures, and different career patterns. This was first discussed in Chapter 2 and at more length in Chapter 3. In these chapters we saw that functional area was one factor that could influence early promotion opportunities. In Chapter 4, we discussed the issue of functional specialization versus general management as the route to the top, and the issue of inter-firm mobility in relation to upward mobility. Here we will examine the issues of how career paths differ across industries and how they change over time.

DOES FUNCTIONAL AREA MAKE A DIFFERENCE IN GETTING TO THE TOP?

Much of the information on the functional backgrounds of CEOs comes from reports on the profile of the "typical" top manager. These studies look at all chief executives regardless of industry and imply that there is a tendency for CEOs to be chosen from particular areas. Conventional wisdom on this issue says that the functions of CEOs change with the critical challenges facing industry. For example, over the past 40 years the following functions have been emphasized: first production, then marketing, then finance, and most recently there has been a return to the production and technical areas. For example, in the early 1980s, much attention was paid to the replacement of financial expert Reginald Jones with the more technical- and operations-oriented Jack Welch as chairman of General Electric (Landro, 1982). As the 1990s begin, this trend continues with the breaking of a long-term tradition at General

Motors. The new CEO will not have a background in the financial area. The top executive, Robert Stempel, is an engineer with a background in product development and operations (Standish, 1990). Given the competition facing the automotive industry in general, and General Motors in particular, the preference was for a "car man," not a "numbers man." We will describe Stempel's career in more detail at the end of this chapter.

When we started the research described here, it was our feeling (and it still is) that statements about "the" background of the CEO were generally misleading and that there was little hard data on changes in CEO background over time. Furthermore, we felt that differences in functional background across industries had largely been ignored.

If different functions are the path to the top in different industries and if the critical functions change over time, how do these differences and changes come about? One explanation is contained in a model of executive succession developed by Pfeffer and Salancik (1978). This model sees executive selection and removal as the means by which the organization's environment affects its structure and strategy. Contingency theories of organizational design and strategy propose that the firm must adapt to different environments (e.g., Lawrence & Lorsch, 1967; Miles & Snow, 1978). However, these theories do not explain how this adaptation takes place. Pfeffer and Salancik (1978) propose that environmental demands determine which functional areas are the most important in dealing with the organization's critical problems. This ability to cope with environmental uncertainty, constraints, and contingencies gives particular groups greater power and control within the organization. This influence then affects the selection and tenure of top executives.

Some of the earliest research in this area showed that there were relationships between environmental contingencies and the backgrounds of top hospital administrators (Perrow, 1961; Pfeffer & Salancik, 1977). Other studies have shown that the importance of various business functions is related to operating conditions or strategies. Hitt, Ireland, and Palia (1982) found that ratings of functional importance depended on the firm's strategy. Gupta and Govindarajan (1984) found that functional experience (specifically the extent of marketing/sales experience) influenced the effectiveness of general managers in strategic business units with "build" versus "harvest" strategies. Our research, described in Chapter 4, showed that early upward mobility in a large oil and gas company was greater for those with a technical background. Slocum and Cron (1988) have proposed that in stable defender firms the powerful functions will be the financial, accounting, and production areas; while in analyzer firms (which search for new opportunities while protecting established areas) there will be more of an emphasis on marketing and engineering. Finally, a study by Sheridan and associates (1990) showed that entry into a powerful department has a positive effect on career mobility (this study is described in more detail in Chapter 3). Environmental demands force the organization to value most highly those with the skills and experience to handle those demands.

Previous Studies of the Functional Backgrounds of CEOs

Some might argue that the CEO of a large business firm is a general manager or a long range strategic planner and early functional experience should not matter here. Harold Geneen, the former chief executive of ITT, believes that if you can manage one business, then you can manage any business (Geneen, 1984). If all that CEOs needed were universal management skills that apply in any setting then we would see all functional backgrounds equally represented at the top of our business enterprises. Numerous studies of the backgrounds of chief executives indicate that functional area does matter.

One of the most comprehensive studies of CEOs was carried out by Newcomer (1955). She compared the three time periods of 1900, 1925, and 1950. Presidents and chairmen of the board of the largest railroads, utilities, and industrial firms were studied. Data on the functional backgrounds of top executives were available only for the 1925 and 1950 time periods. At both times the dominant functional area was clearly operations and production (46 percent in both periods). From 1925 to 1950, the number of chief executives chosen from finance and from sales/advertising increased and those chosen from legal departments decreased.

The research of Dommermuth (1966) overlaps the Newcomer time period. Dommermuth studied the presidents of 239 major industrial firms from 1945 through 1964. This data showed very little variation in functional background representation over the 20 year period. Overall, most presidents were from general management or production; followed by marketing and finance. Although the samples and the definitions of some functions differ, the two studies generally support each other and support the conclusion that through the first half of the twentieth century the path to the top in industrial firms, utilities, and railroads was through production/operations and then general management.

In both of these studies, engineering and technical personnel were included in the production/operations function. However, more detailed analyses by both researchers showed that this background was increasing in frequency among top executives. Newcomer's data shows engineer (as an occupation not a function or department) rising from 12.5 percent in 1900 to 15.6 percent in 1925 to 19.3 percent in 1950. In Dommermuth's study, an engineering or technical background was found for 43.1 percent of the production specialists (10.6 percent of the total) in 1945. This increased to 70.4 percent (or 15.6 percent of the total) by 1964. The slightly higher percentages in the Newcomer study may be due to the fact that her sample included railroads and utilities in addition to the industrial firms studied by Dommermuth.

Dommermuth (1966) also compared the functional background of the successor CEO with that of the predecessor and found that 75 percent of the time the backgrounds were different. He reasoned that there was a tendency to change areas when choosing a new president because of the corporate political structure. Also, the new president is most often the man who has been serving as executive vice president and this person is usually from a different function area in order to have a balanced team at the top.

A number of more recent studies are available; however, most are analyses done at one point in time. It is generally misleading to attempt to compare studies done at different times with different samples and different definitions of functions. For example, Burck (1976) surveyed 800 chief executives. These included the 500 largest industrial firms, plus the 50 largest banking, utility, life insurance, retailing, transportation, and financial companies. His data showed that marketing and distribution were the backgrounds of the largest number of chief executives. However, a 1980 analysis of a similar sample by the firm of Arthur Young (1980) concluded that most chief executives came up through general management. In this study, the marketing and sales function was listed as the background of the fewest chief executives.

A number of factors may account for these large and confusing differences. First, there was about 30 percent turnover of CEOs in the time between the studies. However, it is not likely that this would cause such a drastic change. A second possible explanation lies in the fact that both studies relied on responses to surveys for their data and therefore may actually be describing different samples. The most likely problem here is that the definitions of functional area differed (more will be said about this later).

The Arthur Young report also concluded that technical and production/operations backgrounds as well as financial and legal backgrounds were on the decline. They noted, however, that classification was a problem in that CEOs with early legal and financial backgrounds may have been considered as advancing through general management. This study (Arthur Young, 1980) also touched on the issue of industry differences; noting that both technical and sales/marketing backgrounds were more likely to be found in the industrial than in the non-industrial firms.

Other studies support the contention that general management is the most common background of chief executives. A Conference Board survey of the presidents and chairmen of the *Fortune 1300* firms concluded that the primary functional experience of over 50 percent was in general management. All other functional areas were far behind (Bonfield, 1980).

Research from the University of Michigan may help us understand some of the inconsistencies noted above. In their surveys, they ask more specific questions about prior experience that do most researchers on this topic. For example, in one survey, when newly promoted high level executives were asked the area of their first job, most reported marketing/ sales or finance/accounting (21–22 percent of the total). But when they were asked where they spent most of their time, general management/ administration gained a slight edge as the leader with 25.9 percent. Finally, when asked where they were "last employed," 46 percent reported general management/administration (Bond, Hildebrandt, Miller, & Swinyard, 1981). This is consistent with our data presented in Chapter 4 showing that general management was the most common path to top management. It should be noted, however, that since general management usually means a position with responsibility for multiple functions (Kotter, 1982) some might not consider it to be a "functional area."

From our review of previous studies of the functional areas of chief executives we identified a number of issues concerning the research methodology that had been used. First, no longitudinal studies had been conducted since 1966. Second, research conducted by different authors at different points in time is difficult to compare due to differences in sample composition (i.e., different industrial segments studied or different response rates from different areas) and due to differences in the meaning of "functional background" (first job, last job, most time spent, etc.). Third, we know that firms in different industries face very different environments and adapt very different strategies to cope with their environments. Furthermore, we know that external environments change over time and that organizations must adapt to those changes. It is a major proposition of this book that organizational strategy and structure affect career paths and opportunities. Previous research on the backgrounds of top executives had largely ignored the possibility that there were significant differences across different industries. In addition, there had been no recent longitudinal studies to determine changes over time in functional backgrounds of top executives. Therefore we carried out two studies to examine these issues.

DOES CHANGING FIRMS HELP IN GETTING TO THE TOP?

In general, the answer to this question must be a resounding "NO!" As we have previously noted, 89 percent of CEOs are promoted from within (Shetty & Peery, 1976). In addition, over 50 percent have worked for only one employer (Tuckel & Seigel, 1983). Shetty and Peery (1976) also found that return on investment and sales growth were greater when there was succession from within. They believe that success as a CEO depends largely on the ability to deal with the organization's external environment and that extensive experience in a particular company is crucial in developing this "institutional skill." However, there is other evidence that a pattern of inside succession is associated with slower organizational growth and outside selection is often the result of poor organizational performance (Helmich, 1974, 1977). Helmich feels that a pattern of succession from within leads to a philosophy of "Let's not rock the boat," which may be nonadaptive for an organization which must deal with a dynamic environment.

In addition, as we showed in Chapter 4, there is more movement from the outside into the top management team than there is into the CEO spot. Also, functional specialists seem to be more able to jump from firm to firm and from industry to industry—even at relatively high levels (such as corporate vice president of finance).

Industry differences in this career parameter are proposed by the Sonnenfeld and Peiperl (1988) typology of career systems. They remind us that not all firms make a practice of developing and promoting from within. Some firms are more open to the external labor market than others. Firms in which a premium is placed on innovation and individual talent ("baseball teams") and firms that are struggling for survival ("fortresses") are likely to look outside for personnel at all levels. Our first study of chief executive career paths also examined the issue of time with the firm.

Changing firms is generally a poor strategy for personal advancement, despite the widely held belief that this is the way to move up. Lester Korn, chairman of the executive recruiting firm of Korn/Ferry International, who would seem to have a vested interest in more people moving, has argued strongly against too many moves. This recommendation is based on the results of a survey of over 1,300 senior executives (up to but not including CEOs or chief operating officers). These executives had an average of 17 years experience with their current employer. Twenty-four percent had worked for only one firm; and the average number of employers was only two. In addition, those who had moved more frequently than the average earned less than their less mobile colleagues (Korn, 1988).

Graphs of the relationship between salaries for high turnover (three or more employers) and low turnover (one or two employers) groups by age are very interesting. The data show that high movers are paid more than low movers early in their career, but by about age 30 to 35 those who moved less than the average gain an advantage that generally increases with age. There were industry differences in this data, such that the low movers gain the advantage at about age 30 in banking and insurance; while it takes until age 40 for this changeover to occur in the industrial and diversified financial sectors. A unique pattern was found in the retailing industry, where low movers gained an advantage in their late 20s but lost it again in the early 40s. Retailing is an area that Sonnenfeld and Peiperl (1988) identify as having a "fortress" career system which relies heavily on external recruitment for higher level executive talent.

Korn (1988) notes that this issue involves more than money—"I constantly see people eliminated from consideration for desirable jobs because they have moved 'too often'—which may mean three or four times in the past ten years" (p. 71).

STUDY ONE: INDUSTRY DIFFERENCES IN CEO BACKGROUND AND TENURE

The data for this study were collected from the May 28, 1978, issue of *Forbes*. The industry groupings were based on *Forbes' Annual Report on American Industry* of January 9, 1978. The data were grouped by industry, with industry group sizes ranging from a low of seven (Fire and Casualty Insurance, and Household Products) to a high of 156 (Regional Banks).

Functional Area

A very detailed analysis of this data may be found in an earlier report (Piercy & Forbes, 1981). Here we will give the highlights of our analyses of functional area and time with the firm. When we initially looked at the functional area of the chief executives we found that the most common background was finance (19.2 percent), followed by general administration (17.0 percent), legal (12.6 percent), and marketing/sales (12.3 percent). We felt that these figures might be misleading however, due to the large number of regional banks in the sample. These firms represented one-fifth of the total sample and 38 percent of the CEOs with financial backgrounds. The removal of the regional banks resulted in general administration becoming the background of the largest number of CEOs, followed by finance, marketing/sales, and legal, in that order.

In general there was a wide distribution of functional backgrounds within each industry; however, there were exceptions. In nine industries, one-half or more of the CEOs had the same functional background. These are shown in Exhibit 7.1. The data clearly indicate that certain industries favor those with particular functional backgrounds. These backgrounds are related to the critical competitive issues in the industry. All seven firms in the household products industry were headed by CEOs with a background in marketing and sales. This functional area was also strongly represented in information processing, personal prod-

Exhibit 7.1
Industries in Which One-Half or More of the CEOs Had the Same Business Background

Industry Group	Functional Background	Percentage
Household Products	Marketing/Sales	100
New York Banks	Banking	78
Automotive Supplies	General Administration	63
Electric Utilities (S.E.)	Legal	60
Fire & Casualty Insurance	Insurance	57
Information Processing	Marketing/Sales	55
Supermarkets (Major Chains)	General Administration	54
Electrical Equipment	General Administration	50
Department Stores	Retailing	50

ucts, and health care. Although these four industry groups represented only seven percent of the total, they had 28 percent of the CEOs with marketing/sales backgrounds. In a similar fashion, a high concentration of CEOs with legal backgrounds was found in the regulated industries such as utilities and transportation. While these two combined industries represented only 14 percent of the total sample, they had 30 percent of the CEOs with legal backgrounds.

There were also industry groups in which two different functional areas made up the majority of CEO backgrounds. For example, conglomerates were dominated by CEOs with backgrounds in finance and general administration. In forest products, two-thirds of the top people had backgrounds in either production/operations or marketing/sales. Also, two-thirds of the CEOs in natural gas utilities came from either the technical or legal areas. Within the chemical specialists grouping, most top executives had backgrounds in the technical area or in marketing and sales. In surface transportation, half of the top executives had backgrounds in either the legal or the operations areas. Finance and marketing/sales accounted for half of the CEOs in industrial equipment.

General administration and finance were the predominant backgrounds of CEOs hired from outside the firm. Of the 80 outside appointments, 25 CEOs had backgrounds in general administration and 24 had finance backgrounds. These two areas accounted for 61 percent

Exhibit 7.2
Industry Groups in Which 90 Percent or More of CEOs' Worklives Spent with a Single Firm

Industry Group	Percentage
Electric Utilities (Southeast)	94
Banks (New York)	94
Construction Contractors	92
Apparel	91
Electric Utilities (Southwest)	91
Electronic Equipment	90
Steel (Basic Producers)	90

of the outside appointments but only 35 percent of the total sample. It seems that when firms look outside for top management personnel they prefer general management or financial backgrounds.

Mobility versus Tenure with the Firm

One indication of mobility would be the percentage of the working life spent with one firm. Although specific information on this was not available, we felt that it could be reasonably deduced from other data. The average age of all CEOs was 57. Therefore, it was assumed that most had served in World War II or Korea. In addition, most had college degrees and many had graduate degrees. Thus it was assumed that the average age for entering full-time employment would be about 25 years. To determine the percentage of worklife spent with the same firm, the number of years with the company was divided by the current age minus 25. Based on these assumptions and calculations, the percentage of worklife spent with the same firm equalled or exceeded 90 percent for the average CEO in seven industry groups. These are shown in Exhibit 7.2.

These are utilities, banks, and basic industries which operate in stable environments, have long time perspectives, and typically adapt a defender strategy (Miles & Snow, 1978), or a steady state growth strategy (Leontiades, 1980) and develop the internally-oriented career systems of the "club" or the "academy" (Sonnenfeld & Peiperl, 1988).

At the opposite extreme are the firms in the air transportation industry. Here the average CEO had spent only 47 percent of his work life in the firm. The next lowest category on this measure was the conglomerate group where the average top executive had spent 61 percent of his life with the company. The airline industry was facing the uncertainties of deregulation at the time of this study, and firms were bringing in outside experts, particularly legal experts to deal with the new environment. Conglomerates are typically analyzer firms with respect to strategy. That is, they have certain stable businesses that they defend and other risky, potentially high growth ventures where they are trying new products and markets. Here we typically see Leontiades' (1980) evolutionary strategy of growth by merger and acquisition. The diversity of the conglomerate makes internal development of top executive talent more difficult. The person at the top may not know all the businesses and will manage by the numbers. He will typically have a background in finance or general management. In fact, in the data analyzed here, of 33 firms in the conglomerate category, ten CEOs had backgrounds in finance and eight came from a general administration background. As we noted earlier, these are the backgrounds of most of the CEOs who were selected from outside the firm. It is in this category that the notion of the universal professional manager is most likely to prevail. Conglomerates are much like baseball teams (Sonnenfeld & Peiperl, 1988) in recruiting the best talent available anywhere. Even here, however, the average time spent with the firm was over 60 percent of the worklife.

We also looked at the total time with the firm. The typical CEO had been with his firm for 26 years. Industry differences generally paralleled the findings on percentage of time with the firm. In six industry groups, the average tenure with the firm was 30 years or more. Basic steel and New York banks led with 32 years average tenure, followed by Midwest utilities with 31 years, and international oil companies, food specialists, household products, and apparel with 30 years average tenure. In only two industry groups was the average length of service with the firm less than 20 years. These were air transportation (16 years) and electrical equipment (17 years).

Prior to appointment as CEO, individuals had served an average of 18 years with their firm. In two industry groups (conglomerates and air transportation), the average was only nine years; while in three industry groups (Midwest electric utilities, basic steel, and New York banks) the CEOs spent an average of 25 years or more with the firm prior to appointment as CEO.

In some industries it apparently takes longer to reach the top. This is reflected in the average ages of the CEOs in different industries and differences in the age when appointed CEO. Overall, the average age was 57 (the same found in other studies, e.g., Burck, 1976). However, this varied from a low of 54 in the consumer finance grouping to a high of 62 in the food specialists group. CEOs in basic steel and international oils had mean ages of 61; while the average age was only 55 in electrical equipment, regional banks, life insurance, and diversified chemicals. The average age of appointment to the CEO position was 49. This ranged from a low of 45 (discount and variety stores, and regional supermarkets) to a high of 55 within the international oil companies.

Also of interest here was the extent to which the firms went outside to find a new CEO. Excluding the 25 firms in which the founder was still serving as the chief executive, 724 firms remained for analysis. Of these, 644 CEOs (89 percent) were appointed from within the firm. Seventy-two (11 percent) were outside appointments. Our figures matched exactly those found earlier by Shetty and Peery (1976). In eight industry groups all the CEOs were selected from inside. These were electronic equipment, basic steel, New York banks, Southwest utilities, Midwest utilities, regional chain supermarkets, household products, and apparel. On the other hand, three industry groups had much higher than average selection of CEOs from outside the firm. Here air transportation was the clear leader with 45 percent of the CEOs coming from outside. The others were conglomerates with 21 percent and natural gas utilities with 20 percent of their CEOs coming in from outside the firm.

Summary and Conclusions

The data from this study were very supportive of the general proposition that career paths and opportunities reflect the needs of the organization in managing its environment. Strategic contingencies affect the functional backgrounds found at the top of business corporations and also influence whether the firm selects its highest executives from inside or outside the firm.

We saw that the attempt to identify "the" functional background of chief executives is not as meaningful as describing the relationships between industry groupings and functional areas. For example, sales and marketing backgrounds were very common at the top of consumer-oriented industries such as household products, personal products, and health care. Legal backgrounds predominated in regulated industries such as transportation and utilities. We also saw that firms in stable industries are very likely to promote from within (e.g., basic steel and New York banks), while those firms that are facing more uncertainty, diversity, or complexity may go outside to find the top talent that they need. The tendency to go outside was strongest in the air transportation industry, followed by conglomerates. In addition, those who are chosen from outside are likely to have a background in either general management or finance.

STUDY TWO: FUNCTIONAL DIFFERENCES ACROSS TIME AND INDUSTRIES

This second study had two purposes. One was to gather additional data to support our findings of functional differences in CEO background across industries. The other was to examine changes in the backgrounds of chief executives over time. Here we sought to determine whether environmental changes are so broad as to affect CEO selection across all industries. Ideally, we would have examined changes in each industry but this was not feasible due to the small numbers of CEO appointments within each industry during the five year periods that were studied. We also decided to reexamine the frequency of change in chief executive background upon succession as reported by Dommermuth (1966). He had found that 75 percent of the executive successions result in a change in functional background.

Research Method

Data describing the nation's most highly paid chief executives were obtained from *Forbes*' annual listings for the years 1971 through 1982. Initial analysis showed that among the large number of banks included in the listings, the predominant functional background was finance or banking (more than 75 percent of the total). Since such concentration was not typical in other industry groups it was felt that inclusion of these firms would make it appear that finance and banking were much more common as CEO backgrounds than was actually the case. Therefore, further analyses did not include the banking industry. We also decided to exclude from this study those CEOs who were founders of the firm. These are not typical managers and "founder" is not a functional background. Also, we noticed that founders had a much greater tenure in office than the typical CEO (20 years versus six to eight years for other CEOs). We felt that this fact would influence our analyses of changes in functional backgrounds over time.

Following these exclusions, we still had data on 1,313 CEOs representing 927 firms in 28 industry groups. Firms were again categorized into industry groups according to the classification used by *Forbes* in its Annual Report on American Industry. Group composition ranged from a low of 17 CEOs (1.3 percent of the total) from the construction industry to a high of 140 CEOs from electric utilities (10.7 percent of the total).

Changes in CEO Functional Background over Time

For the 1,313 CEOs listed by *Forbes* over a 12 year period, functional area background was analyzed in relation to year of appointment. This allowed us to examine changes over three decades. Five year periods were used from 1951 to 1981, with a general category for all those appointed before 1951. The detailed results are presented in our earlier research paper (Piercy & Forbes, 1986). Here we will summarize the findings.

Consistent with the first study (when banks were excluded), the largest percentage of CEOs had backgrounds in general administration. This was followed by marketing, finance, and production. Overall, the least common backgrounds were in the technical and legal areas.

The percentages changed over the years in interesting ways, however. General administration seems to have generally declined over the past 30 years. However, the very high percentage in this category for appointments prior to 1951 may be partially due to problems of interpretation of the meaning of functional background. Finance has generally been the third most common functional background, except in the late 1950s when marketing and legal were particularly strong, and in the early 1970s when it rose to number two. Marketing was the second most frequently listed background until the 1960s when it became number one. Its ranking dropped significantly during the 1970s, however. A legal background rose as high as third in the rankings in the late 1950s but is generally near the bottom of the list. Production was generally fourth or fifth until the late 1970s when it rose to second in frequency behind the technical background. The most drastic change was in the ranking of the technical background. Typically at the bottom of the list, it rose to the top in the late 1970s.

Summarizing these trends, it seems that general administration and marketing were the most common background of non-banking CEOs through the 1950s and 1960s. Marketing was particularly strong during the 1960s, which was a time of rapid economic expansion. The most successful firms were those that took advantage of new opportunities. An emphasis on marketing is often seen in firms that adapt such prospector or analyzer strategies (Slocum & Cron, 1988). The early 1970s saw economic contraction and with it the rise of CEOs with financial and production backgrounds who could help bring costs under control. These functions are typically emphasized by defender firms that are trying to protect their niche (Slocum & Cron, 1988). Finally, the rise of the technical CEO in the late 1970s may have been due to the realization that just cutting costs was not enough to regain the competitive edge in the world economy. New high quality products and processes were needed in order to counter the inroads being made by foreign competitors such as the Japanese.

The emphasis on technical and production/operations backgrounds has continued to the present time, particularly among industrial firms. During the 1987 through 1989 period, 59 changes were made in CEOs of industrial firms. Almost one-third (32.2 percent) of the new CEOs had technical backgrounds and 16.9 percent came from production/operations backgrounds. The data strongly support the proposition that the critical competitive issues of the day influence the selection of corporate CEOs.

Industry Differences in CEO Functional Background

Our findings here were generally consistent with the results of the earlier study. The data in this study covered 12 years as opposed to the one year "snap shot" reported in the first study and therefore may be more representative of industry tendencies. Again, certain industries clearly preferred particular business backgrounds. In 26 of the 28 industry groups (92.9 percent) one-quarter or more of the chief executives had the same business background. Two different business backgrounds accounted for one-half or more of the CEOs in 21 of the industries (75 percent).

As noted in the earlier study, marketing was predominant in the consumer goods industries. It was the background for one-third or more of the CEOs in the household products, health care, personal products, and diversified food industries. Marketing also provided the highest percentage of CEOs in the information processing, department stores, and automotive industries.

A similar concentration was found in the basic industries where production was the most common functional background. This area provided more than one-fourth of the chief executives in steel, energy, forest products, and building materials. Production also dominated in multi-industry companies and in surface transportation.

General administration was the leader in five industry groups: leisure, electrical equipment, air transportation, supermarkets, and apparel. A technical background appeared most frequently in the chemical, construction, and electric utilities industries. Finance was the most common background in conglomerates, consumer finance, and natural gas utilities. Legal was the most evenly distributed business background; ranging from eight to 17 percent in 17 of the 28 industries. However, in the regulated industries (insurance, utilities, and transportation) about one-fifth of the chief executives had a legal background.

Statistical Tests

We conducted two types of statistical analyses on this data. Statistical tests fall into two categories: inferential and descriptive. The former are most appropriate when examining a sample from a larger population. They allow us to infer whether differences found in the sample are representative of the entire population. In this study, our data represented virtually the entire population of the most highly paid CEOs in the United States (from 1970 through 1981), and therefore inferential statistics were not necessary. We did, however, conduct tests to estimate the probabilities that the differences in functional backgrounds described here might have occurred by chance. In both cases (functional background differences over time and functional background differences across industries) the results would have occurred by chance less than one time in 10,000.

Two descriptive statistics were also computed which measure the strength of the association between nominal variables (categorical data). The two measures were: lambda, which indicates the percentage of improvement in predictive ability given that we know the value of one of the variables; and the uncertainty coefficient, which gives the proportion of the uncertainty about one variable which is reduced when we specify the other variable (Hays, 1963). Assuming that we would like to know whether knowledge of either year appointed or industry group improves our ability to predict the functional background of a chief executive, then these measures will give us the degree of this improvement.

With functional business background of CEOs as the dependent variable (the variable to be predicted) and year of appointment as the independent variable (the predictor), lambda equaled 0.028 and the uncertainty coefficient equaled 0.015. This indicates that knowing the year of appointment improves our ability to predict functional background by only 2.8 percent and reduces our uncertainty by 1.5 percent. However, with industry group as the predictor of CEO functional background, lambda equaled 0.140 and the uncertainty coefficient equaled 0.128. These figures indicate a 14 percent improvement in predictive ability and a 12.8 percent reduction in uncertainty. This establishes that industry group is a much stronger predictor of CEO functional background than is the year of appointment. Or, the variation in CEO background across industries was much greater than the variance over time.

Changes in Functional Area upon CEO Succession

Although certain industries prefer particular functional backgrounds, there is still a very strong tendency for firms to change functional background when replacing their top executives. In our data, one or more changes were recorded in 362 firms accounting for 504 successions. In 385 instances (76.4 percent) the successor had a different functional area background than that of his predecessor; a finding almost identical to that of Dommermuth (1966). In only five industry groups did the successor have the same functional area background as the predecessor in one-third or more of the appointments. These were automotive (36.0 percent), information processing (37.5 percent), consumer finance (33.3 percent), gas utilities (35.7 percent), and energy (34.3 percent).

Update and Conclusions

First we must note that any statement that purports to identify the functional background of American CEOs is a misleading overgeneralization. Industry differences are very real and even including certain industries in the analysis can lead to questionable conclusions. For example, one recent study of CEOs stated that banking was the most common business background of today's CEOs (Boone & Kurtz, 1988). This study was based on data from *Forbes* and apparently included all the many banking institutions which we chose to exclude. Our data indicated that banking was a leading functional background only in the banking and consumer finance industries. While the authors of such studies carefully describe their data sources and statistics, such conclusions are often cited out of context by other writers.

Another issue complicates the discussion of CEO background when different industries are included in the analysis. First, it should be reiterated that there is little inter-industry movement at the highest levels of management. For example, it is rare for a banking executive to move to a manufacturing firm, or for a manufacturing executive to go to a public utility. Rather, there is a tendency for an individual to specialize in an industry; and then within that industry to spend a good part of their career within a particular functional area.

In a manufacturing firm, an individual may start in finance, marketing, or other specialty, and then move upward through a series of positions in that function until reaching the vice president level. From there, the individual might move to a position of group vice president with general management responsibilities, to executive vice president and finally to CEO (see Chapter 4 for more on these career paths). Generally when functional area is reported, we would expect it to be indicated as finance or marketing, as the case may be.

On the other hand, an individual entering the banking industry might also start in a particular specialized area, such as corporate loans, prior to moving into the upper echelons of management; however, in most listings of backgrounds his would be shown as "banking." Thus when we combine or compare backgrounds across industries, we are actually using the "functional" backgrounds for industrial firms but the "business" backgrounds of those in such businesses as banking, insurance, and retailing.

Unless this distinction is made, the results will be lacking in clarity. For example, to conclude that banking is the business background of the largest number of CEOs, while true, is misleading unless it is realized that banks comprise a large component of the sample and that the backgrounds of most bank CEOs are likely to be listed merely as banking. In the industrial firms, on the other hand, one of several functional areas may be listed as the professional background of the CEO.

We did our own update on the backgrounds of all CEOs by comparing the data for 1978 and 1989 from the *Forbes* listing of the highest paid CEOs for those years. The percentages seem to indicate decreases in the number with backgrounds in finance, administration, legal, and marketing. There is a strong increase in banking and small increases in production/operations and technical backgrounds. The inclusion of the banking industry clouds these conclusions, however. In 1978, banks accounted for one-fifth of the firms represented while in 1989 this figure had risen to almost one-quarter. Also, a much higher percentage of bank CEOs were listed as having backgrounds in finance in 1978 than in 1989 (38 percent versus 15 percent). A change in the sample plus a change in one industry (or possibly just a change in reporting within one industry) might result in inaccurate conclusions about CEO backgrounds in general.

When we look at the totals for each of the functional/business backgrounds without regard for the industry within the 1989 data, banking emerges as the leader. It is followed by administration, finance, technical, production/operations, and marketing. A closer examination of specific industry groups, however, is revealing. Of the 142 CEOs with banking backgrounds, all but six (96 percent) head banks. Four head industrial firms and two are chief executives of insurance companies.

A high degree of concentration also exists for those with backgrounds in insurance, retailing, and journalism. Only four (15.4 percent) of the CEOs with insurance backgrounds head firms outside the insurance industry. Two head industrial firms, one is the CEO of a bank, and one heads a financial services firm. One CEO with a background in retailing is the head of an industrial firm and one heads a service firm. The remainder all lead retail organizations. All five CEOs with backgrounds in journalism head publishing companies.

Within other industry groups, the trends that we had identified in our earlier studies are continuing through 1989. In the industrial firms, most CEOs have technical backgrounds (21.4 percent), closely followed by production/operations (19.1 percent), marketing (18.8 percent), and general administration (17.4 percent). Finance ranks fifth (13.8 percent) and the legal area is a distant sixth (4.9 percent).

Technical backgrounds have a wide lead in utilities with over one-third (34.6 percent). The legal background is the second most popular with 19.2 percent, followed by general administration (16.7 percent), finance (14.1 percent), and production/operations (12.8 percent). Only two CEOs in the utility industry had a background in marketing (2.6 percent).

In the transportation industry, over 50 percent of the CEOs have a background in either the finance (28.6 percent) or legal areas (23.8 percent). Also well represented here are general administration (19.0 percent) and production/operations (14.3 percent).

Rarely does any one functional area account for more than 20 to 25 percent of all CEO backgrounds. In the last of the five year periods that we studied earlier, three functions (finance, technical, and production) were virtually tied for the lead with about 17 percent of the CEOs in each category. Averaging more recent data (from 1984 through 1988), we found four functions within one percentage point of each other. Operations/production, technical, administration, and finance all represented 18 to 19 percent of the CEOs. Marketing was slightly lower (at about 16 percent) and legal averaged nine to ten percent. When we hear statements that one area is the functional background of most chief executives, we must realize that this also means that approximately 80 percent of the CEOs came from other functions.

Boone and Kurtz (1988) were careful not to advise aspiring CEOs to choose the functional background that happens to be most common at any one point in time—noting the tendency for this to change and the tendency for firms to change functional areas 75 percent of the time. Our data show that shifts in the relative importance of functional areas are consistent with changes in the general economic environment. For example, marketing was strong in the 1960s; finance in the early 1970s; and technical backgrounds have become more important since the late 1970s.

More significant, however, were the differences across various industry groups. Since the environments faced by business firms are largely defined by the industry (Lawrence & Lorsch, 1967) and since different functional areas possess the expertise to deal with different environmental challenges, we would expect to find industry differences in the functional representation at the top. However, environments and organizations are only "loosely coupled" (Orton & Weick, 1990), so the magnitude of such effects may not be very large. We did find substantial evidence in both studies to support the notion that many industries favor those functions that are able to perform the most critical tasks for their business. According to Pfeffer and Salancik (1978), this important ability will result in greater power within the organization, which in turn is used to gain more and more influence and representation at the top of the organization. An alternative explanation is that the outgoing CEO and the board of directors make a careful and rational decision to select the candidate most likely to be able to handle the critical strategic contingencies (Vancil, 1987).

The role of power in such selections is suggested by the fact that functional areas change so often (75–76 percent of the time). In most situations, no one function is all powerful. Therefore coalitions are needed at the top and the executive committee consists of representatives of all the most powerful areas. When a change in leadership occurs, the number two man (or hopefully soon, woman) who is from a different background normally ascends to the top. This phenomenon may also be due to the nature of the succession event in many companies. Vancil (1987) has documented the fact that most CEOs "pass the baton" to their successor as in a relay race. The heir apparent is given a position such as president or chief operating officer two or three years prior to becoming the new CEO. The two executives then manage the corporation in tandem while the successor is brought up to speed. There may be a tendency to avoid having two people with the same functional background at the top during the transition period.

Our advice for the aspiring CEO is that he or she plan to gain early experience in one of the functions which will be considered most important to the firm when he or she is 45 to 50 years of age. This may sound like an impossible task; however, we believe that there are steps that anyone can take to increase the chances of having the right background.

First, since rising to the top will require extremely high levels of on-the-job performance, you should try to gain an edge by obtaining an undergraduate or graduate education in an area that matches your interests and abilities and is of relevance in the business world. Do not attempt to major in engineering or finance just because it was listed in some book or article as the background of many chief executives. Choose such majors only if you enjoy and are skilled in quantitative analyses. If number crunching is not your thing, major in other relevant areas such as marketing or management. If you major in liberal arts, consider going on for your MBA or law degree.

Next, choose an industry in which your background has traditionally represented a critical skill. For example, a background in law has been important in regulated industries such as public utilities. A technical background is also important in the utility industry. In industrial firms, backgrounds in the traditional line functions of production and marketing are always strong and these have been joined recently by the technical function. Marketing is likely to remain strong in consumer industries, while production will continue to be important in basic industries such as steel. Finance will continue to be a critical function in conglomerates. Start out in a key area, but do not be afraid to move across functions to gain broader experience as you move up in the firm.

The difficult task is predicting changes in functional importance such as the rise of the technical function during the 1970s. The key here is to observe the changing business environment. Functions become more or less important in relation to the needs of the firms. Experience in the international arena or in human resource management (both considered dead ends in many companies in the past) will become much more critical in the future. We will discuss the process of strategically planning one's career in more detail in Chapter 9.

TOP EXECUTIVE PROFILES

Robert C. Stempel, General Motors Corporation

Robert Stempel's selection as chairman and CEO of General Motors in 1990 illustrates the major point of this chapter, as well as several points from other chapters. The choice of an engineer with no experience in the corporate financial area was a major break with a long-standing tradition at GM. In the 1920s, General Motors faced a financial crisis due to overextension by William C. Durant. Therefore, Pierre duPont and Alfred Sloan set out to reorganize the company. The, then radical, idea of setting up decentralized product-based divisions was introduced. However, a system was needed to balance the power of the operating executives with controls from the financial area. Therefore finance people were placed in the chairman and vice chairman positions, while operating executives typically held the president's post (Pfeffer, 1981).

According to Pfeffer (1981), the finance area consolidated their power over time through strategic appointments and reorganizations. The power of operating management and the presidency declined. The financial area rightly came to power to deal with a financial crisis, but the ensuing institutionalization of their power may have hindered the organization's ability to change.

The new CEO is clearly not a finance man. Robert Stempel was born in 1933 and was educated at Worcester Polytechnic Institute (B.S.) and at Michigan State (MBA). He began work for GM in 1958 in the Oldsmobile chassis design department. In the early 1960s he was first noticed by his superiors for his work on the front-wheel drive Oldsmobile Toronado (Ingrassia & White, 1990). Stempel became director of engineering in the Chevrolet Division in 1975, and vice president and general manager of the Pontiac Division in 1978. He was made managing director of the European Adam Opel subsidiary in 1980 and was brought back two years later as the head of the Chevrolet Division. In 1984, he was named the group vice president in charge of the new Buick-Oldsmobile-Cadillac group; and in 1986, he became an executive vice president in charge of the worldwide truck and bus group and the overseas car group. He was promoted to president and chief operating officer in 1987 and appointed chairman and CEO in 1990.

Stempel had been credited with making needed changes in the Buick-Oldsmobile-Cadillac group and in overseas operations, and the appointment of an innovative, technical/operations man was generally considered the right move for GM (Ingrassia & White, 1990). Our data indicate that General Motors is merely the latest company to follow a broad functional trend that started over a decade ago.

8

Bottom to Top: The Career of the Chief Executive Officer

In the previous chapters we have examined the research and the issues surrounding career mobility in the early years (Chapters 2 and 3) and then in the middle and later years of the career (Chapter 4). We next explored the problems and the opportunities facing women in management today (Chapter 5). Then we turned to the studies of the early backgrounds of CEOs (Chapter 6), and the issue of how the paths to the top depend on the industry and how they change over time (Chapter 7).

What we have not yet done is to examine the entire careers of CEOs. While a good picture of top executive careers may be obtained by piecing together studies that focus on the various phases of a career, some different insights may come from research that focuses on the entire careers of the same individuals.

THE CAREERS OF CEOs IN INDUSTRIAL FIRMS

Research Method

Industries differ in many ways that affect careers. They face different strategic contingencies, utilize different organizational structures, assign similar titles different meanings (e.g., vice president is typically a much higher position in an industrial firm than in a bank), and, as we have seen in the last chapter, vary in the opportunities provided to those in different functional areas. Therefore we chose to analyze CEO careers by industry, starting with manufacturing.

CEOs of all basic industries and manufacturing firms in *Forbes'* 1988 listing of corporate America's top CEOs were selected as the sample for the first part of the study. Biographical and career data were obtained from the 1988/1989 edition of *Marquis' Who's Who in America*. The elimination of company founders and CEOs for whom career information was too sketchy left a data set describing 230 CEO careers. In some cases we retained career data that was incomplete. For example, a period of years might only be identified as "various positions," or early career data might be missing. If most of the information was available, we included the case.

We verified the *Who's Who* data by obtaining approximately 50 CEO biographical data sheets directly from the firms. No significant differences were noted.

Results

Entering the Workplace. The average age of entry into the workplace was 24 (the same as the average for all CEOs—see Chapter 7). As we noted in the last chapter, the late entry is attributable to education and military service. Upon graduation from high school, only eight of the CEOs (3.5 percent) immediately entered the workforce. One-quarter (25.5 percent) either chose or were drafted for military service, while 71 percent (164) entered college. After completing their undergraduate work, those who had entered college chose one of three options upon graduation in almost equal numbers: entry into the workforce (57), military service (54), and graduate education (53). A large majority of those who joined the military from high school entered college immediately upon their release (89.8 percent). Only 10.2 percent entered the workforce without at least an undergraduate degree. These figures are very comparable to those for all CEOs as reported in Chapter 7.

Education. The level of education of these manufacturing CEOs is slightly higher than for all CEOs. About 45 percent have bachelor's degrees, while about one-third have a master's degree and 12 percent have law degrees. CEOs with either no college degree or with doctorates are relatively rare (only 4 and 5 percent, respectively) but are not unknown.

Entry-Level Assignments. Engineering was the area where almost one-third (32 percent) of the manufacturing CEOs were first assigned. This was followed by marketing (17.4 percent), finance and accounting (15.1 percent), legal (11.0 percent), and production/operations (4.7 percent). All but three of the engineers joined a manufacturing firm initially. However, one-third of the accountants had experience with a major accounting firm; and all but three of the attorneys had experience in private practice, with a law firm, or with a governmental agency before joining a manufacturing firm.

Inter-Firm and Inter-Industry Mobility. These industrial CEOs have shown relatively little inter-firm mobility. Over half worked in only one or two firms, while another one-third of the group were employed by three or four different firms. Only ten percent had more than four employers. The greatest mobility occurred early in their careers. Of the two-thirds who served in more than one firm, 59 percent moved at least once during the first five years (18 percent made two or more moves in this early time period). Only 19 percent of the CEOs who moved did so in the second five years of their career. This proportion drops further to 7.6 percent in years 11 through 15 and then levels off at just under five percent per five year period thereafter.

Nearly three-quarters (71.0 percent) of these CEOs joined an industrial firm upon entering the workforce and remained in that or another industrial firm throughout their careers. Another 7.4 percent started their career in an industrial firm; left for brief stints with a government agency, educational institution, or a legal or consulting firm; and then returned to industry. The remaining one-fifth (21.6 percent) started their careers with non-industrial firms. Here the largest initial employers were governmental agencies and legal firms, followed by educational institutions, accounting firms, and banks. The average length of time in a non-industrial setting was 3.6 years. Only five CEOs had over ten years of experience prior to joining an industrial firm.

A few major industrial firms appear to be training grounds for CEOs. Thirty-three CEOs had periods of service averaging 11.6 years in one of nine firms. These were IBM and Ford with six each; GE with five; P&G with four; AT&T and ITT with three each; and Xerox, United Technologies, and TRW: two each. In addition, 15 CEOs had stints averaging 6.6 years with one of the major oil companies.

Timing of Movement up the Career Ladder. The typical ages and the number of years that it took to reach various career levels are shown in Table 8.1. The first management position was reached after about five years at age 29. Ten years later, at age 39, the typical chief executive became either a functional vice president (e.g., vice president of marketing or finance) or attained their first general management position (heading a division or region). Higher level positions quickly followed: executive vice president at age 45, top management (other than CEO) at 47, and finally chief executive at 50. The category of "top management (other than CEO)" includes positions such as chief operating officer, president, or vice chairman. It must be emphasized that these are averages with large variances. Half of the executives attained these positions at an earlier age and half at a later age—often much later, as indicated by the standard deviations and ranges shown in the table.

Early Career Development. Beyond the first management position and prior to reaching the vice president or general management level there tends to be a fair amount of functional diversity. Fewer than one-third (31.9 percent) of the CEOs remained in one area during this time. The

Table 8.1
Age and Years to Reach Organizational Career Levels

Career Level	Age			Years		
	Means	s.d.	Range	Means	s.d.	Range
Management	28.99	3.75	20-37	4.99	3.26	1-13
Functional Vice-President	38.61	5.78	25-53	14.89	5.94	3-29
General Management	38.84	5.99	25-52	14.93	6.24	3-28
Executive Vice-President	44.79	5.67	26-58	20.88	6.07	4-35
Top Management (Other than CEO)	47.44	6.19	29-58	23.63	6.47	4-37
Chief Executive Officer	50.42	6.38	31-65	26.58	6.69	9-40

norm was experience in two different functions (44.7 percent), but almost one-quarter (23.4 percent) moved through three or more different areas. Those who specialized in only one function were most likely to be in the financial area (14), closely followed by legal and marketing with ten each, and then engineering with nine. Keeping in mind that almost one-third of the industrial CEOs started in engineering, the most common secondary areas for assignment were production/operations (23) and marketing (21). These were followed by administration (19), finance (15), and planning (14). Most CEOs in manufacturing companies start to increase their breadth of functional experience fairly early in their careers.

Although not a functional area, at least 36 CEOs had an assignment as an "assistant to" a senior manager during this time. This number is probably very conservative since these were relatively brief assignments and over one-quarter of the CEO career path data contained some gaps. Such assignments usually occurred eight to nine years after the CEO entered the workforce and they averaged 2.5 years in duration.

Another common developmental assignment was in the international area. Almost one-quarter (22.5 percent) of the CEOs had one or more assignments either in a foreign country or with the international division of the firm. International experience came as early as the initial assignment upon entering the workforce or as late as 28 years into the career. The norm was early mid-career (after 13 to 14 years of service). Over 40 percent of the international assignments involved multiple positions.

Table 8.2
Years to Career Levels in Relation to Entry Functional Area

		Career Levels				
Area	Mgmt. (n=89)	Functional Vice Pres. (n=99)	General Mgmt. (n=124)	Executive Vice Pres. (n=98)	Top Mgmt. (n=125)	Chief Exec. (n=172)
Finance/Acctg.	4.36	13.11	13.69	18.92	22.25	24.58
Legal	4.50	10.23	10.83	16.91	19.23	20.95
Engineering	6.42	17.48	16.76	23.66	25.82	29.80
Marketing	4.53	13.41	13.77	18.11	23.41	26.30
Production/ Operations	4.83	16.50	15.17	17.50	22.14	27.50
Other	3.79	14.22	14.36	20.33	22.21	25.24
	n.s.	$p < .01$	n.s	$p < .01$	$p < .05$	$p < .001$

n.s. = Not statistically significant.

Each such assignment averaged almost three and one-half years in duration.

Divisional Assignments. Manufacturing CEOs did not spend their careers in corporate headquarters. Four-fifths had one or more assignments with a division/subsidiary. Over half had two or more such assignments and almost one-third (31.9 percent) had three or more. The first of these assignments came after about ten years of service; and they typically lasted four to five years.

Functional Fast Tracks. Analyses of variance were conducted to determine whether the functional area within which a CEO entered the firm affected the time to reach upper management positions. The results appear in Table 8.2. While most chief executives in manufacturing started in the engineering function, this group took the longest to reach the top. The quickest route to the top was the legal path. Significant differences between engineering and legal backgrounds appear as early as the functional vice president level. The differences in the age at which various levels were reached were not as pronounced due to the additional education required of lawyers. However, those with a legal background still reached the top (CEO level) at a significantly earlier age than those with an engineering background (47.1 versus 53.2).

Education and the Fast Track. A similar analysis was done for educational background. A law degree is associated with the quickest path to

Table 8.3
Years to Career Levels in Relation to Level of Education

		Career Levels			
Education	Mgmt. (n=95)	Functional Vice Pres. (n=132)	General Mgmt. (n=167)	Executive Vice Pres. (n=128)	Top Mgmt. (n=161)	Chief Exec. (n=230)
Non-baccalaureate	4.00	15.50	16.40	22.00	23.43	31.22
Bachelors	5.65	16.00	16.56	22.80	25.12	28.42
Masters	4.69	14.37	13.38	18.60	22.61	24.72
Law Degree	3.69	12.28	11.95	18.83	20.91	22.62
Doctorate	5.63	14.88	15.18	24.80	24.11	29.18
	n.s	n.s	p<.01	p<.01	n.s	p<.001

n.s. = Not statistically significant.

the top, as shown in Table 8.3. A master's degree also helped shorten the path to the top, in comparison to the time that those with only bachelor's degrees took. Again, age differences were not as strong. However, despite the additional years of education, those with a master's degree reached the chief executive level at an earlier age than those with only the baccalaureate (48.7 versus 52.9).

Different Career Paths. One of our most interesting findings was the existence of a number of distinctively different career paths taken to reach the top. Not all CEOs progressed through each of the levels studied in this research. In fact, eight different paths were discovered, as shown in Figure 8.1. Some executives first became functional vice presidents and then general managers. Others were general managers first and then functional vice presidents. Some had experience in only one of these positions before becoming executive vice presidents, while still others moved directly from either general management or functional vice president to top management. The number of executives following each path was fairly evenly distributed: ranging from 15 to 28.

Surprisingly, analyses of the times needed to reach top management or to become a chief executive in relation to these eight paths revealed no statistically significant differences. That is, even if one skips the general management and executive vice president spots and moves directly from functional vice president to top management, it takes approximately as long as if one serves in all possible positions. It seems

Figure 8.1
The Paths to the Top in Industrial Firms

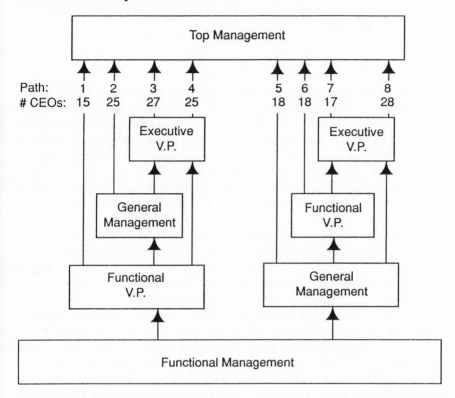

that those who serve in fewer different positions spend more time in each of those positions.

Impact of Early versus Late Movement. We carefully examined the intercorrelations among the times taken to reach the various levels of management. These statistics shed some light on the question of the importance of early upward mobility (see Chapters 2 and 3). Quicker promotion into the first management position was significantly associated with quicker promotion all the way to the top. However, the time to reach either functional vice president or general management was a much stronger predictor of time to the top. These intermediate times (to functional vice president and general management) were much better predictors of all of the higher level times (executive vice president, top management, and chief executive) than was the time to reach the first management position. In addition, promotion to management did not predict promotion to the intermediate positions as well as the intermediate positions predict the time to reach the CEO level. This despite the fact that slightly more time typically passed between the intermediate positions and the CEO spot than passed between the first management position and general management or functional vice president. The importance of reaching these intermediate positions will be discussed further in the next section.

Discussion

Perhaps the most striking finding from this study of the entire careers of manufacturing chief executives was the great diversity of backgrounds and paths to the top. Starting with education, we found that the typical CEO in an industrial firm has been educated at the bachelor's or master's level. However, there are CEOs of major firms with no baccalaureate degree, e.g., Marion Gregory at Snap-On-Tools, as well as CEOs with doctoral degrees, e.g., Jack Welch at General Electric. In addition, a fair number (about 12 percent) of CEOs in manufacturing firms possess law degrees.

The most common entry-level function for CEOs was engineering, which at 32 percent accounted for about as many chief executives' backgrounds as the second and third most frequent areas (marketing and finance/accounting) combined. All initial functional areas are well represented among the chief executive group, however.

Those who have reached the top in manufacturing firms have followed different paths depending on their early background. The engineer has typically spent his entire career in manufacturing. While more CEOs started as engineers than in any other area, they are on the slowest track to the top. In contrast, those with a legal background typically started their careers outside of manufacturing, but were promoted very rapidly once in the manufacturing industry. On the average, lawyers reached the top nine years earlier (total career time) than engineers. The next fastest path to the top was the finance/accounting route. Many of these executives also started their careers outside of manufacturing (one-third had been previously employed by major public accounting firms).

It would seem that in recent years, manufacturing firms have valued those with early experience in the engineering area. This experience provides a background in manufacturing fundamentals: product and process design and production and operations. The typical route to the top has been one that starts in an engineering function, then crosses over into important line functions such as production or marketing. If the typical manufacturing executive changes companies it is likely to be early in the career. He may have started his career with a major company such as IBM, Ford, General Electric, or Proctor & Gamble. Later in the career, more is learned about the business by serving in one or two different divisions. It is a slow, bottom-up career path, designed to develop a top executive who possesses critical skills but who also knows the entire company. This could be described as the "academy" career system (Sonnenfeld & Peiperl, 1988), which is common in large manufacturing companies.

The legal or financial person who rises to the top of a manufacturing firm may have started his or her career in a law firm or accounting firm and may have risen within their specialized functional area while in the industrial firm. They may not have line experience and may not be familiar with all operations of the company, but when their expertise is needed at the top they may be moved up very quickly.

Other typical broadening experiences may include assignments as an "assistant to" a top executive or an international assignment. These positions usually came during the period before reaching the functional vice president or general management level.

The diversity of career paths was illustrated by the identification of eight different higher level sequences of positions (see Figure 8.1). While many experts emphasize the importance of the general management track to the top (e.g., Kotter, 1982, 1988), our findings indicate that at times, in many manufacturing firms, functionally specialized executives may be needed at the top.

With respect to education, we showed that a law degree shortens the time required to reach the top. Also speeding up the trip to the top is the attainment of a master's degree (most commonly the MBA). Since those with law degrees typically start their careers outside of manufacturing, the master's degree would be the appropriate choice for those whose entire careers have been in manufacturing firms.

We would like to comment here on the concept of "age norms" within business firms (Lawrence, 1984, 1988). These norms are widely accepted beliefs concerning the age at which a person should reach a particular level of management. While we have shown the average ages at which the key positions on the path to the top are reached, we have also noted that large variances exist about these means. Although people may believe that a position must be attained by a particular time, the reality is that, in industrial firms as a whole, these norms are not adhered to very closely. Furthermore, we have shown that functional area and level of education make a significant difference in the average ages at which various levels are reached. For example, a lawyer or accountant who makes functional vice president after 15 years would be behind the norm, but an engineer would be ahead of schedule.

Our intercorrelations among the times to reach the various levels of management suggest that a critical event in the life of a CEO is the attainment of the level of functional vice president or general manager. The time to reach the level of CEO is strongly associated with the time at which this event occurs (typically at around age 39).

The preceding decade, from age 29 to 39, appears to be a critical time of development for the future CEO. Having become a manager at about age 29, the future top executive's horizons were broadened by experience in new functions and/or experience overseas. Awareness of top management issues and behaviors, as well as greatly increased visibility, may have been attained through an assignment as an assistant to a top executive. The period is surely a time of testing and evaluation as well as development. This period seems to represent the critical "contest" which determines who continues on to higher management. Some career research (see Chapters 2 and 3) has stressed the importance of very early job experiences (e.g., Berlew & Hall, 1966) and the necessity of very early promotion (Rosenbaum, 1979). We feel that the relative importance of these early events may have been overstated.

Our findings are confirmed by the survey conducted by Korn/Ferry International and the UCLA Graduate School of Management. Over 1,300 senior executives of *Fortune 500* firms responded to their questionnaires. Although the survey did not include CEOs or COOs (chief operating officers), the respondents were all very successful and many would be candidates for the top positions. Lester Korn reports:

There is general consensus among senior managers as to the existence of the breakout phenomena and the time when it occurs. Only four percent of those we surveyed said they had broken out before the age of 26. Only 12 percent said they had broken out after the age of 40. The largest number broke out between the ages of 31 and 35. (1988, p. 129)

Data on salaries from the same survey also support this breakout phenomenon. The respondents were asked how much they had earned at five year increments throughout their careers. In terms of 1987 dollars, these successful senior executives had been earning about one and one half times their age when they were 25 and 30. However, by age 35 they were earning, on average, about four times their age. It is clear that a major career path breakpoint occurred when these executives were in their 30s.

This period that we see as most critical has received relatively little study. It corresponds to Hall's (1976) Advancement Stage, but it seems that most academic research has focused on the earlier Exploration and Socialization stages and on the later Maintenance (plateau) stage. For the top executive, there is no Maintenance stage, only an extended Advancement stage. Some work that does focus on this stage includes Kotter's book on power and influence among middle managers (1985), his more recent book on developing leadership (Kotter, 1988), and the research by McCall, Lombardo, and Morrison (1988) on important executive development experiences. Next we will describe Hall's stages in more depth, and summarize the findings from our study of manufacturing CEOs by describing the career phases of the CEO.

THE PHASES OF THE INDUSTRIAL CEO'S CAREER

There are several well accepted models of career stages. For example, Hall (1976) has identified the five stages that most people experience and has discussed the typical challenges that occur during each stage. We will review this model before presenting the results of our analysis of chief executive careers.

Hall's Career Stage Model

The first stage is entry or exploration. This stage includes preparatory education and the tentative choice of a job and occupation. Changing jobs and/or occupations is not unusual as the individual searches for a satisfactory fit between his or her abilities and needs and the requirements of various positions. Next comes the socialization or establishment stage in which the individual learns the expectations of a particular job and organization. The newcomer begins to become established in a career. We have discussed this stage in some detail in Chapter 2.

The stage that seems to be most important in the career of a successful top executive comes next. This is the Advancement stage which typically occurs between the ages of late 20s through mid-40s. It is at this stage that the individual's performance and potential are first recognized and he or she begins to move up within the organization. There is a relatively large amount of movement. Some individuals will continue to change companies but, as we have shown, the most successful managers will settle into one organization early in this stage. Internally, there will be frequent vertical as well as lateral movement as the experience base is broadened. Again, we have noted that this was true among the manufacturing CEOs studied in this chapter.

For those who reach the top, the Advancement stage continues until retirement. However, for most managers, a major transition comes sometime during their 40s. To use the terminology that we introduced early in this book, they realize that they have lost the critical contests that occurred during the Advancement stage. They are now out of the tournament in which the prize is the top executive position. A plateau has been reached—for most there will be no further significant upward movement. This realization often contributes to a mid-life crisis (Levinson et al., 1978). A major task for the individual and the organization is to maintain acceptable performance from this point on. As we also noted early in the book, the development of more open contests for movement toward the top would reduce or eliminate this problem. Some individuals adjust well to this transition and become "solid citizens" but others turn into "dead wood" (Ference, Stoner, & Warren, 1977). Those with a propensity for risk taking may change companies and/or even change careers.

Finally, the last of Hall's career stages is the Withdrawal, or decline, stage, which comes as the employee faces retirement and the end of the career. Reactions to this major transition vary, with some adapting very well and moving on to active retirement lives, while others have a very difficult time adjusting.

These are the stages that the typical business person experiences, but what about the extraordinary person who rises to the top of a major corporation? There are few, if any, comprehensive studies of the entire career paths of a large group of top executives. What are the major events and transitions in their careers?

CEO Career Phases

Using the data set previously described, we carefully analyzed the careers of the 230 chief executives of large industrial firms. This analysis revealed certain consistent patterns of career development. While no two executives followed exactly the same path and lines of demarcation were not always clearly drawn, there were identifiable phases of career development and progression. Six distinct phases were identified (see Figure 8.2).

Phase I—Exploration (1–5 years). Due to military service, college, and graduate school, the average chief executive started his career at age 24. As is true with most careers, the earliest phase of a top executive's career was characterized by instability and exploration. The individual entered the workplace uncommitted to any employer or organization. Organizational and industry changes were frequent as the individual searched for identity and job satisfaction. Forty percent of the CEOs changed organizations at least once during the first five years of work experience; and 8.7 percent changed two or more times.

Nearly one-quarter started with a non-industrial firm. However, over four-fifths of these joined an industrial organization within five years and only two waited longer than 10 years to move into industry. The average length of time spent in a non-industrial firm was 3.4 years. Often the early non-industrial experience was in a law firm, an accounting firm, or a governmental agency.

By the end of this phase, organizational and industry stability had been achieved, technical skills were established, and at age 29 the future chief executive attained his first management position.

Phase II—Development (6–10 years). The next phase was one of intra-firm development. Organizational changes declined significantly. In contrast to the 40 percent who changed firms in Phase I, only 12 percent changed employers during the second phase of their careers. In this

Figure 8.2
The Phases of the Industrial CEO's Career

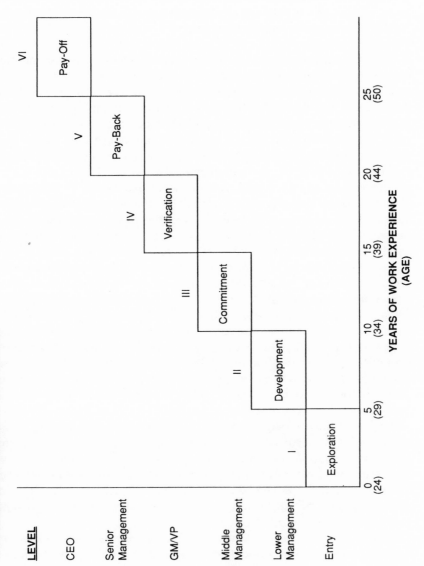

phase, the future executives' experiences were broadened. Fewer than one-third spent all their time in one functional area. Many received additional breadth and visibility through assignments as an "assistant to" a senior manager during this phase. Others started to experience general management and profit center responsibilities as plant manager, product manager, or brand manager.

Phase III—Commitment (11–15 years). Apparently satisfied with their own work and their progress, the young managers identified with and became committed to a particular firm. The frequency of organizational changes declined dramatically. Fewer than five percent of these executives changed employers during this period. Advancement to middle management continued and breadth of experience widened with assignments in the international area. Almost one-quarter had one or more assignments in foreign countries or, at least, assignments with the international division of the firm. These international assignments came on the average after about 13 years of work experience.

By the end of this phase many hurdles have been passed; many contests have been won. The future top executive has gained credibility and visibility. Functional skills have been proven; some general management ability has been demonstrated; and loyalty and commitment to the firm has been established. It is likely that the possibility of top management potential has been recognized and a major career breakthrough either has occurred or is about to occur.

Phase IV—Verification (16–20 years). This phase is best characterized as a period of verification of managerial and leadership capabilities. A major opportunity typically occurred early in the period. The executive was promoted to either the first general management position with responsibility for a division or subsidiary (39 percent made this move) or to a functional vice president position (19 percent had this opportunity). On the average, this occurred at about age 39.

Responsibilities changed frequently during this phase. Ninety-five percent of the executives had two or more assignments; while almost half of the group served in three or more different positions. This was the period of greatest inter-firm stability—only 2.4 percent of the future CEOs changed employers during this time. By the end of this time period, the leading edge of the group (17 percent of the executives) had reached the position of CEO.

Phase V—Payback (21–25 years). Having passed the tests of the Verification phase, the individual was ready to make major contributions to the future of the firm. Job changes came more frequently and were broader in nature. Some assignments may have been based on a specific organizational need. However, it is likely that most assignments were made either in preparation for promotion to the CEO position or at least to place the individual into competition for that position. During the period, over 60 percent served in one or more senior group or division level positions; almost half (48 percent) served as an executive vice president; and about 25 percent served as a chief operating officer or president. By the end of this period, 39 percent had attained the position of CEO.

Phase VII—Pay-Off (Beyond 25 years). On the average, the position of CEO was achieved at age 50, after two and a half decades of long hours, hard work, and intense competition.

These phases describe the career of the average or typical CEO in the manufacturing industry. There was, however, a tremendous amount of variance about these averages. It is unlikely that any of the CEOs actually conformed to every one of the phases as we have described them. The phases do not specify hard-and-fast deadlines for progress to the top. For most, the careers are likely to be similar, but many different time schedules and many different career experiences were found and will continue to be found. Finally, we must note that this study focused on CEOs in industrial firms. The critical phases may vary in other industries.

Summary of Industrial CEO Career Phases

- EXPLORATION (1–5 years)
    - 40% change firms searching for the right fit
    - 25% move into industrial firms from accounting, law, or government
    - Phase ends with promotion to first management position
- DEVELOPMENT (6–10 years)
    - Less inter-firm movement; More intra-firm movement
    - Movement to other functions and/or cross-functional assignments
    - Some assignments as "Assistant to" a senior manager
    - Promotion to lower-middle management
- COMMITMENT (11–15 years)
    - High level of loyalty to one firm
    - International experience attained
    - Advancement into middle management continues
- VERIFICATION (16–20 years)
    - Promotion to either division-level management or functional vice president level
    - Responsibilities change rapidly
    - Executive skills are proven

- PAY-BACK (21–25 years)
  - Frequent, broad job changes
  - Final grooming or competition for the top
  - Experience as senior group or division heads, executive vice president, chief operating officer, or president
- PAY-OFF (Beyond 25 years)
  - Attainment of the position of CEO

THE CAREERS OF CEOs IN OTHER INDUSTRIES

From the same sources as described above (*Forbes'* 1988 listing and the 1988/1989 edition of *Marquis' Who's Who in America*) we will examine the route to the top for CEOs in five other industries and compare them with manufacturing. The industries and the number of CEOs in each are as follows: public utilities (85), transportation (23), banking (127), insurance (27), and retailing (31). Because of the smaller sample sizes, the analyses could not be as detailed as for manufacturing; nevertheless, the data were sufficient to portray the general career paths in these industries.

Pre-Entry Activities

After high school, a combination of military service and post-secondary education, extending from late teens to mid–20s, delayed entry into the workforce for about six years. Overall, 60 percent of the CEOs served in the military—compared to 46.7 percent of the male population of the same age group. There were significant variations by industry, however, ranging from a low of 45.5 percent in retailing to a high of 78.3 percent in the transportation industry. Military service was performed usually after high school or after completion of college. In a few instances it came after initial entry into the workforce.

As a result of the military service and college education the average age at entry into the workforce was 24.3 years. CEOs in public utilities were the oldest (25.3) while those in retailing were the youngest (23.4). The ages in the other industries were very close to the mean.

The level of education was roughly equivalent across all industries, with the exception of retailing. In general, over one-half of the CEOs possessed graduate degrees; however, retailing lagged in this area with less than 30 percent (see Table 8.4). A substantial percentage of retailing chief executives had law degrees but there were relatively few with master's degrees. Retailing had the highest percentage of top executives with only the baccalaureate degree and far surpassed all other industries in the proportion of CEOs without a college degree.

The educational level achieved by CEOs in utilities and in banking

Table 8.4
Level of Formal Education by Industry (Percentages)

Level of Education	Industry Group						
	Mfg. (n=230)	Utilities (n=85)	Trans. (n=23)	Insurance (n=28)	Retailing (n=31)	Banking (n=127)	Composite
Non-bacca-laureate	3.9	1.2	4.3	7.1	16.1	5.5	4.8
Bachelors	44.8	45.9	34.8	39.3	54.8	40.2	43.7
Masters	33.9	20.0	30.4	28.6	6.5	32.3	29.2
Law	12.2	23.5	30.4	21.4	22.6	15.7	16.8
Doctorate	5.2	9.4	0.0	3.6	0.0	6.3	5.5
Totals	100.0	100.0	99.9	100.0	100.0	100.0	100.0

was similar to that of CEOs in manufacturing; however there was a difference in the major areas of study. The percentage of manufacturing and banking CEOs with master's degrees was better than 50 percent more than for those in utilities, while the percentage with law degrees was much lower in the banks and manufacturing firms. Engineering and law degrees clearly dominate in public utilities. One-half of the CEOs here had one or more engineering degrees and almost one-quarter possessed law degrees. Law degrees were also very common in the transportation industry. The highest percentage of corporate leaders with doctorates was found in the utility industry.

Entry-Level Assignments

In the manufacturing industry, entry-level positions were identified by functional areas. We were also able to categorize the first positions in utilities and transportation companies according to similar functions. However, in banking, insurance, and retailing the initial assignments were so diverse that they could not be classified into comparable functions.

In utilities, entry-level positions reflected the educational preparation; with 45.9 percent starting in engineering and 23.0 percent beginning their careers in legal practice. Finance and accounting was the third most popular entry-level position (17.6 percent started here). The remaining 13.5 percent began their careers in a variety of other positions. Finance was the most common entry area in the transportation industry with

30.4 percent, followed by the legal area with 26.1 percent. Administration and operations were other popular starting positions.

While the entry-level assignments were not classified as in the industries discussed above, it seems that knowing the business is critical in retailing. Sales and administration were common first assignments and unlike the other industries, none of the CEOs rose to the top after a specialization in finance or law. Recent financial difficulties in the industry may cause this to change in the near future, however.

Mobility

CEOs in public utilities showed the least degree of overall mobility. Nearly two-thirds (63.6 percent) worked for only one or two companies, while just over one-fifth (21.1 percent) had four or more employers. The pattern was similar in most industries, with the highest percentage of CEOs actually working for only one firm. This proportion generally varied from about one-quarter to slightly over one-third. In all industries but one, as the number of employers increases, the percentage of CEOs in the category decreases. The exception is the transportation industry where almost one-half (47.8 percent) of the CEOs had four or more employers. It appears that the bankruptcies, mergers, and acquisitions brought about by government deregulation of the transportation industry have upset the traditional pattern of promotion from within. These firms are hiring outsiders who have a very high degree of mobility for CEOs.

A closer examination of mobility revealed some interesting differences among industries. In manufacturing, nearly four-fifths of the top executives started in that industry. This would be consistent with the existence of the "academy" career system in which executive talent is developed internally (Sonnenfeld & Peiperl, 1988). However, only about two-fifths (41.1 percent) of the public utility CEOs were initially employed by a utility company. One-fifth started with a law firm or in private practice, while another one-fifth began their careers in either accounting or manufacturing firms. Others started in educational institutions, governmental agencies, banks, or insurance companies.

Another significant difference was the delay in joining a utility firm by those who started outside the industry. CEOs of manufacturing firms who started in a non-industrial setting joined an industrial firm after an average of 3.6 years. Only five (2.2 percent) had over 10 years of work experience before entering the industrial sector. In contrast, the public utility CEOs who started in another industry had an average of 9.7 years of work experience prior to joining a utility firm, and 11 had more than 15 years of experience. In addition, all of these joined the firm in a position of vice president or higher.

This suggests something about how utilities handle internal versus external problems. Normally, the critical concerns of a public utility are the efficient and reliable operation of its physical plant and the reporting of that operation to the satisfaction of the public utility commission. There are times, however, when these regulatory commissions may represent challenges to the firm's profitability. While the typical utility develops its own engineers to manage the operations, it is likely to look outside the firm for financial and legal expertise. When internal operations are most important, an engineer with extensive experience in the firm is likely to rise to the top. However, when external issues become more important, then the specialized expertise needed to deal with outside forces becomes more important than familiarity with internal operations.

This confirms our findings (Chapter 4) concerning the increased external mobility of the functional specialist who is called upon in times of unusual challenges to be CEO. It also implies that public utilities are not always "clubs," as described by Sonnenfeld and Peiperl (1988). They often rely on externally oriented career system that would be better classified in their "baseball team" or "fortress" categories.

In the banking industry, almost three-quarters (71 percent) of the CEOs spent their entire careers in banking, and about one-third stayed with a single firm. Of the 127 bankers studied, 15 started in manufacturing, nine with law firms, and eight with accounting firms. Others started in educational institutions, government agencies, and in retailing. Most entered the banking industry early in their careers. Of the 37 who started outside of banking, about one-third joined a bank within the first two years, another one-third entered the industry within the first ten years, and the remaining one-third had over ten years of experience before becoming bankers. This last group's outside experience was almost exclusively in the areas of finance and law. Like utilities, banks may go outside when specialized expertise is needed.

Although there was relatively little inter-industry mobility, we found a considerable amount of inter-firm mobility in banking. Among those whose careers were entirely in banking, more than half (55 percent) served with two or more banks. More than one-third of those who started in another industry had experience with two or more banks.

The greater mobility in the transportation industry is reflected throughout the careers of the CEOs. Over one-quarter (28 percent) came from outside the firm to assume the top position and another 30 percent had served with the firm of ten years or less when promoted to CEO. It should be noted, however, that, with only one exception, those brought in from outside had transportation experience earlier in their careers. They had been either in a management position in a transportation company or in a senior government regulatory position. Only two-fifths of these CEOs spent their entire careers in transportation and fewer than one-fifth served with only one firm. Over one-third (35 percent) had extensive industrial experience, while others served in senior management positions in accounting firms, legal firms, and government agencies.

These analyses suggest that we need more sophisticated models of career systems that better reflect differences across industries. While two-by-two typologies such as that recently proposed by Sonnenfeld and Peiperl (1988) are a useful step in the right direction, they may be too simple. They classify utilities, banks, and transportation companies (airlines) all as "clubs" with respect to their career system; but as we have seen there are important and significant variations in the career paths of CEOs across these industries.

The insurance industry resembles banking in that over three-quarters of the CEOs (79 percent) had experience only in that industry, and over one-third (36 percent) remained in a single firm. However, those who had experience outside the industry joined an insurance company very late in their careers. They had an average of 18 years of experience and all joined the industry in a position of vice president or higher—with two assuming the CEO role. In this respect, the industry resembles utilities. Three of these outsiders had MBAs and were experienced in the financial area; two had legal backgrounds and extensive government experience; and one had a Ph.D. and over 20 years of experience in the field of education.

Two-thirds of the retailing CEOs had experience only in that industry and one-quarter worked for only one firm. Outsiders were most likely to come from law firms.

Moving Up

The first management position was clearly identified for only one-third of the utility CEOs. Based on this sample, it took 50 percent longer for the future CEO to attain a supervisory position in the utility industry than in manufacturing (7.5 years versus five years). This difference was probably due to the large number of engineers and lawyers. In our study of upward mobility in an oil and gas company, we found that the engineers and scientists did not begin to move up as early as those in other job categories. They were, however, more likely to reach higher levels within the first 11 years of their careers (see Chapter 3). This suggests that while winning the very early contests for promotion may be important in some firms (Rosenbaum, 1979, 1984; also described in Chapter 2), this may not be a universal phenomenon. The important contests may come a little later in the career for the specialized professional. The upwardly mobile in utilities soon catch up to their counterparts in manufacturing, as there was little difference in the time required to reach the vice president level.

The organizational structure of the typical utility firm does not provide the same opportunities for broad general management training as does the large multi-divisional industrial firm. Thus we find more utility executives with a single functional specialty rising to the top. Despite this structural limitation, an estimated 15 to 20 percent of the CEOs did have general management experience as a division or geographical area manager prior to reaching the position of vice president. Also, about three-fifths of these top managers served in two or more different functional areas before promotion to vice president. Those with legal backgrounds were the exception, with almost three-quarters having only legal experience.

Retailing resembled manufacturing in that general management assignments were common. These assignments encompassed such positions as district or regional manager and division general manager or president.

The "assistant to" assignment was used more extensively in the utility firms than in the industrial sector. Over one-fifth of the CEOs had held one or more such positions during their career. As in manufacturing firms, assignments as an "assistant to" a senior manager occurred from as early as the initial job upon entering the workforce to as late as 24 years into the career. One half came after ten or more years of service. Appointments to vice president or higher positions followed the "assistant to" assignments for two-thirds of the CEOs—few of whom had previous experience outside a single functional area. Thus it seems that in public utilities, the "assistant to" assignment is used primarily to broaden an individual's knowledge of the firm's operations in anticipation of promotion to a more senior position.

The Paths to the Top

The average time to reach the various levels of upper management (vice president to CEO) for each industry is shown in Table 8.5. Bankers reach each of these levels in less time than their colleagues in other industries. The average CEO in this industry took only 22.3 years to attain the top position—compared to 27.6 years in the insurance industry, which had the longest times to the top. The second fastest movement occurred in the retailing industry, where the top was reached in 24.4 years. The timing of movement through these positions was virtually even in manufacturing, utilities, and transportation.

One-half of the CEOs in utilities went through the same sequence of job titles to reach the top: vice president, executive vice president, and CEO. Another one-quarter followed this route but also served in the

Table 8.5
Time to Reach Higher Levels of Management (In Years)

	Industry					
Position	Mfg.	Utilities	Trans.	Insurance	Banking	Retailing
Vice-President	14.9	15.8	13.7	13.2	9.1	13.4
Senior Vice-President	a	19.8	a	18.5	13.3	17.3
Executive Vice-President	20.9	20.9	19.5	17.9	15.5	18.0
President[b]	23.6	23.4	21.9	23.4	18.1	20.0
CEO	26.6	26.8	26.6	27.6	22.3	24.4

[a] Position title not frequently used in these industries.

[b] Also includes position of vice-chairman, chief operating officer and chief administrative officer.

intermediate position of senior vice president. More than one-half of those following one of these routes paused for a brief stint as chief operating officer or president before assuming the CEO role. The route which included the senior vice president position resulted in three more years to reach the top than the path which led directly from vice president to executive vice president (29.8 versus 26.8 years). The remaining one-quarter of the utility CEOs took one of five other paths which by-passed some of the intermediate positions. These shorter routes took considerably less time (23.6 years), but the number of CEOs who took each of these paths was small.

These career paths differ in two ways from those taken by CEOs in manufacturing firms. First, two career paths tend to dominate in the utility firms, while the eight different career paths in industrial firms were equally well traveled. Second, in industrial firms the time to reach the CEO level varied little among the eight distinctive career paths, while in utility firms the time to reach the top is lengthened by the number of intermediate positions in which the executive serves beyond the vice president level.

It should be noted that the job titles that we are studying may have different meanings with respect to the level of responsibility and the amount of visibility as we move across industries. This problem with comparing similar titles is perhaps most apparent in the banking industry. Here, concern for customer relations dictates that there will be a very large number of individuals holding officer level titles. In a large bank, there may be hundreds of vice presidents, dozens of senior vice presidents, a dozen executive vice presidents, and even several vice chairmen (Kaplan, 1982; Vancil, 1987). Depending on the size of the firms or banks, a vice president position in a manufacturing company or in a public utility might be comparable to a senior vice president or even an executive vice president in a bank. With this in mind, we will describe the career paths of the banking CEOs.

There were 10 separate paths from vice president to the top in the banking industry. Two of these were followed by 55.8 percent of the CEOs. The most frequently traveled path was: vice president, senior vice president, executive vice president, president, and CEO. This sequence of positions was followed by 36.5 percent. The second path, taken by 19.2 percent, differed from the first in that the individual moved directly to senior vice president, bypassing the vice president position. The other eight career paths were various combinations of three or four of the positions in the first path.

The paths that included four or five different positions resulted in about the same time to reach the top (23–24 years). However, when the executive served in only three of the five positions, the time decreased significantly to 18.4 years.

Those who spent their entire careers in banking required an average of 21.8 years to reach the CEO position. There was no difference in the time required between those who were employed by a single bank and those who had two or more employers. In other words, mobility within the banking industry did not increase or decrease the time required to reach the top. CEOs who started their careers outside banking required about one year longer (22.7 years).

Two positions appear to be keys in upward mobility in the banking industry. The first of these is the executive vice president spot, where 88.5 percent of the CEOs served for an average of 2.6 years. The second is the position immediately below that of CEO. Over three-quarters spent an average of 4.2 years in a position such as president, vice chairman, chief operating officer, or chief administrative officer before being promoted to CEO.

There were 20 thrift institutions in the sample of banks. These were examined separately to determine if there were differences in CEO careers in comparison to the commercial banks. The educational levels and times to reach the position of CEO were the same in both groups. However, a significant difference was noted in banking experience which reflects the problems in this industry. Over one-third of the CEOs of the thrift institutions were brought in from outside to assume the top position or were promoted to that position within two years. None of these outsiders had experience in bank management but three had served in federal regulatory agencies. Two had only real estate development experience; one had broad experience with an accounting firm; and one had spent 22 years with a financial services firm. The other CEOs who were chosen from within had careers similar to CEOs of commercial banks.

No clear pattern of upward movement was found among the CEOs of transportation companies. The 23 CEOs took 11 different paths leading from vice president to the top position. The largest number taking any one path was four. Consistent with our other findings on the nature of careers in transportation, movement within the industry paid off. Those who spent their whole career in transportation but worked for more than one firm reached the top the fastest (21. 7 years). In contrast, those who served with a single firm required 28.7 years, while those with experience in other industries took 28.4 years to reach the top.

Again, in the insurance industry, no clear pattern of movement through the hierarchical positions from vice president to CEO emerged. The senior vice president position was used more frequently than in the other industries studied. It usually replaced either the vice president or executive vice president position. Only two of the 28 CEOs served in the positions of vice president, senior vice president, and executive vice president.

As in transportation, movement within the industry tended to shorten the time necessary to reach the top. Individuals who stayed with a single firm took 29.7 years to reach the top, while those who had only insurance industry experience but served in two or more firms took only 26.5 years. CEOs with experience outside the industry required 28.7 years to achieve the top position.

In retailing, the most commonly traveled route to the top was vice president, senior vice president or executive vice president, president, and CEO. This path was followed by one-third of the top executives and was also the shortest path to the top. The time to reach CEO by this path was almost two years less than the average time for the industry (22.5 years versus 24.4 years). Other paths which bypassed two or more of the intermediate positions actually took a longer time.

Education and the Climb to the Top

In general, the higher the level of formal education, the shorter the trip to the top. The overall average times drop most substantially when the level of education increases from the undergraduate to the graduate level (see Table 8.6). Those with a legal education reach the top most quickly, followed by the holders of master's and doctorate degrees. The level of education is of least importance in retailing, where the nonde-

Table 8.6
Time to CEO Position by Educational Level (In Years)

Level of Education	Industry						
	Mfg.	Utilities	Trans.	Insurance	Banking	Retailing	Composite
Non-Bacca- laureate	31.2	28.0	33.0	26.5	27.8	26.0	27.8
Bachelors	28.4	28.9	29.3	29.5	23.6	24.5	27.2
Masters	24.7	27.3	21.6	25.6	21.3	24.0	24.0
Law	22.6	24.6	28.0	22.0	21.6	23.0	23.3
Doctorate	29.2	20.2	N/A	30.3	18.3	N/A	24.4

N/A Not Applicable.   (There were no CEO's in these industries with doctorate degrees.)

greed CEOs took only three years longer to reach the top than those with law degrees. The strongest effect of education appears in manufacturing, where the climb takes 8.6 years longer for the non-baccalaureate than for law degree holders.

A law degree is the ticket for the fastest trip to the top in the manufacturing, insurance, and retailing industries. In transportation, the master's degree holders reach the top much more quickly than those with any other degree. A doctorate appreciably shortens the path for CEOs in utilities and in banking. We must keep in mind that the quickest path to the top is not necessarily the most common route. Those who reach the top quickly often come in from other firms or industries to solve problems or turn the firm around.

This is well illustrated by examining the transportation industry. This industry has varied from the norms of other industry groups in a number of ways. The CEOs have exceptionally high mobility, having worked for a larger number of firms than is typical. A high number of CEOs were appointed directly from outside the firm. In other industries, those with law degrees reach the top most quickly; in transportation, CEOs with master's degrees had the fastest trip to the top. We will examine the changes in the industry and how they have affected the selection of top executives.

Prior to the late 1970s, the transportation industry was a stable, highly regulated sector. The career systems resembled the "clubs" (Sonnenfeld & Peiperl, 1988) that slowly promote loyal employees from within the organization. In one of our earlier studies (Piercy & Forbes, 1981), we found CEOs in transportation to be among the older age groups at the time of appointment to that position. The average age in surface transportation was 53 and in air transportation was 52. The most common functional background in both industries was legal. The second most popular was operations in surface transportation and general administration in air transportation. This was understandable as the industry had been regulated for almost a century, and the legal background had proved necessary in working with the regulatory agencies.

The transportation acts of 1977 and 1980 dramatically changed the business environment. All economic restrictions were removed from air carriers and restrictions over surface carriers were greatly reduced. As a result, the industry saw more competition and many new entrants, followed by many bankruptcies and a surge of mergers and acquisitions. Taking advantage of the situation, a new breed of CEO arrived on the scene. In air transportation, the financial specialist with an MBA has replaced the legal specialist and the administrative generalist. Names like Icahn, Lorenzo, and Crandall, all with financial backgrounds, are among the most familiar in all of American industry.

Four of the seven airline CEOs in our 1989 analysis had MBAs and backgrounds in finance, one had a legal background, one had risen through operations, and one had a background in general administration. Only one of the seven was brought in from outside; however, the others had an average of only 12 years with their company when appointed CEO. The average age at appointment was 45.6—a decrease of six years in a decade.

These former "clubs" have been transformed into "fortresses"—fighting for market share and survival through fare reductions and drastic cost cutting. Unless there is reregulation of the industry, we would expect to see a continuation of financial experts at the top. If, as is being recommended by some prominent politicians, regulation is reimposed, then those with legal backgrounds will probably return to the executive suite in larger numbers.

Among the nine railroads that we examined, five had adapted a strategy of diversification by acquisitions. They had shifted from "steady state" to "evolutionary" strategies (Leontiades, 1980). Three of the CEOs in these firms were brought in from outside. Two of these had financial backgrounds and the third had government regulatory experience. Of the two promoted from within, one had a financial background, while the other had legal expertise. Again, a shift toward the financial area is evident. The average age of this group at the time of appointment was 49.8 years—a significant reduction from the 53 years of a decade earlier.

The other four railroads chose either not to diversify or diversified to a lesser extent. All four of the CEOs were promoted from within. Three of the four had legal backgrounds, while the fourth had a background in finance. The average age at the time of appointment was 56 years and they had been with the company for an average of 26.8 years. Thus we find the traditional policy of promotion from within and reliance on legal expertise prevailing in those firms that have not changed their strategy. This industry provides an interesting case study of how quickly an industry's environment can change, how business organizations change to try to adapt, and how career paths are altered as a result.

TOP EXECUTIVE PROFILES

Manufacturing: Richard E. Heckert, E. I. duPont deNemours & Co.

Although more highly educated than the average and attaining the top position at a later age, Richard Heckert's career illustrates the typical progression in manufacturing: technical specialist to manager to general manager and finally to senior manager—all within the same firm.

The son of a Miami of Ohio University professor, Heckert was born in Oxford, Ohio, in 1924. He played football in high school and earned a bachelor of arts degree from Miami in 1944. Continuing his education at the University of Illinois, he earned a master of science and a Ph.D. in organic chemistry.

Upon receiving his Ph.D. in 1949, Heckert joined DuPont as a research chemist. From 1954 until 1957, he served as a supervisor in DuPont's Richmond, Virginia, Film department. He became the technical superintendent of the cellophane plant in Clinton, Iowa, in 1957, and plant manager of the Circleville, Ohio, plant in 1959.

From 1963 through 1969, he served in three different assistant general manager positions; and became general manager of the fabrics and finishes department in 1969. He was promoted to the vice president level in 1972, and became a senior vice president and a director in 1973. In 1981, he was named president and chief operating officer. Five months later, when DuPont merged with Conoco, Heckert became vice chairman, and in 1986, he was named chairman and CEO.

Utilities: Robert M. Ginn, Centerior Energy Corporation

Ginn's is an interesting example of a utility company career. He was trained primarily in electrical engineering, but his was a broad education that included the economic applications of engineering principles. His first position allowed him to quickly make use of this knowledge in the important area of rate analysis. This gave him high visibility and his career got off to a fast start.

Robert Ginn was born in Detroit, Michigan, in 1923, and attended public schools. He served in the U.S. Army Air Force from 1943 to 1946; and earned both a B.S. and M.S. in electrical engineering from the University of Michigan in 1948. Ginn joined the Cleveland Electric Illuminating Company in 1948; electing to work in rate analysis rather than engineering. After several staff and management positions in both finance and operations, he was appointed controller in 1959, and became manager of the area development group in 1962.

A year later, Ginn was elected vice president, general service group at the age of 39. He was promoted to executive vice president in 1970. The position of president came in 1977, followed by CEO in 1979, and then chairman in 1983. In 1986, Ginn became the chairman and CEO of Centerior Energy Corporation, the holding company under which The Illuminating Company and The Toledo Edison Company were affiliated.

Transportation: Robert L. Crandall, AMR Corporation

The career of Robert Crandall was profiled at the end of Chapter 4 as an example of the functional specialist who rises to the top. Here we will review the relevant points of his career. He is very typical of today's transportation CEO. A Wharton MBA, his early career was spent in a number of finance-related positions in five different firms and in several different industries. He was hired as senior vice president of finance at American Airlines in 1973 and, after obtaining more general management experience, was made CEO 12 years later.

Banking: Karen Horn, Bank One, Cleveland

Although not yet a corporate CEO, Karen Horn has already broken new ground for women in a number of areas. Her career demonstrates the advantage of a doctorate degree in the banking industry. She has been more mobile than the typical banking executive, especially with respect to movements outside the banking industry.

Born in Los Angeles in 1943, Horn earned a B.A. from Pomona College in 1965, and a Ph.D. from Johns Hopkins University in 1971. She was an economist for the Board of Governors of the Federal Reserve System from 1969 to 1971. After earning her doctorate, she became a vice president of the First National Bank, Boston, from 1971 until 1978; and then Treasurer, Bell of Pennsylvania, 1978–1982.

In 1982, Horn became the first woman to be president of the Fourth District Federal Reserve Bank, Cleveland. She was also the top ranking woman in the Federal Reserve system at the time. During her term of office, she became the first woman to join Cleveland's exclusive Union Club (Wasnak, 1987). She moved back to private banking in 1987 as chairman and CEO of Bank One, Cleveland—a subsidiary of Banc One Corporation of Columbus.

Retailing: William R. Howell, J. C. Penney Co.

Howell's is a very typical retailing career. He started work early in life, stayed with the same company, did not obtain a graduate degree, and moved through a series of general management positions.

Born in Claremont, Oklahoma, in 1936, Howell joined J. C. Penney after earning his B.A. from the University of Oklahoma in 1956. By 1968, he had advanced to store manager; and a year later was appointed district manager for the Treasury Division Stores subsidiary.

In 1971, Howell was promoted to division vice president and director of domestic development in New York City. Five years later, he became regional vice president, western region; and in 1979, was appointed senior vice president, merchandising, marketing, and catalog. Howell was promoted to executive vice president in 1981, vice chairman in 1982, and chairman and CEO in 1983.

Insurance: James T. Lynn, Aetna Life & Casualty Co.

Although not the most common career path in insurance, the history of James Lynn's worklife illustrates a pattern in a fair number of instances—the executive coming into the firm at a very high level and entering from outside the insurance industry.

Lynn was born in Cleveland, Ohio, in 1927, and earned his B.A. from Western Reserve University in 1948, after service in the U.S. Navy. He earned his law degree from Harvard in 1951, and joined the Cleveland law firm of Jones, Day, Reavis, and Pogue, becoming a partner in 1960.

The decade from 1969 to 1979 was spent in public service. First as general counsel—U.S. Department of Commerce, then under secretary of State, secretary of Housing and Urban Development, and director of the Office of Management and Budget.

Returning to Cleveland in 1979, Lynn became managing partner of his former law firm—a position he held until 1984 when he joined Aetna Life and Casualty as vice chairman. In 1985, he was elected to the position of chairman and CEO.

9

The Route to the Top: Climbing on the Decisions of Others

In the first chapter of this book, we described the process of reaching the top of a modern business organization as analogous to climbing a constantly changing volcano. At this point we would like to modify and further elaborate on that picture. A volcano is a physical phenomenon of nature and if two climbers are equally skillful, persistent, and lucky, they may both reach the top at the same time. The volcano does not care who they are, where they came from, nor what they did while on the climb. A business organization, on the other hand, is a creation of men which traditionally has only allowed one person at a time to occupy its highest point. Success in climbing this type of pinnacle depends not only on skill, persistence, and luck, but also on the decisions of those who have already climbed higher than you. It is as if reaching the next highest level requires that someone above lower a rope; and those above must choose one person at a time who may attempt to climb that rope.

As a corporate climber, you must realize that upward mobility in a hierarchical business organization depends on the decisions of those above you. They are attempting to base their decisions on your ability to perform at the higher level. However, since you have never been at that level before, they are forced to make a prediction. As we have shown throughout this book, there are certain signals that promotion decision makers look at. These signals are assumed to be predictors of the type of manager that you will be. In fact, they are largely a reflection of your background, particularly your career history. Some signals are more important at particular stages of the career and some are more important in certain situations.

In this chapter, we will first review and summarize the signals that have been identified in the previous chapters and then discuss some of the additional considerations that surround the choice of the top executive—the CEO. This discussion will focus on past and present practices. Next we will make recommendations for changes that are needed in the processes of management development and evaluation in order to meet the continually shifting challenges of the 1990s and the twenty-first century. Finally, we will make suggestions about how to strategically plan an individual career.

SIGNALS FOR SUCCESS: PAST AND PRESENT

Although this is an oversimplification, we will divide the career of a top executive into two major competitions. The first contest takes about 15 years and determines who will reach the threshold to top management: the positions of general manager (at the division or regional level) or functional vice president (at the corporate level). This level appears to be a natural breakpoint in career progression. The salaries of senior executives take a big jump at about this point (Korn, 1988). The time taken to reach this level is a strong predictor of the time to reach the top (Chapter 8). Those who have reached this level suddenly have much more responsibility and are much more visible to top management. They have a major piece of the action and are now close enough to the top to be considered seriously as contenders for CEO. The second major contest takes on average another ten years and decides who will be the leader of the entire corporation.

The Early Years

Here we will define the "Early Years" to extend from the time the individual enters the workforce (at about age 24) through the time of promotion to the level of general manager or functional vice president (at about age 39). One very important signal that is typically attained before beginning the career is the level of education. We will discuss this further in relation to advancement during the Middle Years, however, it can also affect a person's credibility from the very beginning of the career.

In some firms very early performance and promotion seem to be prerequisites for further upward mobility (see Chapter 2). This has been described as tournament mobility and was first documented in an old, well established firm in which the most successful managers quickly moved into and then out of foreman positions (Rosenbaum, 1979). In a public utility, those who moved early continued to move more frequently but not necessarily to higher levels (Sheridan et al., 1990). Ratings of job performance and promotability from the first three years on the job predicted the timing of later promotions in a Japanese firm (Wakabayashi et al., 1988). Those who performed well on early challenging assignments moved up more quickly in the early Bell System studies (Berlew & Hall, 1966).

Other research, however, indicates that technical personnel in an oil and gas company need not start moving up in the hierarchy as early as non-technical employees in order to reach the same or higher levels (Chapter 3). Our study of the entire careers of chief executives revealed that, on the average, they attained their first management position after about five years, however, there was a great deal of variance about this mean (Chapter 8). We also found that many future chief executives changed employers at least once during the first five years of their career (the Exploration Phase).

Other signals begin to come into play as early as the first ten years of the career. Those whose functional background is related to the critical problems facing the corporation begin to move ahead. We saw this in Chapter 3: the technical employees moved more quickly in an energy company. In this same study we also found that breadth of experience was related to upward mobility. The importance of this factor was confirmed by our study of the CEOs' entire careers and by our study of the general management promotion decision. Over two-thirds of the top executives changed functional areas during the Development Phase of their careers (years 6–10). In addition, some began to obtain more general experience and visibility through cross-functional positions such as product or brand managers or plant managers (Chapter 8). Breadth of experience was by far the most important variable in predicting the choice of a general manager by the top executives in our simulation exercise (Chapter 4). The signals of early upward movement and functional area did not consistently influence the general management promotion decision. Instead, they varied with organizational strategy.

Others have shown that entering the company through a prestigious training program and starting work in a powerful department can provide an early boost to the career (Sheridan et al., 1990). This is also the time when a young manager may have the opportunity to be evaluated in a corporate assessment center. A positive evaluation will be a strong, long-lasting signal to promotion decision makers (Thornton & Byham, 1982). The more successful managers in the Japanese study were those with better vertical exchanges who became members of the supervisor's in group (Wakabayashi et al., 1988). Many of the chief executives in our study (Chapter 8) were assigned as an "assistant to" a senior manager early in their career.

Towards the end of this period, many top managers receive assignments in the international area, further increasing their breadth of experience. Also, those who reach the top are not likely to have changed employers during the last five years of the early career period. It seems that the organization is looking for evidence of loyalty and commitment among those being considered for higher level positions.

These signals may be described as indicators of ability, or may be evidence that important developmental experiences have been success-fully completed (see McCall, Lombardo, & Morrison, 1988 for more on developmental experiences). They also provide an opportunity for the young manager to learn more about the company and to begin devel-oping important networks (Kotter, 1982, 1988). In addition, one other function is served which is equally important: they provide increased visibility for the young manager. He or she becomes more familiar to more higher level executives, who, in turn, become more comfortable with these people.

The important signals at this early stage seem to be telling higher management that the employee is a competent professional or manager, that he or she is trying to learn different aspects of the business, and that he or she is becoming known by others in the organization, partic-ularly those in the upper echelons. The successful future top executive has begun to build credibility and visibility.

The most successful young managers will be simultaneously enhanc-ing both their credibility and their visibility. Tremendous performance and credibility will not foster career progress if no one knows about it. Likewise, tremendous visibility with no credibility will surely kill a ca-reer.

The Middle Years

The "Middle Years" of a top executive's career will be defined as from the time that general management or functional vice president is reached (approximately age 39) until the time when the appointment as CEO occurs (approximately age 50). Our story ends after this stage; however, the CEO's tenure as the top manager may continue another ten to 12 years. This second major phase of the top executive's career has not yet been extensively researched. Our identification of the relevant signals will depend heavily on the descriptive, archival research conducted by us and others which was presented in Chapters 6, 7, and 8. We will also draw from the books by Melvin Sorcher (1985) and Richard Vancil (1987), both of which were based on direct personal communications with numerous senior executives.

At this level, those at or near the top may become very much involved in monitoring and/or managing the careers of promising subordinates. We suspect that the decision to sponsor a senior executive and possibly select that person as chief executive is much like the decision to support and to vote for a candidate for high public office. Both can be explained

Exhibit 9.1
Important Promotion Signals during the Early Years

Signals Indicating Credibility

Successful Early Performance in a Critical Functional Area

Tenure With The Firm

Education

Signals Indicating Credibility

And Enhancing Visibility

Entrance Through A Prestigious Training Program

First Assignment In A Powerful Department

Early Promotion Into The Managerial Ranks

Moving Through Various Functional Areas

Positive Assessment Center Evaluation

Cross-Functional Assignments

Assistant To A Senior Executive

International Assignments

by attitude theory—particularly the theory of cognitive dissonance (Festinger, 1957). In psychological theory, an attitude represents a tendency to respond in a particular way toward some person or object. Attitudes have three related components: 1) the rational or cognitive component (or do we believe in the person?), 2) the emotional or affective component (do we feel right about the person?), and 3) the behavioral component (what action will we take towards this person?). When we choose to vote for political candidates we do so not just because we believe in them or their positions but also because we feel good about them. The concept of cognitive dissonance says that we try to maintain consistency among these attitudinal components. Or, conversely, that cognitive dissonance is uncomfortable and will be avoided if at all possible. We try to behave in ways that are consistent with both our beliefs and our feelings. This same process affects the selection of corporate candidates.

A person is not chosen just because he or she is logically the best alternative but also because the decision makers feel right about the individual at a non-cognitive level.

Sorcher (1985) boils it all down to the fundamental question, "Can he or she run things the way we want them run?" (p. 5). This query addresses not only bottom line performance but also "soft" issues such as values and culture and process and even personal chemistry. Henry Ford's reason for firing Lee Iacocca was simply, "Well, sometimes you just don't like somebody" (Iacocca, 1984, p. 127). A powerful halo surrounds the candidate with whom senior managers and directors are familiar and comfortable (Sorcher, 1985).

At this level, credibility is still very important. It is a measure of the strength of the belief that a manager can do the job that needs to be done. This depends on the track record and the area(s) of expertise of the candidate for promotion. In some cases it may also reflect the belief that the person will be loyal to the organization and its culture. In other situations it may involve the belief that the candidate can transform the organization and its culture. Visibility becomes much less important. Everyone inside the corporation at this level is highly visible. The issue seems to be one of getting to know the higher level decision makers on a personal basis and allowing them to become familiar with you.

The Early Backgrounds of CEOs. Turning control of a multi-billion dollar corporation over to a single individual requires a great deal of trust. We trust those with whom we are familiar. Familiarity slowly increases with personal contact and communication, but it can develop almost instantaneously for those who have very similar backgrounds and experiences. Therefore it is not surprising that those who choose top executives often select individuals who are very much like themselves. Approximately 50 percent of CEOs are the sons of business executives and about 20 percent had fathers who were professionals. Remarkably, these figures have not changed significantly in over 100 years. Also, since 1900, the percentage of CEOs from a middle- or upper-class background has ranged from 80 to 90 percent (Chapter 6).

Top executives are a well educated group, with a large number of the undergraduate degrees coming from a small number of elite universities and colleges. Graduate education is increasing and here also there is a strong concentration of alumni from elite institutions—especially Harvard. The most common undergraduate majors are business and engineering; while at the graduate level, CEOs tend to hold MBAs or law degrees (Chapter 6). Education and social origins seem to be interchangeable with respect to their effect on upward mobility. For those with undergraduate or graduate degrees from the right schools, social origins do not seem to matter. For those of elite social background, education is not that important a factor in predicting success (Useem &

Karabel, 1986). This seems to support our familiarity thesis. Those with similar backgrounds or experiences are trusted more readily by high level decision makers.

CEOs also tend to come from larger metropolitan areas and from regions of the country that are more heavily industrialized. This may be due to self selection into competition for executive positions or it may be due to cultural similarity and again increased familiarity among people from comparable backgrounds.

Familiarity may come very quickly as the result of similar backgrounds or very slowly through social interaction. Credibility in the context of selection for a top management position is more complex. Of course it depends on an outstanding track record, but it also requires that the track record contain evidence that you are the type of person needed at this particular point in time. Three major career history parameters will influence the match between the candidate and the needs of the organization. These career signals are: generalist versus specialist, area of functional expertise, and the timing and extent of inter-firm mobility. We will discuss each in light of the research described in Chapters 4 through 8.

Generalist or Specialist? Our study of executive promotions (Chapter 4) dealt with the career paths of individuals during these middle years. The data indicated that there are two distinct paths into top management: a generalist path and a specialist path. The generalists are those who have had previous responsibility for an entire division or business within the company. These managers have spent most of their careers within the same firm or at least the same industry. They may have managed a number of different divisions before moving into an executive vice president or senior vice president position. The specialist has spent most of his career within one functional area while climbing to the position of corporate functional vice president. Those following this path are more mobile with respect to changing employers. They have skills that transfer more easily to new settings. As Kotter (1982) has noted, the general managers specialize in a particular firm or industry. Our data show that this limits their opportunities outside that setting. Mobility is greatest for those who specialize in the finance or legal functions. Before reaching the top executive position, these specialists are given general management experience as senior or executive vice presidents. When it is believed that specialized expertise is needed at the top, usually when change is needed, the firm is likely to look for the best talent available anywhere. On the other hand, if it is believed that knowledge of the company or industry is critical and if change is not needed, the next CEO will usually be chosen from among the generalists within the firm.

Our descriptions of the entire careers of CEOs in Chapter 8 generally confirmed these conclusions but also illuminated the differences across industries. In manufacturing, we found CEOs who had been general managers, functional vice presidents, or both. However, in utilities, where basic functional organization is common, more CEOs were functional specialists; although most had some experience in more than one function. In contrast, there appeared to be little specialization in the retailing industry. Early rotation through a variety of areas was common, as was experience as district, regional, or division managers.

Functional Background. A related issue concerns the functional background of the person chosen to be a new chief executive. This also depends on the strategic needs and objectives of the firm. Our research described in Chapter 7 clearly shows that certain industries consistently prefer top executives with particular functional backgrounds. For example, a marketing background is commonly found among CEOs in consumer products firms; while regulated industries often choose CEOs with legal backgrounds. Production/operations backgrounds are common in basic industries such as steel and energy. Conglomerates favor those with backgrounds in either finance or general administration who are able to manage a variety of different businesses.

In Chapter 8, we saw that almost one-third of the CEOs in a broad sample of manufacturing firms started their careers in engineering. An even larger proportion of the CEOs in utilities began work in engineering (46 percent), followed by law (23 percent). A majority of transportation CEOs had backgrounds in either finance (43 percent) or law (30 percent)—reflecting the needs of an industry undergoing deregulation.

Our analyses also indicated that there have been general shifts in the emphasis on various functions (without regard for industry) which reflect general trends in the economy and in the competitive issues facing American industry. During the high growth era of the 1960s, marketing was a very popular background for CEOs. With recession followed by high inflation during the 1970s, finance became a favored specialty for top executives. Most recently, we have seen more CEOs being chosen with backgrounds in the technical and production/operations areas. However, these general shifts do not result in any one function becoming dominant across all industries. The functional area found at the top is much more strongly predicted by the industry than it is by these general trends.

Moving from Firm to Firm. The third major career history variable is the extent and the timing of movement among firms and industries. We have analyzed this issue in several different chapters. In Chapter 4 we noted that although few outsiders are hired directly into the chief executive spot, 29 percent of the promotions into the more broadly defined category of top management were from outside the firm. The large majority of these appointments were from within the same industry, and were moving from another top management position. At the corporate general management level (executive vice presidents and senior vice presidents), one-quarter of the appointments went to outsiders and again these were typically people in similar positions in the same industry. For division-level top management, 22 percent were outside appointments, usually from within the industry. A significant difference was noted at the senior functional vice president post. Here, more than half were from outside the firm and one-third were even from outside the industry. Financial and legal vice president positions were most likely to be filled from outside the firm.

In Chapter 7 we examined industry differences in CEO mobility. The firms most likely to promote from within were utilities, banks, and basic industries. In these firms, the average CEO spent more than 90 percent of his worklife in the same firm. Overall, 89 percent of the new CEOs came from within, but this varied from 100 percent in several very stable industries to a low of 55 percent in the air transportation industry. The data in this study indicated that the outside appointees were most likely to be individuals with backgrounds in either finance or general administration.

Within the manufacturing sector, we found that almost 80 percent of the chief executives started in that industry. Those CEOs who started as engineers generally spent their entire careers in manufacturing. However, those who started as accountants or lawyers were likely to have begun their careers in accounting or law firms—moving into manufacturing early in their careers (Chapter 9). In general, CEOs in manufacturing do not change firms frequently after the first five years of their worklife. Utility company CEOs were much more likely to have begun their careers in other industries—especially within law firms or accounting firms. These executives did not enter the utility firm until ten years into their career and then came in as vice presidents. The disruption in the transportation industry is evident in the fact that 26 percent of the CEOs were hired directly from outside the firm and another 34 percent had ten years or less tenure with their firm before reaching the top. In both banking and in insurance, about three-quarters of the CEOs spent their careers within one industry. The timing differed for those who moved, however. In banking, two-thirds of those starting elsewhere moved into banking within ten years of the start of their careers (one-third within the first two years). While in the insurance industry, the movers came in late (with an average of 18 years experience) and as vice presidents or higher. Finally, in retailing, two-thirds of the CEOs were retail industry specialists; and most of those from outside the industry came from law firms.

The general finding with respect to movement is that early changes in employment are typical. However, most future top executives quickly

Exhibit 9.2
Important Promotion Signals during the Middle Years

<u>General Signals Of Familiarity And Trust</u>

Socio-Economic Origins

Geographical Origins

Education

<u>Situational Signals Of Credibility</u>

Generalist Or Specialist

Functional Expertise

Mobility

settle into and begin learning about one industry. The exceptions are those who bring specialized expertise from law firms or accounting firms. Specialists in the legal and financial areas seem to have more inter-firm mobility throughout their careers. Their skills are more easily transferred. In industries where success depends on knowing the basic products and markets, such as manufacturing and retailing, we see more generalists being promoted from within the firm or industry. Where outside regulatory forces (or deregulatory issues) are critical, such as in utilities and transportation, more firms rely on outside legal or financial expertise.

The major signals that influence promotion decisions during the middle years are summarized below.

Promotion Signals for Women

Until very recently, there was only one signal that mattered when women were considered for upper management positions. The signal was their gender and it flashed a bright red. Decision makers were not familiar with the concept of female manager or executive. They had never known women who held positions of high responsibility in business organizations. They were not sure whether they could trust women in traditionally masculine roles. The problem is partially one of negative stereotyping, but perhaps more importantly it is due to a lack of information.

As argued in Chapter 5 and elsewhere, business organizations need to broaden the pool of candidates for top management. The quality of the leadership at the top will be strengthened if businesses encourage those who were previously excluded (such as women, minorities, and even white males from lower socioeconomic origins) to fully participate in the competition for the high executive positions. We will discuss this point more fully later in this chapter, but for now let us assume that the rules of the game do not change dramatically. If that is the case, women will be promoted to the degree that they present the same signals as men (although the signals may have to be a little clearer and brighter).

First, let's look at the early career signals which indicate credibility and enhance visibility. Higher education, particularly job-relevant graduate education such as an MBA or law degree will signal credibility. The point of entrance into the firm should signal high potential. A woman must avoid, if at all possible, beginning the career in a clerical or secretarial position. Instead she should enter a highly regarded management training program. Performing well in critical functions is also important. The best human resources person will not go far if the company believes that only engineering expertise is important. Investigate these issues before accepting a job. Try to discover the fast track within each culture.

It is difficult for many women to follow the typical top executive career path because of the conflict between the timing of important career events and the childbearing years. The average CEO first became a manager in his late 20s, and reached the vice president or general management level by the late 30s. Women who put their careers on hold during these years, in order to start their families, may miss out on important contests in the top executive tournament. This is also a time when future top managers often gain breadth by moving into new functions and through international assignments.

The fact that a woman may take a maternity leave and possibly never return sends a very negative signal to promotion decision makers. Business organizations want to invest in human resources who will provide an acceptable payback. If they believe that an employee is likely to soon leave the company then the investment becomes much more of a risk.

During the middle to later years of the career, education, especially a diploma from a very prestigious institution, seems to be very important. Credibility and familiarity are greatly enhanced by the right schooling. Again, promotion decision makers hesitate in the face of uncertainty. They do not know how women, or even males from lower social classes, will behave in executive positions. Elite education seems to help overcome this uncertainty.

While most top executives under stable operating conditions move slowly through the hierarchy, learn the business and industry, and become generalists, we have seen that functional specialists are frequently needed at the top during times of change. The functional specialist track requires more formal education, allows more inter-firm and inter-industry mobility, and is faster than the generalist path.

The woman who does not anticipate any career interruptions may choose either path. However, given the rules of this game as we presently see them and the conflicts faced by women executives, we would suggest that those women who might leave the workforce for a time consider the specialist route. This route to the top does not necessarily require early promotion into line management. It does not require extensive experience within the firm or industry nor the associated long tenure with the same firm. This path is more tolerant of discontinuities of employment, allowing an individual to drop out of the workforce for several years and then get back up to speed more quickly upon reentry.

Judy C. Lewent is an example of a very successful functional specialist. Armed with a B.S. in economics from Goucher College and an M.S. from MIT's Sloan School of Management, she held a series of early positions at E. F. Hutton, Bankers Trust, and Pfizer, before joining Merck & Co. in 1980. In 1990, at age 41, she was named vice president and chief financial officer of Merck. She is considered to be the first woman chief financial officer of a company of this size—Merck is a $6.6 billion company (Weber, 1990).

This is a critical position for a company in the drug industry in the 1990s. CEO P. Roy Vagelos reports that Lewent was the best candidate and that gender had nothing to do with the decision. Lewent describes Vagelos as her mentor—they both came up through the lab division where he was director and she handled the financial problems. She was clearly a familiar, highly credible candidate for the job.

Lewent describes herself as "intense, aggressive, and definitely hard-charging" (Weber, 1990, p. 58). She is also described as very well organized and hard working. Lewent is married, but she and her husband have decided against having children due to the demands of their careers.

Our prognosis with respect to the opportunities for women in business is very positive. The data presented in Chapter 5 indicates that Judy Lewent's case is not an isolated example—more younger, highly educated women are reaching the critical vice president and general management level at the appropriate times in their careers. Business firms are slowly but surely filling the pipeline. The number of women in these highly responsible and visible positions is growing, and as a result the questions about credibility, familiarity, and trust should begin to disappear. The red light associated with being a women will fade in comparison to the green lights associated with a successful career history and women will become serious candidates for top management positions. Later in this chapter we will make recommendations for changes in career systems that will open things up even further. At this point we will review other observations on the nature of the top management succession decision.

The Nature of the CEO Succession Decision

The selection process for top business executives does not always result in the best choice. Melvin Sorcher (1985) estimates that, based on performance, one-third of the choices would not be made again. Richard Vancil (1987) reports that ten percent of CEOs are fired, but that due to the difficulty of deposing an incumbent CEO, "most boards have a high tolerance for mediocrity" (p. 5). What is wrong with the process and how might it be improved?

Sorcher (1985) has emphasized how the halo effect that accompanies familiarity and comfortable predictability influences many top executive choices. To many, the process appears very systematic and objective, but Sorcher's insights show that to not always be the case. Starting with early identification of managerial potential, Sorcher notes that: "of all the long shot bets in the world, surely one of the most presumptuous is predicting which young person will become a chief" (p. 45). The strengths and weaknesses of supervisor evaluations and assessment centers are discussed, as is the role of sponsorship in early identification. These are all useful techniques, but all may lead to premature judgements about candidates.

Our data (Chapter 8) supports Sorcher's assertion that most chief executives are identified during what he calls "the crucial third stage". This stage extends from the time of acceptance as an accomplished individual contributor through middle management. The critical signals here are that the person be perceived as 1) very good at their job and 2) able to communicate their ideas well. Or, in the words that we have been using: high credibility and visibility. Many companies carefully plan experiences to test potential CEOs but usually the process " . . . is not systematic or even planned much in advance . . . " (Sorcher, 1985, p. 122). The typical practice of selecting the new CEO from within leads to the danger that loyal, long-term employees become candidates for the top position because they are familiar, predictable "good soldiers".

Relay Races or Horse Races? Further insight into the CEO selection process can be gained from the work of Richard Vancil (1987). His book was produced with the collaboration of 29 businessmen, most of whom were present or past CEOs. Much of the information came to light during a series of seminars on the subject at the Harvard Business School.

Vancil (1987) states that the objective of chief executive succession is usually two-fold: to find the best candidate while minimizing the disruption to the firm. There are two basic patterns that are followed: a relay race and a horse race. The former is by far the most common. In the relay race, the heir apparent is chosen and placed into a senior management position such as president. For several years the outgoing CEO gradually shares more power and responsibility with the newly selected leader. This is also a time of further testing of the selected candidate. When the new man has gotten up to speed, the baton is passed, and he is named the CEO. The old CEO may remain as chairman for another two or three years. Vancil notes that the title of CEO has become increasingly popular within the past 30 years to allow for this type of orderly succession.

The horse race occurs when a number of viable candidates are placed into positions where they compete for a period of time before the final selection is made. This method may lead to increased disruption within the organization, both during and after the competition. The choice between the two seems to be based mainly on the firm's culture. For example, a horse race would be more easily accepted in a highly competitive meritocracy such as General Electric, and in fact this is what occurred during the selection process that led to Jack Welch becoming the CEO.

The General Electric succession was very carefully and systematically planned and is described in detail in Vancil's (1987) book. We will review some of the key points. Reginald Jones, who did not retire until 1981, began planning the selection of his successor in 1974, two years after he became CEO. At that time the executive manpower staff presented ten contenders for the position. It is informative to note how that number was determined. They started with 96 officer level executives. Then they eliminated 44 who were over age 55 and another 34 who were judged to not have top management potential. Next, one new hire was added to the list; and nine were dropped who "were not highly rated against the specs" (Vancil, 1987, p. 38). At that time, Jack Welch was a 37 year old division manager and not on the list.

In 1977, General Electric was reorganized into six sectors composed of similar businesses or strategic business units. The reasons for this change were to reduce the number of strategic plans that required review at the top, and to allow "radical reassignment of key candidates to businesses with which they were not familiar" (from a plan prepared by Reginald Jones—reproduced in Vancil, 1987, pp. 40–41). At this time, Welch was a candidate assigned to head one of the sectors. During the period Jones conducted a series of "airplane interviews" (i.e., if Jones and the interviewee were killed in an airplane crash—who should be the next chairman?) with each candidate in order to examine the "chemistry" within the group. Jones and the board then chose three contenders who were promoted to the vice chairman level for a period of 15 months for additional evaluation by the board.

Vancil's analysis of this final "contest" is somewhat different from Jones' version. It seems that a number of contenders were threatening to resign if not named chairman. At the same time, others were building coalitions of those with whom they would work even if not given the top position. In order to not further exacerbate the existing turmoil, the final group of three was in fact a team, headed by Jack Welch. The appearance of a contest was presented to allow the board time to get to know and accept Welch, who was considered a "risky maverick". It also gave the board the option of choosing one of the other vice chairmen if Welch did not prove satisfactory. A unique process was created which allowed the board "to select an 'outsider' from inside" (Vancil, 1987, p. 194).

Vancil (1987) credits Henry Schacht, CEO of Cummins Engine, with introducing him to the concept of the relay race, and describes the executive succession process within that company. The story starts in 1960, when J. Irwin Miller, at age 50, began thinking about a successor to run the family-owned business. Actually, the team of the chairman/CEO and the president/COO were to be selected. Two young Harvard MBAs, Schacht and James Henderson, were identified very early as potential leaders, and in the late 1960s, the decision was made to skip a generation and appoint Schacht as president. During the next five years, Miller worked with Schacht preparing him to become CEO and the retiring president, Don Tull, worked with Henderson. In 1973, Schacht was named president and CEO, but Miller remained chairman until 1977, at which time a transfer of power that had taken almost ten years was completed.

The following points about Cummins Engine are important to note. It is a family-owned company with revenues of over $2 billion that is focused on one product line—diesel engines. As such, it is functionally organized. There are no product-oriented divisions which might serve as testing grounds for general management skills—as there are in larger or more diversified firms. This makes it difficult to train and evaluate executive talent. The first general management job is the president, and therefore the company must choose carefully and develop thoroughly. The major strength of the relay race is that it allows general management skills to be developed and tested at very high levels of the firm (Vancil, 1987). The method is appropriate in this type of organization and would also be suitable in a larger, product-oriented firm when a functional specialist, without general management experience, is selected for the top position.

Both Sorcher (1985) and Vancil (1987) argue the need for improved selection through a wider search for executive talent. However, both see that search as focused outside the firm. Vancil notes that there is a trend in that direction, but that an outsider is usually only chosen when change is needed and even then only if it will not be overly disruptive to do so. This is the explanation given for why AT&T chose an insider, Jim Olson, as CEO in 1986. They wished to avoid adding to the disruption being brought about by deregulation (Vancil, 1987). More recently, despite reports of outside pressures to the contrary, a troubled General Motors selected an insider, Robert Stempel. Here, however, the company did break with tradition by choosing a man with an engineering rather than a finance background (see Chapter 7).

REFORMING TOP EXECUTIVE DEVELOPMENT AND SELECTION

Top executives are human beings chosen by other human beings. The objective of the decision process is to find the person who can help the organization to be most effective for the next eight to ten years. We know that the quality of any decision depends on a number of basic factors. Among these are the number of alternatives considered, the quality of the information available about each alternative, and the criteria for evaluating each alternative (Bass, 1983). It is our conclusion that the top executive selection process is flawed and therefore the best selections are often not being made. Typically only a small number of candidates are considered and the information used is often very subjective and possibly biased. The new CEO is usually picked by the outgoing CEO from among those who report directly to him (Vancil, 1987).

Even in the very systematic process followed by Reginald Jones at General Electric, the initial list contained only ten names. Jack Welch was not included because he was only a division manager at the time. It is to Jones' credit that Welch was identified and despite his young age was ultimately chosen to be the new CEO. In most companies little consideration is given to those below the officer level. If a suitable candidate is not found immediately below the CEO level then the search typically shifts to outside candidates.

What information is considered and how is it used? Although thorough, well thought out guidelines for choosing chief executives exist (e.g., Levinson, 1980), our research has identified a series of simple signals that influence the decision. An even smaller number of underlying dimensions were proposed as important promotion criteria. Early in the career, the keys are visibility and credibility. Visibility is not actually a decision criterion, but rather it determines whether an individual is even included as a known candidate. Later, the critical variables are credibility and familiarity (and the trust it engenders). In both cases, the evaluation of the candidate at the rational, cognitive level is determined by credibility—which, in turn, should be closely related to performance in a series of appropriate managerial assignments. Outstanding performance on critical tests may not be enough, however. The incumbent CEO and the board must trust the candidate. The chemistry must be right.

We saw earlier how the "risky maverick," Jack Welch, had a 15 month trial period as vice chairman during which he gained the support of the board (Vancil, 1987). For similar reasons, it seems that another innovator decided to play it safe during his trial period. *The Wall Street Journal* reported that Robert Stempel successfully introduced major changes in the two assignments that preceded his appointment as president of General Motors, but became much more cautious during the three years before being named CEO (Ingrassia & White, 1990). Even when change is clearly needed, the successful candidate for the top position must avoid making any mistakes until the final passing of the baton.

A new system for identifying and developing top management talent is desperately needed. In less volatile, less competitive times, CEOs could be chosen from among a small group of loyal, familiar candidates. If the selection were not the best, well, the company would still survive. Today, even the best CEOs face the threat of hostile takeovers and drastic restructuring of the firm. Even at lower levels the costs of incorrect promotion decisions are considerable. It has been estimated that the cost of a failed general manager is $500,000. This figure includes only the costs of selection, relocation, outplacement, and replacement of the failed executive, not the business costs of poor performance (McCall, Lombardo, & Morrison, 1988). The total costs would easily run into the millions of dollars.

Returning to the basic principles of decision making, better selection of executives requires the following:

1. A much wider search for executive talent—especially inside the firm,
2. Collection and utilization of more relevant measures of performance on key jobs,
3. A greater willingness to base promotion decisions on objective performance measures.

In the past, the search has been very limited; much of the information which is actually used has been anecdotal; and as a result the final decisions have been based on simple signals of ability, plus personal chemistry and familiarity.

The new system that we propose will place greater demands on both line managers and human resource professionals. The knowledge and the techniques to improve the process are available; however, they must be applied differently. Major changes will be occurring in business management in general and in human resource management in particular during the 1990s. Perhaps the most pressing need is for change in our methods of deciding who leads our business corporations. The proposed system fits in well with other ongoing and anticipated changes.

The traditional organization of the past was a tall, many-layered structure. Communication flows were typically up and down—mostly down. Various functional areas were isolated from one another, except when forced to interact. All important decisions were made at high levels of the firm. The larger firms adapted product divisions which were, in theory, decentralized, self-contained units. However, even here elaborate information and control systems were designed to manage these units from the top. Internally the organization was very efficient, but it was not particularly good at recognizing or responding to changes in the external environment.

Human resource practices evolved in this context. Top management could not possibly get to know many personnel at the lower, or even at the middle, levels of the company. Therefore they established "objective" procedures to identify the most promising young people at the lower levels and to develop these high potential employees. It was important to expose these future executives to a variety of functional areas and to begin moving them up quickly so that they would soon reach a level at which meaningful decisions could be made. As a result, the most common path to the top became one that involved a fast start, breadth of experience, and often responsibility for a division at a relatively early age.

The problem with this traditional method is that it is based upon early identification of and commitment to a small number of serious contenders. Much is invested in these individuals. They are sponsored and mentored and given developmental assignments—all of which is highly appropriate assuming that the very best people have been chosen. In any case, the phenomenon of the self-fulfilling prophesy begins to play a part. Both the individual and the organization become committed to seeing early predictions come true. This process can prove very costly. The company may be betting on the wrong horses and may not discover its mistake for quite a long time. No business firm would consider an investment strategy in which a decision was made to continue investing in the same small number of promising stocks for a period of 20 years, and yet that is what many firms do in the area of management development.

Another problem with this strategy is the effect it has on those who are passed over. We discussed this in Chapters 2 and 3 in relation to the tournament mobility model. The motivation and productivity of the employee who knows that he has not won the early contests, and is therefore out of the running for higher level positions, will fall dramatically. The problems of the plateaued mid-career employee and the conflicts faced by women (among others) can be linked to the existence of this system (Rosenbaum, 1984; see also chapters 2, 3, and 5).

The feasibility of an alternative system increases as we examine the direction in which business organizations are heading. In order to reduce costs, increase organizational flexibility, and improve employee involvement and motivation, many firms are moving toward flatter, less hierarchical structures. They are pushing decision making authority down to the lowest possible level and eliminating communication barriers among the functional areas, among the remaining levels of authority, and between the firm and its environment (its customers, suppliers, communities, etc.). They are allowing product divisions to become more autonomous than ever before.

Some fear the chaos and confusion of such organizations, while others praise the simplicity. One of the latter is Jack Welch, who has transformed General Electric. According to Welch, the excessive layers of the traditional business organization just hide weaknesses and mediocrity (Tichy & Charan, 1989). Conversely, we would add, they also hide talent. In the flatter, more open organization, employees at very low levels have meaningful responsibility and can make important decisions. Everyone is more visible. It will become commonplace for engineers to interact with marketing managers, for production workers to communicate with customers, for salespeople to share information with the president. In this type of organization, the need for early identification of management potential, and rotational assignments, and early upward mobility will no longer exist.

Two other factors support a major change in the way we promote and develop executives. The first is demographics. As the "baby bust" continues, business firms will have fewer and fewer new young employees from which to choose future managers. They will have larger numbers of more experienced personnel in the lower and middle levels of the organization. There is concern over the frustration that may be felt by all these employees, who, in a flat organization, have nowhere to go. However, let us consider why people desire to move up in an organization. Most report that they want more responsibility and authority or more challenge; some admit that they want more power and esteem. Many realize that in order to move up later, they must often begin to move up early and so they get on the treadmill. In the organizational forms that are emerging today many of these things are coming down— you do not have to move up to get them. If, in addition, it were possible to move up later without moving up early, then most people might be satisfied to remain in middle or lower level positions until they get their chance to prove themselves as a leader. It would also be possible for women to leave the workplace for several years, return as an older employee, and not have been left so far behind.

The skeptical reader may ask: "What about money? All of these people cannot be paid that much." We would agree but would argue that if they perceive a very real (even though very small) chance to reach the top, they will be extremely well motivated. Today, very few people believe that they have any chance of becoming a corporate leader, and so they invest their money in the state lottery rather than investing their time and effort in the corporate game.

The other supporting factor is technology. More people at lower levels will have the information and the tools to make important decisions; and those at the top will have better measures of who is making the good calls. Improved communications technology will also give more employees higher levels of visibility. Enhanced human resource information systems will not replace personal contacts but will supplement these with a variety of measures of performance.

How will this new system work? We are proposing a much more open contest for top positions than has ever existed before. This system will reward performance, not necessarily social origins or formal education or gender or a career history that includes all the right moves. The distinction between evaluation and development will fade but there will be much more of both.

We envision the wider application of assessment center methods. However, these would be for developmental purposes only. The results would be available only to the individual and to top management. The assessment center might be repeated at various points in the career and also would be used with senior managers (White & De Vries, 1990). Positions within the organization would be evaluated with regard to their use as "assessment positions" or on-the-job assessment centers (Gaertner, 1988). The learning that comes from various types of career experiences has been identified (McCall, Lombardo, & Morrison, 1988). Job assignments would be based, at least partly, on the developmental needs of each individual. There would be greater use of team management and peer and subordinate evaluations. All performance evaluations would include assessments of future potential and recommendations for development. Employees would be evaluated by outside contacts: customers, clients, suppliers, community leaders, etc.

The company would encourage new learning and development at all levels and at all ages. Formal education would be supported but not required. Cross-functional training and movement would be encouraged but not necessary. There would be room for the functional specialist. Employees would be realistically informed of career opportunities for those in various functional areas.

More entrepreneurial or "intrapreneurial" activities would be encouraged. These make excellent developmental and evaluative opportunities. Risk taking would be encouraged and failure tolerated. High levels of performance would be ensured by gain-sharing reward systems.

The key is that in an open career mobility system everyone would be considered a "high potential" employee. The probability of further promotion would no longer decrease over time. It would remain constant or increase. The firm would have a much larger pool of more qualified, more motivated employees from which to select its executives. Upward mobility would no longer depend on signals such as socioeconomic origins or degrees from elite universities, but instead on actual performance within the organization. Both individuals and organizations would be more healthy and more effective.

This is only a vague sketch of what may appear to be a radically different approach to management assessment and development. Our challenge to human resource managers and to top executives is to begin to try these ideas. Discover what will work and what will not. Continually fine-tune the system. New organizational structures and management styles require new approaches to human resource development.

STRATEGICALLY PLANNING AN INDIVIDUAL CAREER

Faced with all this change and uncertainty, how might a young prospective CEO plan his or her career? We would suggest a technique similar to that used by business firms when they plan long-term strategy. The firm will start by carefully defining its mission. This will be formulated by first identifying the company's strengths as well as its weaknesses. Also considered will be the firm's traditions and its values. Next, external forces are brought into the picture. The company will attempt to analyze the opportunities and threats that currently exist within the external environment. They will consider what they have done well in the past and what they can learn to do well in the future. The fit or match between the firm's capabilities and the needs of the environment will be studied. This will be done for the present situation and then they will project themselves five or ten years into the future and repeat the analysis. A mission statement will emerge from this process which will define what the organization is and what it wishes to be. The statement will provide general direction with respect to what opportunities or businesses the firm should pursue.

Normally, there will be a gap between what the organization is now and what it needs to become in order to realize its future aspirations. Therefore long-range strategic plans must be devised. How do we get from Point A to Point B? The strategic plans map out the long-term changes needed. Next, the firm identifies the general activities that must be accomplished in order for these changes to occur. These activities in turn become intermediate-range objectives. Finally, the firm will specify the more immediate, more concrete steps that must be carried out to achieve the intermediate-range objectives. These are the short-term plans or objectives.

If we substitute the word "individual" for "firm" in this process, we would have an excellent system for career planning. The procedure is fairly straightforward. The only real difficulty is forecasting the future. The business organization attempts to predict the future economic, technological, social, and political environments in order to plan its important future activities. The individual must not only try to forecast these future environments but must also attempt to predict how business firms will adapt. The key to success within a business firm is the ability to help the company solve its critical problems. This may, however, depend on the particular strategy that has been adapted. As we have seen, strategies change as the environment changes.

In the formerly highly regulated transportation industry, rates and service were critical issues, and therefore we saw many CEOs with backgrounds in the legal or operations areas. With deregulation, issues such as cost cutting, diversification, and mergers and acquisitions have become more important and so we now see a majority of CEOs with backgrounds in finance. The career planner's strategy must be flexible. In the future, experiences in the international area and in human resource management are likely to become more important (Bennett, 1989; Solomon, 1990). The individual must engage in constant "environmental scanning," attempting to gain an early warning of coming threats and opportunities, and adapting as needed.

We have described a general process and argued that success "all depends" on events that may not develop for another ten to 20 years. This may be realistic but not very satisfying to the young person who wants concrete advice. Are there any specific findings from our research that the corporate climber can use? Although we are urging change, it will come slowly. The career history signals listed earlier in this chapter are likely to continue to be attended to by the top executives who make promotion decisions for some time to come. In addition, many of these are more than just signals. They do, in fact, improve the ability of the individual to perform his or her job. These factors include higher education. At the undergraduate level, those majoring in business and engineering will continue to have an advantage. Graduate training is also very important and here the MBA and the law degree will help to boost the career. The right experiences on the job are helpful also. Early challenge, if successfully handled, leads to increased confidence and the beginning of a success cycle. Broader knowledge of the business can be gained through transfers across functions, by switching from staff to line positions or vice versa, by serving on cross-functional task forces, or by moving into positions such as product or project manager.

Moving up into supervisory and management positions at the right time is important, but we have shown that very early movement is not critical. Those in more professional positions seem to start this climb later in their careers. Our description of the phases of the careers of CEOs gives some rough guidelines for reaching various levels, but there is much variance around these averages and there are different time schedules in different industries. The typical timing of various developmental activities is also described here. A common event in the lives of many CEOs was reaching the general management or functional vice president level by about age 40. Timing becomes more important later in the career. In order to avoid a confrontation over when the CEO should step down, many boards stipulate a mandatory retirement age for CEOs of 65 (Vancil, 1987). This dictates that those over 55 are not likely to be seriously considered for the top position. Candidates for the top should consider the time to retirement for the current chief in relation to their own age. Are they in the right position to be included in the next "wave," or in the one after that? (Sorcher, 1985). If not, they should try to improve their position or they might consider changing employers.

Good managers are still a rare commodity but sometimes things just do not fall into place at one employer. The story of Donald Lennox illustrates how other opportunities arise. When his career seemed to have plateaued at Ford, Lennox left, at age 50, to become a Xerox senior vice president for manufacturing and procurement. He rose to group vice president and was waiting for retirement when contacted by Archie McCardell, then CEO of International Harvester. McCardell was trying to engineer a turnaround at IH and needed help assembling a corporate staff. Lennox made the move and in a year became president and chief operating officer after McCardell's efforts failed. After a six month search, the board chose Lennox to be the next CEO. In five years, Lennox successfully transformed the company, now Navistar International. He then left Navistar to become chairman and CEO of Schlegel Corp., a manufacturer of weather seals (Rice, 1987).

Our study of the paths to the top has lead us to believe that those who are successful do not follow any one particular route, but they do continually endeavor to learn and grow and seek new challenges.

References

Arthur Young & Associates. (1980). *The chief executive: Background and attitude profiles*. New York: Author.

Bass, B. M. (1983). *Organizational decision making*. Homewood, IL: Irwin.

Bateman, T. S. & Zeithaml, C. P. (1990). *Management: Functions and strategy*. Homewood, IL: Irwin.

Baum, L. (1987, June 22). Corporate women: They're about to break through to the top. *Business Week*, pp. 72-88.

Bennett, A. (1987, July 17). Losing ground? Surveyed firms report fewer women directors. *The Wall Street Journal*, p. 17.

Bennett, A. (1989, February 27). The chief executives in year 2000 will be experienced abroad. *The Wall Street Journal*, pp. A1, A7.

Berlew, D. T. & Hall, D. T. (1966). The socialization of managers: Effects of expectations of performance. *Administrative Science Quarterly*, 11, 207-223.

Bond, F. A., Hildebrandt, H. W., Miller, E. L., & Swinyard, A. W. (1981). *The newly promoted executive: A study in corporate leadership*. Ann Arbor: Division of Research, Graduate School of Business Administration, University of Michigan.

Bonfield, P. (1980). *U. S. business leaders: A study of opinions and characteristics*. New York: The Conference Board.

Boone, L. E. & Kurtz, D. L. (1988). CEOs: A group profile. *Business Horizons*, 31 (4) 38-42.

Boone, L. E., Kurtz, D. L., & Fleenor, C. P. (1988a). CEOs: Early signs of a business career. *Business Horizons*, 31(5), 20-24.

Boone, L. E., Kurtz, D. L., & Fleenor, C. P. (1988b, March). The road to the top. *American Demographics*, pp. 34-37.

Borucki, C. & Barnett, C. K. (1990). Restructuring for self-renewal: Navistar International Corporation. *Academy of Management Executive*, 4, 36-49.

Bray, D. W., Campbell, R. J., & Grant, D. L. (1974). *Formative years in business: A long-term AT&T study of managerial lives*. New York: Wiley.

Burck, C. G. (1976, May). A group profile of the *Fortune* 500 chief executive. *Fortune*, pp. 173-177, 308-312.

Cain, J. P. & Stahl, M. J. (1983). Modeling the policies of several labor arbitrators. *Academy of Management Journal, 26,* 140-147.

Campbell, J. P., Dunnette, M. D., Lawler, E. E., & Weick, K. E. (1970). *Managerial behavior, performance and effectiveness.* New York: McGraw-Hill.

Cawsey, T. F., Nicholson, N., & Alban-Metcalfe, B. (1985). Who's on the fast track? The relationship between career mobility, individual and task characteristics. *Proceedings of The Academy of Management,* 51-55.

Cohen, J. & Cohen, P. (1975). *Applied multiple regression/correlation analysis for the behavioral sciences.* Hillside, NJ: Erlbaum.

Cooney, J. G. (1978). A woman in the boardroom. *Harvard Business Review, 56*(1), 77-86.

Daft, R. L. (1986). *Organizational theory and design.* St. Paul, MN: West.

Deaux, K. (1984). From individual differences to social categories: Analysis of a decade's research on gender. *American Psychologist, 39,* 105–116.

DeVenuta, K. (1990, February 9). Education: Openers. *The Wall Street Journal,* p. R5.

Dobbins, G. H. & Platz, S. J. (1986). Sex differences in leadership: How real are they? *Academy of Management Review, 11,* 118-127.

Downey, R. G. & Lahey, M. A. (1988). Women in management. In M. London & E. M. Mone (Eds.), *Career growth and human resource strategies* (pp. 241-255). Westport, CT: Quorum.

Dommermuth, W. P. (1966). On the odds of becoming company president. *Harvard Business Review, 44*(3), 65-72.

Erickson, E. H. (1963). *Childhood and society.* (2nd ed.) New York: Norton.

Fagenson, E. (1987). [Review of *Breaking the glass ceiling*]. *Academy of Management Executive, 1,* 351-352.

Feldman, D. C. (1988). *Managing careers in organizations.* Glenview, IL: Scott, Foresman.

Feldman, D. C. & Arnold, H. J. (1978). Position choice: Comparing the importance of organizational and job factors. *Journal of Applied Psychology, 63,* 706-710.

Feldman, D. C. & Brett, J. M. (1983). Coping with new jobs: A comparative study of new hires and job changers. *Academy of Management Journal, 26,* 258-272.

Feldman, D. C. & Brett, J. M. (1985). Trading places: The management of employee job changes. *Personnel, 62,* 61-65.

Ference, T. P., Stoner, J. A., & Warren, E. K. (1977). Managing the career plateau. *Academy of Management Review, 2,* 602-612.

Festinger, L. (1957). *A theory of cognitive dissonance.* Palo Alto, CA: Stanford University Press.

Forbes, J. B. (1987). Early intraorganizational mobility: Patterns and influences. *Academy of Management Journal, 30,* 110-125.

Forbes, J. B. & Piercy, J. E. (1983). Rising to the top: Executive women in 1983 and beyond. *Business Horizons, 26*(5), 38-47.

Forbes, J. B., Piercy, J. E., and Hayes, T. L. (1988). Women executives: Breaking down barriers? *Business Horizons, 31*(6), 6-9.

Gaertner, K. N. (1988). Managers' careers and organizational change. *The Academy of Management Executive, 11,* 311-318.

Geneen, H. (1984). *Managing*. Garden City, NY: Doubleday.

Graen, G. & Cashman, J. (1975). A role making model of leadership in formal organizations: A developmental approach. In J. Hunt & L. Larson (Eds.), *Leadership frontiers* (pp. 143-165). Kent, OH: Kent State University Press.

Greenhaus, J. H. (1987). *Career management*. Chicago: Dryden.

Gregory, F. W. & Nau, I. D. (1962). The American industrial elite in the 1870s. In W. Miller (Ed.), *Men in business* (pp. 193-211). New York: Harper & Row.

Gupta, A. K. & Govindarajan, V. (1984). Business unit strategy, managerial characteristics, and business unit effectiveness of strategy implementation. *Academy of Management Journal, 27,* 25-41.

Hall, D. T. (1976). *Careers in organizations*. Pacific Palisades, CA: Goodyear.

Hays, W. L. (1963). *Statistics*. New York: Holt, Rinehart & Winston.

Heidrick & Struggles, Inc. (1980). *Profile of a woman officer*. New York: Author.

Helmich, D. L. (1974). Organizational growth and succession patterns. *Academy of Management Journal, 17,* 771-775.

Helmich, D. L. (1977). Executive succession in the corporate organization: A current integration. *Academy of Management Review, 2,* 252-266.

Hitt, M. A., Ireland, R. D., & Palia, K. A. (1982). Industrial firms grand strategy and functional importance: Moderating effects of technology and uncertainty. *Academy of Management Journal, 25,* 265-298.

Hobson, C. J. & Gibson, F. W. (1983). Policy capturing as an approach to understanding and improving performance appraisal: A review of the literature. *Academy of Management Review, 8,* 640-649.

Howard, A. & Bray, D. W. (1988). *Managerial lives in transition: Advancing age and changing times*. New York: Guilford.

Hunt, D. M. & Michael, C. (1983). Mentorship: A career training and development tool. *Academy of Management Review, 8,* 475-485.

Iacocca, L. (with W. Novak). (1984). *Iacocca: An autobiography*. New York: Bantam Books.

Ingrassia, P. & White, J. B. (1990, April 4). The two styles of GM's new chairman. *The Wall Street Journal,* pp. B1, B5.

Jennings, E. E. (1971). *Routes to the executive suite*. New York: Macmillan.

Kanter, R. M. (1977). *Men and women of the corporation*. New York: Basic Books.

Kaplan, G. (1982). *The big time*. New York: Congdon & Weed.

Katz, D. & Kahn, R. L. (1978). *The social psychology of organizations* (2nd. ed.). New York: Wiley.

Kelley, J. (1973). Causal chain models for the socioeconomic career. *American Sociological Review, 38,* 481-493.

Kerr, J. L. & Slocum, J. W. (1987). Managing corporate cultures through reward systems. *Academy of Management Executive, 2,* 99-108.

Korn, L. (1988). *The success profile*. New York: Simon & Schuster.

Kotter, J. P. (1982). *The general managers*. New York: Free Press.

Kotter, J. P. (1985). *Power and influence: Beyond final authority*. New York: Free Press.

Kotter, J. P. (1988). *The leadership factor*. New York: Free Press.

Landro, L. (1982, July 12). Electric switch: GE's turning from the bottom line to share of the market. *The Wall Street Journal,* p. 1.

Lawrence, B. S. (1984). Age grading: The implicit organizational timetable. *Journal of Occupational Behavior*, 5, 23-35.

Lawrence, B. S. (1988). New wrinkles in the theory of age: Demography, norms, and performance ratings. *Academy of Management Journal*, 31, 309-337.

Lawrence, P. R. & Lorsch, J. W. (1967). *Organization and environment: Managing differentiation and integration*. Boston: Harvard University Press.

Leontiades, M. (1980). *Strategies for diversification and change*. Boston: Little, Brown.

Levinson, D. J., Darrow, C. N., Klein, E. B., Levinson, M. H., & McKee, B. (1978). *The seasons of a man's life*. New York: Knopf.

Levinson, H. (1980). Criteria for choosing chief executives. *Harvard Business Review*, 58(4), 113-120.

Livingston, J. S. (1971). The myth of the well-educated manager. *Harvard Business Review*, 49(1), 79-89.

Loden, M. M. (1985). *Feminine leadership or how to succeed in business without being one of the boys*. New York: Times Books.

London, M. & Stumpf, S. A. (1983). Effects of candidate characteristics on management promotion decisions: An experimental study. *Personnel Psychology*, 36, 241-259.

Louis, M. R. (1980). Surprise and sense making: What newcomers experience in entering unfamiliar organizational settings. *Administrative Science Quarterly*, 25, 226-251.

Mai-Dalton, R. R. & Sullivan, J. J. (1981). The effects of manager's sex on the assignment to a challenging or dull task and the reasons for the choice. *Academy of Management Journal*, 24, 603-612.

March, J. & Simon, H. (1958). *Organizations*. New York: Wiley.

McCall, M. W., Lombardo, M. M., & Morrison, A. M. (1988). *The lessons of experience: How successful executives develop on the job*. Lexington, MA: Lexington Books.

McComas, M. (1986, April 26). Atop the *Fortune 500*: A survey of the CEOs. *Fortune*, pp. 26-31.

Miles, R. & Snow, C. (1978). *Organizational strategy, structure, and process*. New York: McGraw-Hill.

Miller, W. (1962). Historians and the business elite. In W. Miller (Ed.), *Men in business* (pp. 310-328). New York: Harper & Row.

Moorhead, G. & Griffin, R. W. (1989). *Organizational behavior*. Boston: Houghton Mifflin.

Morrison, A. H., White, R. P., & Van Velsor, E. (1987). *Breaking the glass ceiling*. Reading, MA: Addison-Wesley.

Naisbitt, J. (1982). *Megatrends: Ten new directions for transforming our lives*. New York: Warner Books.

Newcomer, M. (1955). *The big business executive*. New York: Columbia University Press.

Nieva, V. F. & Gutek, B. A. (1981). *Women and work: A psychological perspective*. New York: Praeger.

Nystrom, P. C. & McArthur, A. W. (1989). Propositions linking organizations and careers. In M. B. Arthur, D. T. Hall, & B. S. Lawrence (Eds.), *Handbook of career theory* (pp. 490-505). New York: Cambridge University Press.

Orton, J. D. & Weick, K. E. (1990). Loosely coupled systems: A reconceptualization. *Academy of Management Review*, 15, 203-223.

Ouchi, W. (1981). *Theory Z: How American business can meet the Japanese challenge.* Reading, MA: Addison-Wesley.

Pascale, R. (1984, May 28). Fitting new employees into the company culture. *Fortune*, pp. 28-43.

Peters, T. (1987). *Thriving on chaos: Handbook for a management revolution.* New York: Harper & Row.

Perrow, C. (1961). The analysis of goals in complex organizations. *American Sociological Review*, 26, 854-866.

Pfeffer, J. (1981). *Power in organizations.* Marshfield, MA: Pitman.

Pfeffer, J. (1977). Effects of an MBA and socioeconomic origins on business school graduates' salaries. *Journal of Applied Psychology*, 62, 698-705.

Pfeffer, J. & Salancik, G. R. (1977). Organizational context and the characteristics and tenure of hospital administrators. *Academy of Management Journal*, 20, 74-88.

Pfeffer, J. & Salancik, G. R. (1978). *The external control of organizations: A resource dependency perspective.* New York: Harper & Row.

Piercy, J. E. & Forbes, J. B. (1981). Industry differences in chief executive officers. *MSU Business Topics*, 29, 17-29.

Piercy, J. E. & Forbes, J. B. (1986). The functional backgrounds of chief executives: Differences across time and industries. *Akron Business and Economic Review*, 17, 27-32.

The power and the pay: The 800 best paid executives in America. (1989, May 29). *Forbes*, p. 237.

Rice, F. (1987, August 31). Lessons from late bloomers. *Fortune*, pp. 87-91.

Robertson, W. (1978, July 17). The top women in big business. *Fortune*, p. 59.

Roche, G. R. (1979). Much ado about mentors. *Harvard Business Review*, 57(1), 14-28.

Rogan, H. (1984, October 25). Top women executives find path to power is strewn with hurdles. *The Wall Street Journal*, pp. 35, 44.

Rosenbaum, J. E. (1979). Tournament mobility: Career patterns in a corporation. *Administrative Science Quarterly*, 24, 220-241.

Rosenbaum, J. E. (1984). *Career mobility in a corporate hierarchy.* Orlando, FL: Academic Press.

Russell, C. (1985). Individual decision processes in an assessment center. *Journal of Applied Psychology*, 70, 737-746.

Salancik, G. R. & Pfeffer, J. (1974). The bases and use of power in organizational decision making: The case of the university. *Administrative Science Quarterly*, 19, 453-470.

Salancik, G. R. & Pfeffer, J. (1977). Who gets power and how they hold on to it. *Organizational Dynamics*, 6, 3-21.

Sathe, V. (1985). *Culture and related corporate realities.* Homewood, IL: Irwin.

Schein, E. H. (1964). How to break in the college graduate. *Harvard Business Review*, 42(6), 68-76.

Schein, E. H. (1968). Organizational socialization and the profession of management. *Industrial Management Review*, 9, 1-15.

Schein, E. H. (1978). *Career dynamics: Matching individual and organizational needs.* Reading, MA: Addison-Wesley.

Schein, E. H. (1986). A critical look at current career development theory and research. In D. T. Hall & Associates, *Career development in organizations.* San Francisco: Jossey-Bass.

Schwartz, F. N. (1980). 'Invisible' resource: Women for boards. *Harvard Business Review, 58*(2), 6-14, 8.

Schwartz, F. N. (1989). Management women and the new facts of life. *Harvard Business Review, 67*(1), 65-76.

Sheridan, J. E., Slocum, J. W., Buda, R., & Thompson, R. (1990). Effects of corporate sponsorship and departmental power on career tournaments. *Academy of Management Journal, 33,* 578-602.

Shetty, Y. K. & Peery, N. S. (1976). Are top executives transferable across companies? *Business Horizons, 19*(3), 23-28.

Slocum, J. W. & Cron, W. L. (1988). Business strategy, staffing, and career management issues. In M. London & E. M. Mone (Eds.), *Career growth and human resource strategies* (pp. 135-151). Westport, CT: Quorum.

Slocum, J. W., Cron, W. L., Hansen, R. W., & Rawlings, S. (1985). Business strategy and the management of plateaued employees. *Academy of Management Journal, 28,* 133-154.

Solomon, J. (1990, March 9). People power: Corporations are beginning to see personnel professionals as strategic managers of a major asset: human beings. *The Wall Street Journal,* p. R33.

Sonnenfeld, J. A. & Peiperl, M. A. (1988). Staffing policy as a strategic response: A typology of career systems. *Academy of Management Review, 13,* 588-600.

Sorcher, M. (1985). *Predicting executive success: What it takes to make it into senior management.* New York: Wiley.

Spence, M. (1973). Job market signaling. *Quarterly Journal of Economics, 83,* 355-374.

Standish, F. (1990, April 4). Stempel is named GM's top executive. *The Beacon Journal,* pp. D4, D8.

Stewart, L. P. & Gudykunst, W. B. (1982). Differential factors influencing the hierarchical level and the number of promotions of males and females within an organization. *Academy of Management Journal, 25,* 586-597.

Stumpf, S. A. & London, M. (1981). Capturing rater policies in evaluating candidates for promotion. *Academy of Management Journal, 24,* 752-766.

Taylor, M. S. (1981). The motivational effects of task challenge: A laboratory investigation. *Organizational Behavior and Human Performance, 27,* 255-278.

Taylor, M. S. & Ilgen, D. R. (1981). Sex discrimination against women in initial placement decisions: A laboratory investigation. *Academy of Management Journal, 24,* 859-865.

Taylor, R. N. (1975). Preferences of industrial managers for information sources in making promotion decisions. *Journal of Applied Psychology, 60,* 269-272.

The power and the pay: The 800 best paid executives in America. (1989, May 29). *Forbes,* p. 237.

Thompson, P. H., Kirkham, K. L., & Dixon, J. (1985). Warning: The fast track may be hazardous to organizational health. *Organizational Dynamics, 13,* 21-33.

Thornton, G. C. & Byham, W. C. (1982). *Assessment centers and managerial performance*. New York: Academic Press.

Tichy, N. & Charan R. (1989). Speed, simplicity, self-confidence: An interview with Jack Welch. *Harvard Business Review*, 67(5),112-120.

Trost, C. (1990, May 2). Women managers quit not for family but to advance their corporate climb. *The Wall Street Journal*, pp. B1, B2.

Tuckel, P. & Siegel, K. (1983). The myth of the migrant manager. *Business Horizons*, 26(1), 64-70.

Turner, R. (1960). Modes of social ascent through education: Sponsored and contest mobility. *American Sociological Review*, 25, 855-867.

Useem, M. & Karabel, J. (1986). Pathways to top corporate management. *American Sociological Review*, 51, 184-200.

Vancil, R. F. (1987). *Passing the baton: Managing the process of CEO succession*. Boston: Harvard Business School Press.

Van Maanen, J. (1976). Breaking in: Socialization to work. In R. Dubin (Ed.), *Handbook of work, organization, and society* (pp. 67-130). Chicago: Rand McNally.

Vardi, Y. & Hammer, T. H. (1977). Intraorganizational mobility and career perceptions among rank and file employees in different technologies. *Academy of Management Journal*, 20, 624-635.

Veiga, J. F. (1983). Mobility influences during managerial career stages. *Academy of Management Journal*, 26, 64-85.

Veiga, J. F. (1985, August). *To the beat of a different drummer: A comparison of managerial career paths*. Paper presented at the annual meeting of The Academy of Management, San Diego, CA.

Vroom, V. H. & MacCrimmon, K. R. (1968). Toward a stochastic model of managerial careers. *Administrative Science Quarterly*, 13, 26-46.

Wakabayashi, M., Graen, G., Graen, M., & Graen, M. (1988). Japanese management progress: Mobility into middle management. *Journal of Applied Psychology*, 73, 217-227.

Wanous, J. P. (1980). *Organizational entry: Recruitment, selection, and socialization of newcomers*. Reading, MA: Addison-Wesley.

Warner, W. L. & Abegglen, J. C. (1955). *Big business leaders in America*. New York: Harper & Brothers.

Wasnak, L. (1987, July). Women head for the top. *Ohio Business*, p. 55.

Weber, J. (1990, April 30). 'I am intense, aggressive, and hard-charging.' *Business Week*, p. 58.

What's needed to become a company superstar. (1980, September 15). *Business Week*, p. 146.

White, R. P. & DeVries, D. L. (1990, Winter). Making the wrong choice: Failure in the selection of senior-level managers. *Issues and Observations*, pp. 1-5.

Williams, C. H. & Van Sell, M. (1985, August). *How generalizable is the relationship between first jobs and later career outcomes?* Paper presented at the annual meeting of The Academy of Management, San Diego, CA.

Index

About the Authors

J. BENJAMIN FORBES is a Professor of Management at John Carroll University in Cleveland, Ohio. He holds the degrees of Bachelor of Science and Master of Management Science, both from Stevens Institute of Technology, and a Ph.D. in Industrial/Organizational Psychology from the University of Akron. His research interests include career mobility models, executive careers, management skills assessment and development, and motivation for creativity and productivity. His publications have appeared in journals such as *Academy of Management Journal, Akron Business and Economic Review, Business Horizons, Group and Organization Studies, Journal of Applied Psychology,* and *Organizational Behavior Teaching Review.*

JAMES E. PIERCY retired from John Carroll University in 1988 as a Professor of Management. He holds the degrees of Bachelor of Arts (University of Maryland), Master of Science (Air Force Institute of Technology), and Ph.D. (Case Western Reserve University). He retired from the U.S. Army in 1973, in the grade of Colonel, after 33 years of military service; he joined the faculty of John Carroll University in 1977. He has researched and written numerous articles in the areas of Business Logistics and Management.

DUE DATE			
FEB 22 1995			
APR 17 1997			
FFR 05 2002			
FEB 28 2002			
			Printed in USA